CorelDRAW
for Non-Nerds

Gary David Bouton

NEW RIDERS PUBLISHING

New Riders Publishing, Carmel, Indiana

CorelDRAW! for Non-Nerds

By Gary David Bouton

Published by:
New Riders Publishing
11711 N. College Ave., Suite 140
Carmel, IN 46032 USA

Printed in the United States of America 1 2 3 4 5 6 7 8 9 0

Library of Congress Cataloging-in-Publication Data

Bouton, Gary David, 1953-
    CorelDRAW! for Non-Nerds / Gary David Bouton.
        p.   cm.
    Includes index.
    ISBN 1-56205-174-1 : $18.95
    1. Computer graphics. 2. CorelDRAW! I. Title.
    T385.B683   1993
    006.6'869—dc20   93-22383
                                                 CIP

Publisher
Lloyd J. Short

Associate Publisher
Tim Huddleston

Acquisitions Manager
Cheri Robinson

Acquisitions Editor
Rob Tidrow

Managing Editor
Matthew Morrill

Marketing Manager
Brad Koch

Product Director
Cheri Robinson

Production Editor
Steve Weiss

Editors
Patrice Hartmann
John Kane
Phil Worthington

Technical Editor
William R. Schneider

Book Design and Production
Roger Morgan
Dennis Clay Hager
Carla Hall-Batton
Juli Pavey
Angela M. Pozdol
Michelle Self
Kelli Widdifield

Proofreaders
Terri Edwards
Mitzi Foster Gianakos
Howard Jones
Sean Medlock
Linda Quigley
Linda Seifert
Tonya Simpson
Dennis Wesner
Donna Winter

Indexed by
Suzanne Snyder
Tina Trettin

Acquisitions Coordinator
Stacey Beheler

Editorial Secretary
Karen Opal

Publishing Assistant
Melissa Keegan

About the Author

Gary David Bouton was once described by a now-famous Hollywood director as a "jack of all trades," although Gary insists that Jack is his *father's* first name. Illustrator, designer, writer, and art director are all hats he has worn in the print and film industries. This made him an obvious choice to write about a program as diverse as Corel.

Gary's interest in creating many different types of published material—illustrations, articles, logos, and so on, led him to using a personal computer to broaden his scope and increase his personal productivity. "Gosh, I just designed an annual report in a weekend that would've taken 1,000 man-hours without my PC" is a gleeful proclamation often heard around the Bouton household. One of Gary's convictions is that other designers who began like himself, with physical design tools on a wooden drawing table or easel, can benefit from today's computers and the software that's being written for them, like CorelDRAW.

Gary spent 17 years in Manhattan as an art director at advertising agencies before returning to his hometown, Syracuse, New York. In charge of his own company now, Gary is very flexible in accomodating his clients' needs. The attitude of "What would you like us to be? Yeah, we do that" has led his company to create computerized video shows, newsletters, posters, maps, optimized configurations for other designers who use PCs, and a lot of unusual system failures while running Windows.

In 1992, Gary won second prize in the Corel World Design Contest in the miscellaneous category. His work, titled *Astrotext*, can be seen in New Riders Publishing's *CorelDRAW! Special Effects*; the author gives step-by-step, detailed instructions on how the piece was designed.

Besides the two or three he colored in as a child, *CorelDRAW! for Non-Nerds* is Gary's first book. He did the illustrations, the writing, most of the puns, and even offered to do the saddle-stitch binding before realizing New Riders has a machine that does that.

Gary and his wife Barbara live in Liverpool, New York, and frequently get mail addressed to the Beatles. The author can be reached at this address: Gary David Bouton, Exclamat!ons, 7300 Cedar Post Road, No. A31, Liverpool, NY 13088-4843.

Dedication

This one's for Barbara, who ran the business while I wrote the book, often made sense out of my meandering on paper, and who gives me the spirit and encouragement to always try something new. She has been both my guide and co-creator in the PC world, and never let me become a nerd for the wisdom she's bestowed upon me. And I forgive her for not having laughed once while she proofread my first drafts. "But Barb, that was supposed to be *funny*!" "I know, Gare."

Acknowledgments

This book would be nothing more than a dream if it wasn't for the invaluable help of other dreamers like myself. I'll try real hard not to miss anyone. Thanks and a tip o' the hat to:

Cheri Robinson, who called me after seeing my work in the Corel Design Contest coffee table book. She asked me whether I knew how to write, then let me do this book anyway. Cheri, I can't thank you enough for letting me do my thing, and your hours on this project made it all as worthwhile as my own.

Steve Weiss, who played lead editor, lightning rod, and the better half of a comedy team most of the time on *CorelDRAW! for Non-Nerds*. His editorial comments on my manuscript would make a terrific book alone. The world should be thankful the two of us live in different states. The universe would implode somewhere over the northeastern U.S. continent otherwise.

Patrice Hartmann, John Kane, and Phil Worthington, for making sure the technical aspects of this book were in sync with the editorial licence I freely abused while writing it. And for being gracious enough not to snicker.

William Schneider, technical editor on this Non-Nerd book. Most technical editors have to correct keyboard commands and such. William had to check sizes of dinosaurs, the width of mechanical pencil leads, and generally verify all the screwball tutorials so this book could be technically accurate, albeit a little silly.

Jeannie Sullivan, Bill Cullen, and Kerry Williams at Corel, for providing us with information and beta copies of CorelDRAW 4.0. This material helped make this book as fresh and accurate as humanly possible. Nice people and friends, if I've had a little fun with your product in this book, then I apologize. Because I honestly do have a lot of fun with CorelDRAW.

PHCP Production staff for making the Corel artwork in this book look as good as I envisioned it.

My mother, Eileen, for putting up with a store-bought card from her oldest son on Mother's Day. You see, since I was around 7, I'd always designed them myself. This was the exception in an exceptional year, Mom, and I dedicate Chapter 6, and the Mother's Day card I teach others to design in it, to you with all my heart.

My dad, who has a profound understanding of how things work in the universe. He's explained a lot of it to me over the years, while sparing me all the nerdy details. He also bought me my first computer, so there's a very direct cause-and-effect that can be found in this book. His generosity, kindness, and unconditional love are a Bouton trait. He inherited them from my grandmother, and I hope Effie is smiling down on me for writing this.

Louis Misenti, who got me my start in publishing. Lou, I hope we have many fine years together putting out our user group newsletter, and the command for Copy in CorelDRAW version 4.0 is now **CTRL+C**, not **CTRL+INS**ert like we've grown used to.

The Central New York PC Users Group (CNYPCUG). A bunch of incredibly patient, wise, and sharing volunteers who help the novice user. Everyone is a novice at some time when it comes to PCs, and my ability to write a book like this wouldn't have been possible without having gone to the meetings, classes, and events the Group holds. I've learned that there's still more to learn through being a member of CNYPCUG. I hope we can all make nerdy details as palatable to the new user as New Riders does in their books.

Trademark Acknowledgments

New Riders Publishing has made every attempt to supply trademark information about company names, products, and services mentioned in this book. Trademarks indicated below were derived from various sources. New Riders Publishing cannot attest to the accuracy of this information.

CorelDRAW! is a registered trademark of the Corel Corporation.

Windows and MS-DOS are registered trademarks of the Microsoft Corporation.

Autodesk is a registered trademark of Autodesk, Inc.

Freelance Graphics is a registered trademark of Lotus Development Corporation.

Hewlett Packard is a registered trademark of Hewlett-Packard Co.

Macintosh is a registered trademark of Apple Computer, Inc.

PageMaker is a registered trademark of Aldus Corporation.

PC PaintBrush is a trademark of Z-Soft Corporation.

PostScript is a registered trademark of Adobe Systems Incorporated.

Hickory Farms is a registered trademark of Hickory Farms, Inc.

MasterCard is a registered trademark of MasterCard Intnl.

Star Wars and associated characters are trademarked and licensed by LucasFilms and 20th Century Fox.

The Munchkin characters are protected by U.S. copyright and Glynda the Good Witch, and were conceived by L. Frank Baum in his Wizard of Oz series.

Frisbee, the original flying saucer, is a registered trademark of Wham-o, Inc.

IBM is a registered trademark of International Business Machines, Inc.

Godzilla is a registered trademark of the Japan Tourist Bureau.

Trademarks of other products mentioned in this book are held by the companies producing them.

Warning and Disclaimer

This book is designed to provide information about the CorelDRAW! computer program. Every effort has been made to make this book as complete and as accurate as possible, but no warranty or fitness is implied.

The information is provided on an "as is" basis. The author and New Riders Publishing shall have neither liability nor responsibility to any person or entity with respect to any loss or damages arising from the information contained in this book or from the use of the disks or programs that may accompany it.

Contents at a Glance

Contents

INTRODUCTION

Dressing Up Your Designs Without Getting Dressed Up

Welcome to the New Riders Publishing Non-Nerds series. We want to make learning about computers and software, in this case CorelDRAW, as easy and as fun as possible. In this introduction, we will:

- Sympathize with your having to learn a new software program

- Berate your boss for a shallow comprehension of this mandate

- Explain why graphic designers are not to be confused with sissies

- Make you laugh, because it'll probably be the last time you do if you have to install CorelDRAW without reading Chapter 2

Why You Were Pushed Into CorelDRAW, and Congratulations!

There is a difference between wanting something and needing something. You want to display a killer bod in your new swimsuit at the beach, but for that to happen, you need to do a lot of muscle-shaping exercises. Let's continue with this train of thought. You, or your boss, want a report cover, diagram, or an art studio in your department at work. Now you need to address this want. It's the common formula of having to do something unpleasant in order to fulfill a wish.

Welcome to the wish fulfillment center

New Riders Publishing is very sympathetic with your plight, and we think we have the solution for you in this book. We wrote it assuming that just as there are some people who achieve a "killer bod" without strict exercise (roughly .02 percent of .10 percent of the population), there are other people who seem to be born with an understanding of the fine points of computer programs. In the politest of company, they are called *nerds*. They know 1,001 ways to plug in a computer and want to show you every one.

This is an example of a nerd. He reads 1,000-page software reference manuals for the sheer pleasure of it. He's forgotten more about computers in the past week than you or I will need to know in a lifetime. To each his own...

You're not like that? Take heart. This book is for YOU. You don't want or need to know 1,001 ways to plug in a computer. *CorelDRAW for Non-Nerds* is 50-percent leaner than other computer books, and contains a minimum dose of overly-long explanations you couldn't care less about.

We're with you all the way

By the way, you just got lucky for the second time today, because you, or whoever bought CorelDRAW for you, made an extremely wise selection. Besides being a ridiculously complete drawing package (which means you can design almost everything with it), it's easier to use than most others. This is what a lot of people don't know when they order Corel.

By the virtue of Corel's easiness, combined with the very best book for technophobes (a nerd term for non-nerds), together we'll get you up and running, fulfilling assignments at a breakneck pace (the pace your boss likes), with plenty of time left to kick back and enjoy the rest of things in life... like getting up and running with WordPerfect.

Don't Get Put Off By the Artiste's Chapeau (Hat)

A lot of people have the hardest time with graphic design because they think it's "not them." They think that you have to be some kind of weird-creative type who dresses funny, lives in a garret, eats strange food, and has even stranger friends.

Au contraire (no way!)

Untrue, untrue. This is a caricature, or cartoon, of an artist. There are plenty of examples of cartoons in this book for reference. Today's graphic designer looks more like a hip businessperson than a beachcomber, so don't worry about any personal lifestyle modifications or prerequisites in order to use Corel.

In fact, the only real hurdle you may have to address is *Creativity*. We all have this notion that some people were born Creative Types, and the rest have to go to work for a living. But what really makes a Creative Type? It's a person who earns the reputation by being creative over and over again. It's that simple; no genetic material is involved.

Is creativity a good idea?

Creativity is as simple as giving a good idea a shape. Corel is excellent at making shapes, borders, headlines, and other stuff. All it's waiting for is a basic understanding of how it works and the application of your Good Idea.

A good idea is usually an original one. It's the foundation of work that gets recognized by the right people. That's not to say you can't build on someone else's ideas; just don't depend on them or present them as your own work. That's called "ripping off a good idea" and will get you recognized by the wrong people.

A 90s Kinda Tool

Corel is a great tool for "creating a look," for doing things that are way too complex for human hands to do, and for generating precise work with a minimum amount of time and effort. If you really get into it, you'll soon regret that you ever had to line up shapes and headlines by hand, use photostats of artwork to resize things, and get artist's glue all over the sleeve of an expensive shirt. Nerds won't appreciate this, because you can usually tell what they've had to eat all week by looking at their shirt sleeves.

You therefore can have all the advantages of feeling like an artist, being praised as an artist, and legitimately turning down nonart work (like doing a spreadsheet on your PC), with none of the disadvantages—if you'll give yourself and us a chance by using this book with CorelDRAW.

... and a 90s Kinda Book

This book won't try to teach you everything about CorelDRAW. You want a guide, not an encyclopedia. A little structure in our lives, however, is sometimes beneficial, so here's how this book is organized:

- You'll get a chance right off the bat to make a simple graphic. No deep studying, no fuss. Quick, painless, and fun. It's kinda like getting to drive when you aren't old enough yet.

- You'll learn how to set up and install CorelDRAW, and at the same time discover you're learning a lot of neat computer stuff that only nerds think they can understand.

- You'll learn how to take command of CorelDRAW, ordering around icons, modules, tools, and utilities (and showing them who's boss).

- You'll go through some simple but cool tutorials to get used to making lines and shapes, filling them with color, and moving them around.

- You'll build on the other stuff you've learned by practicing more advanced CorelDRAW things, like adding text to graphics, moving pictures from one file to another, and experimenting with strange and exotic typefaces.

- You'll discover how CorelDRAW Clip Art can be a lifesaver, or at least a career saver.

You'll learn about the nondrawing features of the CorelDRAW package.

 You'll actually learn how to put everything you've learned together to understand and analyze a complex "killer graphic" (the kind people notice and want copies of). You'll also learn how to print everything you create in CorelDRAW.

The Non-Nerdy Special Info Icons

This New Riders Non-Nerds CorelDRAW book has four little cartoon characters who hang out in the pages. They were hired to get your attention when we want to make a special point. Yes, they were created with CorelDRAW. Here they are:

SECRET

Sometimes you want to know a trick or a tip that'll make life easier for you when learning a program. Or you simply want to know something that's cool. The cartoon in the **Secret** box will clue you in. All you have to do is rap on the top of the carton a few times to shake him out.

PROFOUND REALIZATION

Nothing in the computer world is as simple as putting two and two together. You get nine, or the square root of infinity, or something else. **Profound Realizations** are peppered along the path to your CorelDRAW wisdom to help put one piece of information to work in order to understand another. When you discover the reason why something works, you may look like our cartoon character. Hopefully, you'll be better dressed at the time, though.

UH-OH

It takes a lot of experience, or the mind of a nerd, to know how to work around computer stuff when it screws up. And it will. So unlike our **Uh-Oh** cartoon character, don't feel like you've blown it. Instead, read the little gem to get you out of the jam.

NERDY
NOTE

Whenever you see a pair of unfashionable reading glasses that were mended with electrical tape, chances are there's a nerd's mind behind them. And that mind contains a wealth of computer-related **Nerdy Notes**. In this book, information you may want to know, but not from the face behind these glasses, is condensed so that normal people don't get overloaded while assimilating.

Read Me Fast

If you haven't already installed CorelDRAW on your personal computer (PC), Chapter 2 is for you, and the Introduction, although well-written and entertaining, will probably be confusing and irritating. If you already have CorelDRAW on your PC, but it was installed by a nerd, see the back of Chapter 2, and we'll cover one or two things to correct some nerdy things they most likely chose to do to your system and Corel. If you installed CorelDRAW, and

1.   you're confident you did it correctly, and

2.   you have more than a basic working knowledge of your computer

then you wouldn't benefit in the least by the next sections. You may pass GO, collect $200, and proceed directly to Chapter 3.

CHAPTER 0

Working Out of Sequence

Within the ivy-covered walls of school, we were taught things from the ground up to build to a single pinnacle of "truth." The Pyramid Theory, if you will.

Now that you've graduated to the ergonomically decorated halls of Business, you discover that "getting something out the door" and then arriving at a better understanding of your tools is the order of the day. An inverted Pyramid!

Don't worry! *CorelDRAW! for Non-Nerds* works the way *you* have to, especially this chapter!

In this chapter, you learn the following:

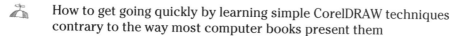

- 🔧 How to get going quickly by learning simple CorelDRAW techniques contrary to the way most computer books present them

- 🔧 How to create a simple drawing without boring you with a long drawn-out explanation

How to actually break the time barrier in terms of producing a drawing in an ultra-sophisticated, mega-complex drawing program

 How to get used to the mouse as a drawing tool, instead of just something to poke a menu bar with

First Things Last

New Riders knows you—you're the kind of person who never reads the instruction manual. Only nerds and engineers do. You rush home with a new gas grill, assemble it, and have four extremely important-looking parts left over.

We can't do much about the gas grill (hint: don't turn it on), but we can take some of the initial frustration and panic out of "assembling" and using a powerful, fun tool: CorelDRAW.

PROFOUND
REALIZATION

Don't panic. CorelDRAW handles impatience very well, your PC handles impatience very well, and so does this book. CorelDRAW is a very different sort of picture-drawing program than the Windows Paintbrush module you probably fooled around with before reading the instructions to Windows. Corel does some very weird things. But they're "good" weird, as opposed to "my VCR keeps blinking 12:00" weird. It's these very same weird qualities that will help you create graphics that will make nerds and humans alike say "awesome" and "Great work, Hobkins. See me in my office about that raise."

You need to start someplace. This chapter gives you a taste of what you can accomplish with Corel's mighty set of design tools. Before you know it, you'll be diving into other chapters, learning all kinds of nifty stuff. Don't be intimidated by the fact that CorelDRAW is used by some of the top computer graphics artists around the globe, and that Corel has won over ninety awards in the software world as best design package—because that's probably not why CorelDRAW landed in your lap.

We'll start simply and make the distinction throughout this chapter (as will follow in the rest of this book) between *what you should know* to work with the program, and *what a nerd would tell you you need to know*. This includes off-the-wall-stuff like Corel's "dithered palette," "PostScript fill options," and the gory details about the nerd's root canal work. You've decided the technical stuff is a crock, and that's why you picked up (and hopefully bought) this book. Let's work together, then, and in a few hours you'll be able to invite friends over to look at your screen, show them a piece of art, and tell 'em, "I did this without *even reading* Chapter 1!"

Getting Presumptuous before Getting Started

In order for this chapter to be of any use to you, there are some things I'm taking for granted. These presumptions are as follows:

That you have this book propped up next to your computer, or it's in your lap as you're sitting in front of your computer—whichever works for you. It's important to have a computer involved.

That Microsoft Windows version 3.1 is properly installed on the computer in front of you. A quick way to tell (and to start Windows), is to type **WIN** at the DOS command line (that's the C:\> with a blinky underline after it that you see at the top of your black computer screen). If Windows is properly installed, you should soon see a pale blue box on your screen with the Windows logo on it. This screen will shortly be replaced by the Program Manager screen.

That CorelDRAW version 4.0 is properly installed on the computer. Figuring this one out is a little trickier. You probably have Corel installed okay if you have a box in the Windows Program Manager entitled Corel Graphics Group with a lot of little pictures in them. Nerds and normal people alike call these pictures *icons*. If all these presumptions are correct, you're ready to go exploring.

If you're not sure whether these presumptions are correct, one or two possible scenarios got you off on the wrong foot. They are:

1. Your computer was set up with a menu system that doesn't list Windows and/or DOS, or doesn't give you a way to get to DOS so you can check for yourself. You're going to have to bite the bullet on this one, and consult a nerd and/or your MIS director, because they're the key-holders in this instance. We can spare you all the nerdy stuff in this book, but we can't nerd-proof your work environment.

2.   Windows 3.1 is not installed. Consult New Riders Publishing's *Windows for Non-Nerds* for guidance on how to install and use Microsoft Windows. If Corel 4.0 is not installed, or you have doubts about how well it was installed, go to Chapter 2 in this book, and then come back here.

Blast Off!

There are five ways to start CorelDRAW. Two of the ways are simple, inviting methods. The other three are nerd methods. Nerds always take the most complicated route. I'll illustrate one of these nerdy methods later, if only because it'll give you some insight into how truly Byzantine the nerd mind can be. If that sounds boring, then skip it; you'll still have two easy ways to go with.

The remaining two nerd methods are so stupid, I refuse to discuss them, but I'll give you a hint. One way is to type a "command line statement" from DOS. We can just hear you saying, "Oh, yeah, *right*! That's why I bought Windows—so that I could go back and work in DOS! Go eat a fish!"

Without further delay, here are the simple, inviting ways to start CorelDRAW:

1.   The first way is to move the mouse (the thing that looks like a "soap on a rope" attached to your computer, which nerds call a *click and point device*) so that the pointer (that little arrow on your screen that moves as you move your mouse) points to the icon in the Corel Groups box labeled CorelDRAW. Not CorelSHOW, or CorelPAINT, and *certainly* not the Read Me First icon. Then very quickly press the left button on your mouse twice, real fast. This action is called *double-clicking.*

2.   If you don't have the knack of double-clicking, try this method: Click *once* with the mouse on the CorelDRAW icon, then press the Enter key on the keyboard. This method works just as well.

The third way to launch (the nerd word for start) CorelDRAW is unnecessarily complicated, and that's why nerds also love it. If you want to know how complicated, read the following Nerdy Note. If two ways are enough for you, skip the following note, and save your gray matter for more important stuff.

NERDY
NOTE

A really groovy way to launch CorelDRAW (or any other Windows program) involves using Windows File Manager. Open the File Manager and then choose the drive you want to look at by clicking the picture (icon) of a drive on the drive bar that runs across the top of the screen. This usually opens up a window with two boxes in it, like in figure O.1.

Figure O.1

The File Manager.
Sort of like
reading a
government form.

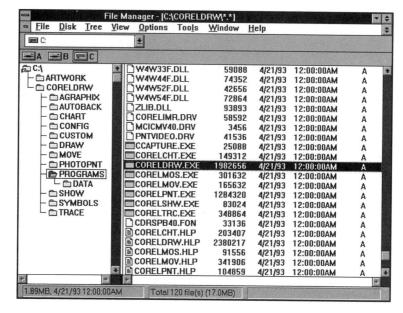

NERDY
NOTE

The left box in the window shows something that looks like an organizational chart with little icons of file folders with names next to them. This is your directory tree. Am I boring you yet? The directory tree represents all of the directories you have on that drive. If you have a file folder with a "+" on it, that means that the directory has subdirectories that aren't being shown. To see them, click on that folder and the directory tree will expand one level.

The other box in this window also has icons with file names next to them. The icons that look like a rectangle with a bar across the top are program files, the sort we're looking for in this idiotic detour to opening a Windows program.

The file that starts a program usually has the extension .EXE after its name. We are looking for CorelDRAW's main program file, called CorelDRW.EXE, that is located in the directory CORELDRW\PROGRAMS.

Scroll down the tree box using the up and down arrows on your keyboard until the CORELDRW directory is highlighted. Click on it to display the directories belonging to Corel if they aren't already showing. Scroll down until the program's subdirectory is highlighted. The other box will now show you the files in this directory. Click with your mouse on this box, and with the arrow keys on your keyboard, move the highlight around until you land on the CORELDRW.EXE file. Double-click with the mouse on this file, or press Enter on your keyboard. CorelDRAW is now launched, and you are in awe that a nerd would expend this sort of energy!

If you *still* don't believe that a non-nerd way is best for you to approach CorelDRAW, there will be other nerd nonsense scattered throughout the book to convince you.

Entering the Corel Zone

You should now have Corel's billboard screen flashing up on your screen. It goes away in a moment, and you are presented with Corel's Workspace, which should look like figure 0.2.

Neat, huh? This place looks like one huge playing field, with benches on the top (called the *Menu Bar*) and on the side (Corel's *Toolbox*), waiting for you to call the players down!

SECRET

It helps to remember that the tools in the Toolbox are hand tools. You use your hands (and eyes and your judgment) to draw shapes and enter text with these hand tools. And you use these tools to modify the objects on-screen. You actively make the changes with tools.

Actions that are picked from the Menu Bar are akin to a menu in a restaurant. They are done (prepared) for you. You select an action (an order from the menu), say how you want it done (rare, medium, well-done), then Corel does the calculations and presents you with the change. Dinner is served!

Figure 0.2

This is
CorelDRAW's
workspace.

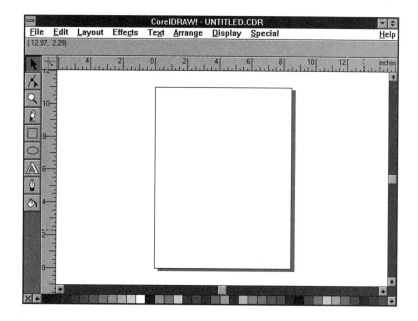

Drawn to the Toolbox

You need to select a drawing tool. Pick the one that looks like a circle by moving your cursor (arrow) so that it is on top of the circle, and click the left mouse button once. You've just selected the *Ellipse* tool.

The *Ellipse* (circular) tool button will look darker and depressed, and that's a good way of remembering which tool you're working with.

SECRET

Now move your mouse, which moves your cursor, onto the box that looks like a piece of paper. This area is called the Printable Page by Corel. It's the *page border* when you get around to printing a masterpiece. You can move, create, even leave objects you draw outside the page border, but they won't print. Remember when you were chastized for coloring outside the lines as a kid? Same theory. Notice that your cursor has changed into a crosshair shape. Wherever you place the crosshair is where CorelDRAW starts drawing the ellipse.

Click and hold down your left mouse button, and then *drag* the mouse so that your on-screen cursor goes from an upper left-hand position on the page (your starting point when you clicked the mouse) to a lower right-hand position. Then release the left mouse button, and voilà... you get the sort of a smooshed circle that figure 0.3 shows!

Figure 0.3

Click, hold, and drag the mouse down and to the right.

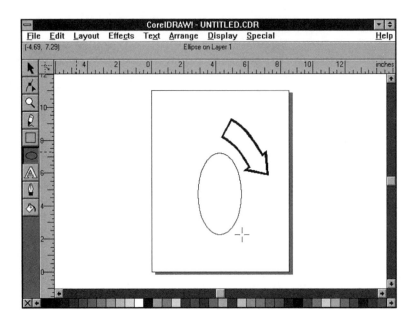

Nerds call these smooshed circles *ellipses* because that's the techno-geek term for a nonsymmetrical circle. I call them ellipses also, because that's what Corel calls them. Corel calls them ellipses because it heard nerds calling them that... it's a vicious circle, you see?

Fill 'er up!

Anyhow, now that you have your ellipse, move your crosshair cursor down to the bottom of the screen where all the colors are lined up, and click on the red square with your left mouse button. You now have an ellipse filled with red.

Congratulations! You have just mastered two very important skills in CorelDRAW. You created a shape, then modified it by filling it with color.

UH-OH

What if you don't have a red-filled ellipse after this last step? There are two big time things that may be interfering with your budding career as an ellipse artist. Here are two scenarios, with accompanying "repair kits":

   SCENARIO #1

You're working in Wireframe view instead of Preview mode, and can only see the outline of your ellipse, and no color. Do this:

Click on the **D**isplay menu item. One of the options on the list is **E**dit Wireframe. If there's a check mark next to it, click on it once, and you'll now be in Preview mode and see your ellipse colored in. When you begin with CorelDRAW, it's important to have **E**dit Wireframe unchecked. Clicking on a checked menu item removes the check. And vice versa.

   SCENARIO #2

You've been experimenting with CorelDRAW prior to reading anything about it, and accidentally changed two of Corel's defaults. Do this:

1. Make sure no objects are selected. Do this by clicking once with the left mouse button over an empty space on your workspace.

2. Click on the Outline tool button, shown in figure O.4.

Figure O.4

The Outline tool button flyout.

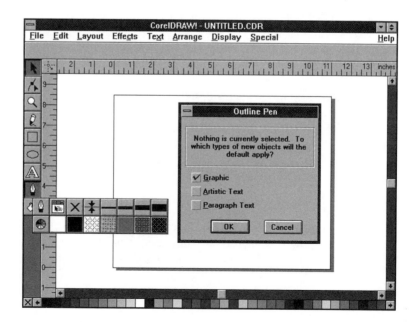

UH-OH

3. Click on the button that "flys out" that has a picture of two arrows pushing inward on a really thin line from above and beneath, as in figure 0.4.

4. You'll get a dialog box like in figure 0.4. Select **G**raphic (for graphic objects), and click on OK.

5. Click on the Fill tool button, the one beneath the Outline tool button, with a little pouring paint can on it.

6. Click on the "X" button on the flyout. You'll get another dialog box like in figure 0.4. Click on **G**raphic again, and click on OK.

7. You're fine now. Make sure you're not in Wireframe view (scenario #1), and try filling the ellipse again.

For a Select Audience

Selecting and *deselecting* are very big in Corel as well as other software programs. And both terms are equally important, especially when you get around to changing something you've drawn.

When you want to move something, you have to *select* it so that CorelDRAW can comply with your command. For all you've heard about computers, they're still pretty stupid, and you have to spell out everything for them. For example, if you want to move your new ellipse to the right, you have to select it first. Otherwise, no go. It helps to think of selecting and deselecting as being similar to an object (noun) in a sentence, as in, "I want to move the *selected thing* to the right." But selecting it is really easy.

Go ahead and move your cursor, which now should be shaped like an arrow, and plant that guy on your no doubt attractively colored ellipse, and click on it with your left mouse button. You should see eight little boxes around your ellipse (see fig. 0.5). Congratulations! You've *selected* it! Dancing has broken out in the streets, and the war has ended!

Move on over

You can move the ellipse to the left or to the right. Actually, you can move it anywhere, as long as you see the eight little black squares around it. We will call these "squares" selection handles. They define the boundary of your shape. Simply place the cursor within the space defined by the selection handles of a filled shape (or directly on the outline of the shape if it's not filled), *hold down* on the left mouse button, and *drag* the ellipse around. Then *release* the left mouse button when you have a good, new location for your shape.

Figure 0.5

Selecting an object is confirmed by eight boxes around its border.

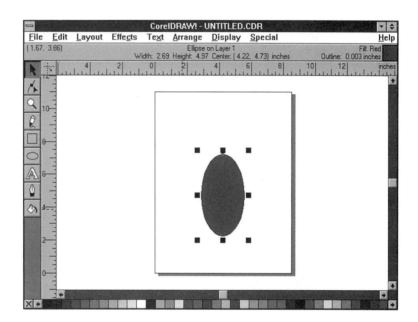

UH-OH

You aren't moving your ellipse. Instead, your ellipse is stretching and shrinking and distorting all over the place, like the Blob that Ate Chicago. You're doing something very common to beginners in CorelDRAW. You don't have your cursor positioned directly on top of the shape, and you are accidentally tugging on one of the shape's selection handles instead of moving the shape. Take a deep breath, then place the cursor in the center of the shape, and try moving it again. *Selection handles*, if you're reading this and have had the misfortune to learn about their properties prematurely in this book, *change the shape of things, and assist in moving things not in the least.*

PROFOUND REALIZATION

Drag and drop is a slang term computer users have for one of several mouse techniques, which are two- or three-step routines you perform to get something done with a mouse. Although nerds have glommed on to this term, drag and drop was originally coined by a cool guy (not named Gates). The guy was working with a Windows program to design the ultimate sports car (neat, huh?), so it's an okay phrase to use.

If you click with the left mouse button anywhere else on the paper-shaped workspace, you *deselect* your ellipse. The squares bordering the ellipse go away, and you pretty much can't do anything else with your ellipse, until you select it again.

If you're like me, the amusement of selecting and deselecting has worn thin by now, so let's move on to neater stuff. If you aren't bored yet, a nerd would love to give you a three-hour dissertation on selecting. Let him get his *own* book!

Click Twice, Then Enter

If you click on your ellipse once, you select it. But what happens if you click on it twice? If you do, you unleash a powerful Corel effects function (and to think we haven't even touched the Effects menu item yet!). This function is called the *rotate and skew* function. Those timid little selection handles surrounding your ellipse have now become curvy double-headed arrows like in figure 0.6. This tells you that you have a new feature activated and ready to work.

If you use the drag and drop technique on these new shapes, screwy things happen to your ellipse other than making it taller or wider. I really like the *rotate* function, because you can now do something with that ellipse you really can't do with a program like Windows Paintbrush. You can *tilt* it! Figure 0.6 shows a tilted ellipse.

To rotate an object in your workspace, do the following:

 Move your arrow-shaped tool to one of the curved, double-headed arrows at the four corners (not the ones in the middle; those are for *skewing* and you'll hate the look).

 Click on it with your left mouse button, and drag and drop in an up or down direction.

Figure 0.6

To rotate an object, pull clockwise or counterclockwise on the corner handle.

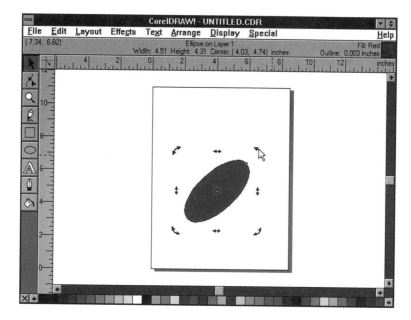

You've got a masterpiece now! Let's call it *Frisbee Hurtling Its Way To Your Neighbors' Roof*. It's really important to savor this moment, because you have arrived at one of the wonderful truths of drawing in Corel—that you can design just about any shape, going in about any conceivable direction, and you can't make mistakes like you already have made when you used Paintbrush.

NERDY NOTE

CorelDRAW is a *vector* art-based drawing program. When you draw a circle or a line or some other shape, a *mathematical algorithm* calculates where the shape is on the page, what the outline of the shape is, and includes references to relative co-ordinates within the shape. This information is then graphed (or mapped) as an object on the screen. This process is called *rasterizing*. Closed shapes like ellipses and rectangles that are produced this way are "hollow" because the math only describes the outline of the shape.

Paint-type, *bitmap* programs produce their images on an imaginary grid, a lot like a sheet of graph paper. When you paint a shape, the paint program either fills in a square on the grid with color, or it doesn't. A closed shape like an ellipse doesn't have an outline. It is composed by filling in squares that are adjacent to each other in a pattern that approximates an ellipse.

This is where "paint" programs fall down over "draw" programs. You start out with a fixed amount of little squares when you start painting, and if you want the picture larger, your only choice is to blow it up, which some paint programs feature tools for, and others don't. And this enlargement is still composed of what are now larger, little squares, and you will detect a "jagginess" to the outline of shapes.

Draw programs let you design stuff with the precision of a mechanical pencil whose point is as fine as a human hair. Paint programs give you a predetermined amount of "canvas" (the little squares in the imaginary grid) which you fill (or don't fill) with paint.

The non-nerd translation of the preceding note is as follows:

   Paint Program=paintbrush

   Draw Program=mechanical pencil

Imagine how impractical it would be to fill in a 10-inch ellipse by hand with a mechanical pencil. Same theory. Think of paint programs as capable of generating soft, pastelly watercolors, and Corel as a powerful, precise, dramatic, earth-shaking, promotion-getting, *drawing* tool. Then check to see how many successful execs have a box of pastels tucked under their desk.

Be Fruitful and...

One of the nice things about a computer is that you can exactly duplicate something you've done right, except winning at solitaire. In CorelDRAW, there are usually at least two ways to do the same thing, which doubles your chances of doing something you like. You're going to duplicate this *Frisbee Hurtling...* masterpiece by using the simplest way Corel has to multiply objects. If you want to learn about *other* ways to do it, you'll have to go beyond Chapter 0 (see Chapter 8).

First, click on the ellipse to select it. Then drag the ellipse away from its original position. But before you drop (release the left mouse button), use another finger to click on the right mouse button (yes, you are holding down on *both* buttons for the moment), then release both buttons. Bombs away!

You should now have the ellipse you originally drew, in its original position on the page, and a second, identical ellipse where you dragged the first one to and released both mouse buttons (see fig. 0.7). While we're at it, why not color this second ellipse a different color?

Figure 0.7

Your first optical illusion.

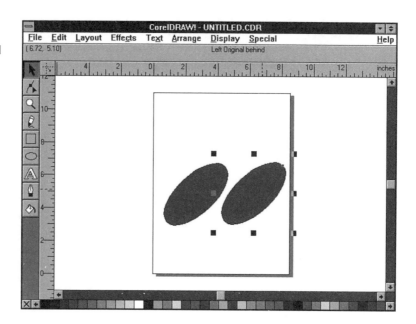

SECRET

Corel objects remain selected once you create them, and stay selected as you work on them. Most of the time, well-adjusted, average adults (non-nerds) have a more difficult time deselecting items.

Imagine their surprise when they find out how simple it is. To deselect an item, click on an empty area outside an object's borders.

Get on a collision course

While this second ellipse is still selected, go down to the strip of colors on the bottom of the screen. If your first ellipse is red, fill the other one with blue. Picking a contrasting color seems to be a *tutorial* sort of thing, so let's play the part.

Now, the blue ellipse is still selected, right? Click on it one more time to call up the *rotate and skew* function, and get those weird shapes on the corners of the ellipse going. Rotate the blue ellipse in a direction opposite to the red one.

Now your masterpiece should look like *Two Frisbees On A Collision Course* (see fig. 0.8). You've created two masterpieces without even reading Chapter 1 yet! Hey, if all this practice and learning is going to make you late for work, call in and tell the boss what you've accomplished so far. If he has any sense of humor, he'll only dock you *half* a day's pay.

Figure 0.8

The art world's finest hour.

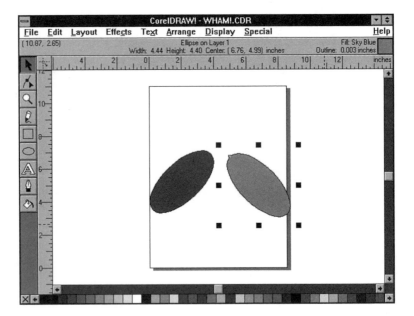

Experimental Art

If you really want to push the envelope, as our first astronauts used to say when they were flung farther and farther from the earth's atmosphere, let's kick out all the jams in this trial-size chapter and move the blue ellipse on top of the red one.

Select the blue ellipse and move it with your cursor to on top of the red one. What happens? What were you expecting to happen? Did you expect that the area where the two shapes overlap would turn purple? Black? Some other color?

The result is that *squat* happened. The reason is that these are vector shapes with solid fills. It is the same reason that you can move them around as separate objects, and that they will never intermingle like shapes in a paint program. You can do exceptionally neat and fun stuff with this property of vector art, with a minimum of understanding why.

NERDY NOTE

When you move a chunk of paint-type bitmap picture of a red ellipse onto a chunk of paint-type bitmap of a blue ellipse, you're replacing the blue ellipse, not hiding it from view. Your bitmap "canvas" (composed of several squares which form an imaginary grid that makes up the "canvas") can only hold one color at a time. Paint-type pictures are dependent on what's occupying another piece of the grid/canvas it's in when you move it. These pictures get changed really easily when you move them onto another piece of filled-in grid/canvas.

Vector drawings, however, contain all the information about themselves discreetly as objects, and they travel around your workspace unaffected by other objects. Vector drawings can be built in layers because of this unique property. Vector drawing is also called object-oriented drawing because of its discreet handling of separate shapes.

Do you really believe that Norman Rockwell knew how they got those tiny little erasers on his pencils?

So Is This Toy Fun, or What?

Hopefully, this chapter has revealed a little about the *Zen* of CorelDRAW. In other words, you've maybe experienced the program's feel and physicality; an idea of what can be produced with a few simple commands.

NERDY NOTE

Nerds also use the word *command*, but it usually refers to typing a string of meaningless blurbs at a DOS command line or teaching their pet frog not to wet the carpet.

This book is for fun, not for sweating bullets over. There's nothing wrong with being entitled to *experience* stuff before you *learn* it. What you've actually learned in this prechapter chapter is the following:

 The basic handling of the mouse, which is important, because you can't do much drawing without it

 A fraction of the Ellipse tool's usefulness

Granted, we've barely scratched the surface of learning how to use a fairly sophisticated computer program. I haven't even touched on the treasure-trove of dazzling effects contained in the menu bar yet. There indeed is a lot to learn. But the good news down the pike is that all of Corel's tools and modifiers can be used in combination with each other to produce original, eye-catching effects and designs.

Who knows? You might even get to *like* art.

Wanna continue?

CHAPTER 1

Taking the Toys Out of the Box

T he very first thing you'll notice when you take CorelDRAW out of its box is that there are two tons of manuals, cards, reference guides, and other literature. You also see the installation (or program) disks and two CD-ROMs, which are compact laser discs, somewhat like, but not identical to, your stereo CDs. It's interesting that your car didn't come with as much information, isn't it?

What do you do with all this stuff? Well, this chapter answers that question, plus lets you do the following things:

- You can dawdle around a little before you actually install CorelDRAW. It's important to understand what you're getting into.

- You get to learn how to prepare disks so that you can make a backup copy of CorelDRAW.

- You'll discover why no one can truly "own" software, and the legal implications of making too many backup copies of CorelDRAW.

- You'll even evaluate whether you need to put all of CorelDRAW on your computer.

The Adventure Begins

Okay, so you've found the nerve to open up the CorelDRAW package. You are looking at all the stuff and wondering what to do next. At this point, it is vital to your mental well-being that you follow these guidelines:

 Don't throw a shred of paper away, except perhaps the UPS wrapping and the cellophane shrink-wrap on the Corel box. Then again, don't even throw out the wrapping. If anything is defective with your copy of CorelDRAW, adjustments with whomever you bought it from will be really tough to negotiate if you toss out *anything*.

 Find the registration card, but don't fill it out yet. Again, it's hard to return something if you've written on it. You can fill it out later after you install CorelDRAW and are certain that the disks the software comes on work.

 Take out the big, fat envelope in the CorelDRAW box that contains the disks and the CD-ROM discs, and put the envelope next to your keyboard. **DO NOT OPEN** the big, fat envelope yet.

UH-OH

The disks computers use to store information on, whether it is CorelDRAW's program or copies of the masterpiece you create with it, are quite sturdy. But like most things in life, you have to take care of them.

Disks are particularly sensitive to sources of magnetism. Your computer uses magnetic impulses to put information on a disk. This is good.

It is bad, however, if something other than your computer hits your disk with a magnetic "blip"—this will scramble the information and make it worthless to you. These are dicey places to put your disks:

 On top of, or behind, your PC monitor or TV set.

 Next to, or on top of, anything with a speaker—your stereo, radio, telephone. They all have magnetic coils in 'em.

 Near magnets, obviously. Common information corruptors in your life are refrigerator magnets, magnetic whiteboards, and those paper clip holders that hang on to clumps of clips. Watch out for the paper clips, too. They've been zapped when they cling to the paper clip holder.

 Electric motors: fans, shredders, the motor that drives the fluoroscan device (the conveyor contraption that checks out your luggage) at the airport.

If you *do* accidentally zap a disk, you'll have to buy a replacement disk from the software manufacturer or make a new copy of the disk from the backup set you'll learn to make later in this chapter.

What does the fine print mean?

You'll see a lot of fine print, which looks extremely nerdy and official, on the big, fat envelope. This is common with most commercial software. This book was written to spare you a lot of unnecessary details, so here's the *Reader's Digest* version of what the fine print means:

 By the act of opening the flap (breaking the seal, as they sometimes write it) on the envelope (which is basically the only way to get the software out), you agree, by law, to a license agreement with Corel.

 A *license agreement* says that you don't actually *own* CorelDRAW. Strange thought after shelling out several hundred dollars, huh? What you *do* own is the right to *use* CorelDRAW on your computer.

Your artistic license begins here

People who build electronic programs for a living have to be careful about protecting their work because it easily can be copied. When that happens, there goes their hard-earned work and profits: down the dumpster. Therefore, it's only right and fair that people who benefit from using the software (and face it, that's everyone) should pay for it. Licensing lets the software maker know that you're a straight arrow and have paid them for the use of their nifty program.

You don't own the software, because you didn't think it up. But just owning a license to use the stuff is okay, too. You're entitled to keep the books and the work you produce with Corel (naturally). You can even mark the Corel installation disks with your name and take them in the shower with you. It's the *information* on the disks that the manufacturer is trying to protect.

PROFOUND REALIZATION

Although it is still a popular notion that most pirates can get away with breaking the law, organizations such as the Business Software Alliance (BSA) and Software Professionals Alliance (SPA) are increasing law enforcement against offenders. In the United States and Canada, pirates can pay fines in the millions of dollars and face serious prison time. What's more, many businesses are adopting tough internal policies regarding electronic security. Software audits can cost a company $100,000 a hit, and you can lose your job.

You help keep prices reasonable on really good software if you play by this slightly strange rule, which is: Make only *one* copy of the installation disks. These copies are called *backup disks*, which I will get to in a moment.

One copy of backup disks means one set that you're sure are good copies. Not *two or more* copies. Not one for a friend, and one to a co-worker who smiled at you, and one for a nerd because he offered you a copy of some software in exchange… See how this stuff gets out of control?

Okay, okay. Now what?

It's best to install CorelDRAW from your one set of backup disks, because that ensures two things:

1. You know how to prepare a disk and copy information to it, which also is useful for saving your work.

2. You're making sure that the copy of the CorelDRAW disks is flawless while you're working on installation. You save yourself time and headaches later, right?

If you are lucky enough to have a CD-ROM player attached to your computer, you can install Corel from a CD. You can stay with us here and learn how to make backup disks or breeze past this, to the next section in this chapter on what parts and how much of CorelDRAW you want to install.

Preparing a Disk for Use

This is an invaluable lesson that, if successfully done, will make you the envy of your friends. A blank disk, as you get it from the store, usually is not formatted, which means you can't use it yet. In simple terms, unless the box specifically says *preformatted*, the disks can't hold copied information in an organized format.

NERDY NOTE

When you format a disk, your floppy drive lays down tiny sectors on the blank disk by marking it with tiny magnetic impulses at regular intervals. These patterns depend on whether the disk is high-density or double-density. These marked sectors allow your computer to put information on the disk, and then find it again when you need it.

To make exact copies of disks, the disks must be the same size and have the same format. Without formatting a disk, your PC would have no way of knowing where to put all the little electronic ones and zeros it must find later. It won't like that, and it will refuse to obey you. When your computer doesn't obey you, you are often forced to ask the office nerd to help you. It irritates nerds when you whine a lot.

Get some disks

If you don't have any disks, go to the store and take two boxes (there are 10 disks to a box, usually) of high-density, 3 1/2-inch disks. Then pay the man. You'll need at least 13 disks because CorelDRAW comes on 13 disks (at the time this was written; aftermarket changes can make this number vary). Since stores don't sell boxes of disks in 13s, because they're superstitious, you'll have a few disks left over, which is okay, too. Sometimes a new box of disks will contain a "clunker" (a non-nerd word for an unformattable disk), and you don't want to have to go the store at this critical phase of Corel installation.

Format some disks

Start up Windows. When you finally see all the Windows group boxes, go to the Main Group, where File Manager usually lives. Double-click on this icon.

Put your first disk to be formatted in drive B, or if your computer only has one floppy drive, it's probably a 3 1/2-inch drive and will be labeled drive A as far as File Manager is concerned.

From the **D**isk menu, choose **F**ormat Disk. The Format Disk dialog box appears (see fig. 1.1).

Figure 1.1

This is the Format Disk dialog box.

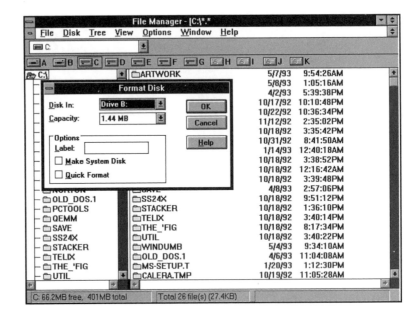

The Format Disk dialog box asks for the following information:

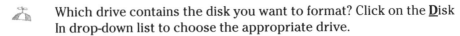 Which drive contains the disk you want to format? Click on the **D**isk In drop-down list to choose the appropriate drive.

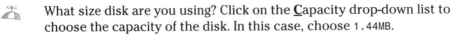 What size disk are you using? Click on the **C**apacity drop-down list to choose the capacity of the disk. In this case, choose 1.44MB.

NERDY
NOTE

Windows default setting in the Format disk dialog box makes the presumption that you want to format a 1.2MB (high-density 5 1/4-inch disk) in Drive A. Not. If you click on the down arrow button next where it says **Drive A**, you now have the choice of selecting Drive B. Do this, and the default in the capacity windows changes from 1.2MB to 1.44MB, which is the capacity for a high-density 3 1/2-inch disk. You may come across different capacity disks in your travels, but this is the **Disk In** and **Capacity** you want this time out.

A default is just a techie term for the option a program always gives you when it first starts up. Manufacturers, like Microsoft and Corel, give you these defaults to present the most convenient options to non-nerds. Nerds love poking and fussing with defaults, however, and that's why their own PCs look like they were sent to the Three Stooges for repairs.

Windows will ask you to confirm your decision by popping up a box explaining that you're going to wipe out previous information on this disk by continuing. It's a fair warning, but these disks are blank, so it's okay. Select Yes. A little box pops up that indicates the progress of the formatting, giving you the percentage of this task completed. It will take a few minutes to format the disk, so be patient.

Because you have 13 disks to format, you might want to manage your time so that you can do something else that requires taking a break every few minutes. Of course, you can sit there and watch the percentage number change, but this is pretty boring. You might want to rearrange your desk or your dresser (if you're at home). Or you can thumb to other chapters in this book. The last option is the best. This book is modular, and you'll find plenty of break points to coincide with your popping fresh disks into the PC.

NERDY NOTE

Nerds relish the term disk jockey to describe themselves when engrossed in copying or formatting disks. And it's a fitting title, because this annoying yet necessary procedure does resemble a guy at a radio station spinning platters one after another. The difference is that a professional DJ gets paid for work that serves to entertain others (okay, okay, work with me on this a little). A nerd, however, simply likes the annoying part of this procedure, and nerds do nothing between changing disks except eat snack foods and drink soda. That explains why their posture is always so poor, among other things.

Your computer will tell you with a dialog box when it is finished formatting a disk, and will ask you if you want to format another. Click on the Yes button, and you will be asked to remove the first disk and put in a fresh one. You'll want to do this to all your disks.

Be certain you keep these formatted disks in a special box or area because blank unformatted disks look a lot like the ones you've just formatted. And you don't want to repeat irritating work more than you have to.

SECRET

What If Something Goes Wrong?

Occasionally, something goes wrong in the formatting process. Typically, three operational culprits tend to be the cause of such formatting woes. All of these problems are easy to fix. Just keep reading.

Oh no, I have bad sectors

"Inspected by #39" is a tag that seems to come in all our new clothing. Inspector #39, unfortunately, doesn't work for a disk manufacturer, and without so much as an "I'm sorry" sticker on it, you may run into a blank, unformatted disk that is a lemon. Nerds will tell you there are bad sectors on this disk. What Windows will tell you, and only after you're done formatting the disk, is that you have a less than typical amount of formatted space on this clunker.

If the total disk space reads 1,457,664 bytes, and the bytes available on disk reads anything less, you got stung. A telltale sign you're formatting a disk that isn't up to par is if you hear abnormal thumping sounds from the floppy drive. No problem. Nothing is hurting your computer. It simply means your PC is telling the defective floppy disk, "Hey, I need to lay down some magnetic roadway for information to go over later," and the clunker disk has a rock in the roadway's path, and it's not gonna move the rock. So you've got the roadway laid down on the disk (sectors, if you want to talk like an adult here), but there's an area that can't be driven over. Which means that you cannot use this disk to make a backup copy of one of Corel's disks, because computers make perfect, identical copies of stuff, and this bum disk is not perfect.

Just do this:

1. The dialog box asks you if you want to format another disk. Click on the Yes button.

2. Remove the defective disk from the drive and put in another blank, unformatted (hopefully perfect) one, like the dialog box suggests.

3. Put a piece of masking tape on the defective disk and write "Bad," "Defective," or "I'm sorry, Dave. I'm afraid I can't do that" on it.

4. You're back to formatting again. When you're done formatting the next disk, click on Yes in the dialog box and put in another blank disk.

Get your money back on the defective disk, use it as a coffee coaster, or sell it to a nerd for as good as new. More advanced users can use these disks for other things, but not to make backup copies of any program.

To write or not to write

You also might have accidentally pushed the little plastic slidey thing on the disk you are trying to format. This plastic slidey thing is the write-protection control.

If a disk is *write-protected*, you cannot format it or store any new information on it. Write-protection is a good feature on 3 1/2-inch disks because it prevents you from accidentally erasing information.

How can you tell whether the disk is write-protected? If you can see the light through the hole like in figure 1.2, the disk is write-protected. If the tab covers the little square hole, it's ready to format or store information. Make sure that when you are formatting and copying, you can't see light through the upper right corner hole (if you're looking at the front of the disk).

This end up

You also might have placed the disk upside down in the floppy drive. The silver metal circle should always be facing the floor when you insert it. Unless you have a really strange machine. Press the eject button on the floppy drive, and put the disk in with the silver metal circle facing down this time.

That's really all you need to know about formatting disks.

Figure 1.2

The back of your
disk, where the
problem may be.

Can't write on

Can write on

Making the Backup

Now you can make copies of those original CorelDRAW program disks.
Making backup copies involves many of the same skills you've just acquired.
Just follow these steps:

1. Write-protect all your original Corel installation disks before you do
   any other steps. Push the little plastic slidey thing on all your Corel
   disks so you can see the light through the holes. You do not want to
   accidentally copy information over the originals. Sometimes Corel
   disks come with the little plastic slidey things already in the write-
   protect position, sometimes they move around when they were
   shipped. The point is, make certain for yourself. See figure 1.2 if in
   doubt.

2. From the **D**isk menu in File Manager, select **C**opy Disk. The Copy
   Disk dialog box appears.

3. In the **S**ource In box, select drive B. In the **D**estination In box, choose
   drive B, and click on OK.

   Windows prompts you to insert the source disk in drive B.

4. Put Corel's Disk #1 in drive B... click on OK, and Windows provides
   you with the status of its copying. Essentially, Windows uses your PC
   to temporarily memorize the contents of the disk, and then spits it
   out onto your *destination* (or target) disk afterwards.

5.   You then will be asked to insert the target disk into drive B. Remove the Corel Disk #1, and take one of your newly formatted disks and put it in drive B.

SECRET

If you have trouble understanding the difference between the source and target disk, just remember this:

Source disk = disk you want to copy

Target disk = disk you want to make the copy on

Use this time now to start marking labels, if you haven't already done so. Boxes of disks you buy generally come with a whole page of perforated sticky labels. Mark them "Corel Disk #1," and so on, copying the titles on the original Corel disks.

SECRET

You should label copied disks *after* the information has been copied to them. You'll screw up, otherwise, if a disk fails to format or copy correctly. Some do, and it's a bear trying to pull a label off a disk. Some of these manufacturers not only go cheap on the amount of blank labels they ship, but they also use an adhesive similar to Crazy Glue. You will lose fingernails, part of the labels, and part of your mind if you have to do this often.

After you've made your copy of Corel Disk #1, it's on to copying Corel Disk #2, but let's tidy up first. Write-protect your copy of the disk, and carefully affix a clearly marked label on your effort here. Make sure the label doesn't overlap any moving parts like the little plastic slidey thing or the bigger metal slidey thing (the disk's shutter), and that it looks quite like the disk in figure 1.3.

Now you can put the original Corel Disk #2 in drive B and repeat the preceding steps for all of Corel's Installation disks. Then you can take two aspirin for your headache, and take comfort in the fact that nerds eagerly charge more than the cost of this book to do something like this. And sometimes they actually get it, too.

Figure 1.3

Your disk should
look like this, but
larger.

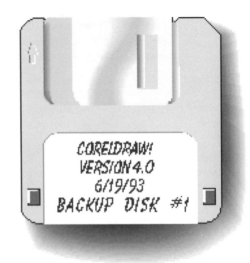

Decisions You Must Make

Corel offers two options for installing the software, **F**ull and **C**ustom, as
shown in figure 1.4. Although we aren't up to this point yet, you do need to
make some decisions now before you actually start installing CorelDRAW.

Figure 1.4

You'll get this
screen after
Corel welcomes
you and asks for
your registration
number.

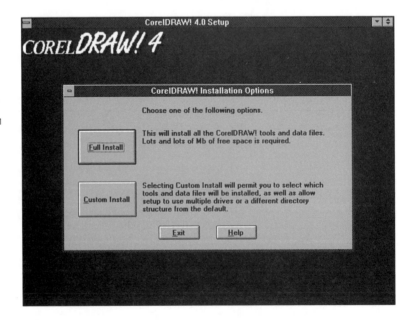

Full Install means you get every mega-inch of CorelDRAW's goodies. Thirty-four megabytes is a little hefty to go putting on your hard drive, especially if you ever want to put any other program on it. It's a sad fact that every time you create a drawing, your hard disk space is eaten up. You are going to need as much space as you can get. In short, do not pick the Full Install.

 Custom Install means that, with our advice and help, you can choose exactly what modules, typefaces, and Clip Art you want installed on your hard drive. It's a fair bet you'll want CorelDRAW itself installed, but what about CorelPHOTO-PAINT, CorelMOVE, and the 750 type-faces that come on the CDs? Think you can cram it all in your hard drive? Think you need everything on your hard drive? It's your choice, and we'll offer some recommendations.

Most custom installations allow you to pick and choose what you want—and more importantly, don't want—the installation routine to put on your hard drive. And because an Install Program generally futzes around with your AUTOEXEC.BAT and WIN.INI files in order to work with Windows, it becomes that much harder for an average user to eliminate the extra program frills later on when you decide they're a waste of hard drive space. So do this non-computer thing *before* you put Corel Disk #1 in your drive.

Pick what you need

Pick up the literature in the Corel box and find the Corel Library Catalog and the typeface guide. With disk installation, you'll have a choice of No Clip Art or Yes, Clip Art. CD-installers install none, because you don't load any clip art onto your hard drive; you simply access it from the CD just like another hard drive.

If you choose to install the Clip Art from the disks, it'll take up a few mega-bytes of hard drive space, but it's worth it. Corel has commissioned a lot of terrific artists to do finished illustrations in CorelDRAW; this is prime mate-rial you can use and modify to suit your business needs. The Clip Art is divided into different categories to address the graphics needs of many different professions, like medical, publishing, and transportation. Hint: General, People, and Celebrate are sure bets for a lot of common business Clip Art needs.

If you're doing Corel install from backup disks and you're really in a bind for hard drive space, install the Clip Art anyway, and we'll show you a trick at the end of the installation chapter to whittle down your Clip Art collection.

SECRET

My recommendation is to install all the Symbols when it comes time. Each symbol category only takes up as much hard drive space as a typeface, and they're very useful for "bullets" in reports. Also, you can combine one or two symbols to create a corporate logo and, with what you'll learn in this book, modify the Symbols to create a full-blown graphic or two! And you can install these symbols as TrueType typefaces that'll work with all your Windows applications.

Last of all, give really careful attention to the typefaces, or *fonts*, you decide to keep on your hard drive. Corel has some beautiful typefaces that are available not only to Corel, but to all your Windows programs. You'll be able to type a letter in Windows Write with the *Cheltenham*, the *Amerigo*, or even the *Amelia* typefaces.

The real question is how often you actually use a typeface like *Amelia*. If you were chief graphics designer on the *Starship Enterprise*, and Worf or Picard needed "Out of Order" signs for the transporter room, you might...well, check out figure 1.5 and see for yourself.

The drawback here is that these TrueType faces each take up an average of 25–40 kilobytes on your hard drive.

NERDY
NOTE

A kilobyte=1,024 bytes. There are 1,024 kilobytes in a megabyte (M). The average PC has a 120M hard drive. Basic math tells us if you store 400 typefaces at 40K apiece, that adds up to 16M, or a whole 12 percent of your hard drive space! Which is larger than a lot of entire programs!

Corel 4.0 comes with 750 bonus typefaces on one of the two CDs. Just a suggestion? Unbiased and dispassionate about choking your hard drive with too many silly, ornamental, one-use only typefaces?

Let them go! At least some of them. The 50 that come on the disk install version of Corel are perfectly adequate. For CD people, there's a FONTINST.EXE program on CD disk #1 that'll let you install all, some, or none of the 750 TrueType and ATM faces at any time. Stick with a few nice, conservative typefaces, like the *Schneidler* set.

Mark down everything you feel is critical to install at this point, and you'll be on your way soon.

Figure 1.5

Don't waste hard drive space with typefaces you'll rarely use.

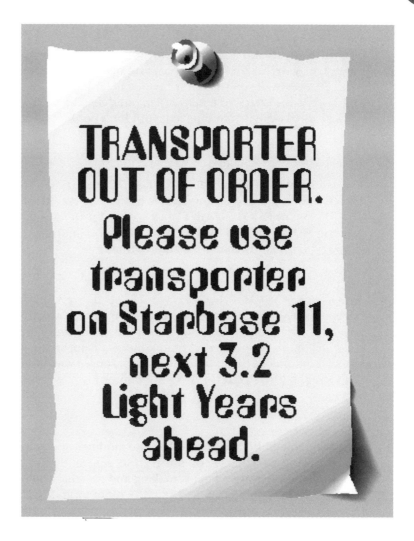

So Many Modules, So Little Time

CorelDRAW is marketed as the Total Business Graphics package, and it lives up to its name. However, there's a slim difference between a Graphic Designer, and a designer of Business Graphics, besides the capitalization.

CorelDRAW and CorelCHART for business

CorelDRAW will help you create terrific graphic designs that may or may not be designs your business has a constant need for. It depends on your business. **CorelCHART**, on the other hand, will let you create a terrific business graphic of a pie chart, or a histogram, but doesn't have the tools in its workspace to design, say, a page layout for a book.

CorelMOVE and CorelSHOW

The same thing is true of **CorelMOVE** and **CorelSHOW**. They are used for presentations, not generating terrific designs. In fact, they depend on CorelDRAW (or **PHOTO-PAINT**) as a source for the designs you then choreograph in **MOVE** and **SHOW**. If you bought Corel in order to do video screen shows, you'll want to install these programs.

CorelPHOTO-PAINT

CorelPHOTO-PAINT is a bitmap, paint-type design, worthy of considering installing even though this book may not contain every detail on its features. It is much more sophisticated than Windows Paintbrush, if you've ever fooled around with that. We'll show you a simple way to actually retouch photographs with **PHOTO-PAINT** in Chapter 11.

CorelTRACE

We briefly touch the periphery of all the modules above in this book. But if your business day is heavy on illustration, sign, and advertisement designing; and light-to-empty on chart-making and creating a little movie to run on your PC, install CorelDRAW and skip the other modules. Except **CorelTRACE**.

CorelTRACE is a conversion program that will let you work with bitmap pictures, such as a cartoon you've scanned into your PC, in CorelDRAW. This conversion utility is an important one to own, because it lets you edit (tinker with) bitmap drawings in a whole new way that we'll discuss in Chapter 10, "Tracing is *Not* Cheating!"

CorelMOSAIC

CorelMOSAIC is sort of a wash all ways around, unless you need a program that will show you a collection of thumbnail sketches of graphical files; not only Corel's, but a whole bunch of other file formats as well. The main reason I don't recommend installing **CorelMOSAIC** is that it takes up hard drive space, and all the other Corel modules offer a thumbnail preview of work before you open a graphical file. Besides, this is only the beginning of the book, and we haven't created a lot of files to make a "collection" yet!

Think hard before you install

So call it Parental Logic ("because I'm the daddy, and I say so, that's why"), but I suggest you examine your need for each program before installing it. Hard drive space is hard to recover once you've loaded a program you later find you don't need. Why? Because father knows Corel, and father knows best.

Graphic designers: Load **CorelDRAW**, **PHOTO-PAINT**, **CorelTRACE**, the Symbols, some typefaces, and the Clip Art.

Business graphics people: Load the modules that best suit your presentation needs, as well as **CorelDRAW**, Symbols, some typefaces, and Clip Art.

Nerds: Install the entire contents of the Corel package, including both CDs, the shrink-wrap, and the cardboard (nerds prefer a "challenge" over getting useful work done).

System Requirements vs. Your Requirements

Every responsible software manufacturer publishes something called suggested (or *recommended*) system requirements. These tell how your system should be *configured* (what equipment you have; for example, a 386DX33 model, with 4M RAM, an 80M hard drive, a video card and Super VGA monitor that supports 256 colors) to run a program successfully.

But "successfully" is a weasel-word, and it's relative. You see, manufacturers also like to *sell* large amounts of their product. I don't know why. I think it has something to do with capitalism or not starving. At any rate, we see a trend in which manufacturers are a little overly optimistic about their suggested system requirements. This gets more people to buy their product.

The following table is a slightly tongue-in-cheek reference guide that you can apply to Corel as well as other full-featured Windows applications. Your mileage may vary, and restrictions in some states may apply...

Table 1.1
Reference Guide

Class	System	Drive	Monitor	Memory
Lavish	486DX, DX2 486SX	200+M	21" Super VGA, capable of 256 colors	16M 8M
Adequate	386DX, SX	120M	14" VGA, capable of 256 or 16 colors	4M
Sorry	286, AT, XT	20M	B&W G.E. 8" portable	Guts from a pocket calculator

This table is meant to provide a sliding scale relating to Corel's performance on your machine. The simplest rule of thumb is that the bigger, faster, and more costly PCs will run Corel in a stupendous way and you'll get more work done. The slower the machine, the slower you'll be forced to work. This descends to the lower rung of PCs, the 286-class, where only a masochist will attempt to run Windows, let alone a full-blown application like Corel. Windows will crash, you'll lose the work you've put a lot of effort into, and you'll wind up blaming Corel instead of the fossil it's running on.

NERDY
NOTE

The latest fashion this season for the terminally PC-power/speed-hungry is the *Pentium* chip. No, it's not a yogurt-and-soy-based snack food. It's an Intel-based processor chip that handles roughly twice the MIPS (millions of instructions per second) of the earlier 486 machine that tops the list on the preceding chart. Manufacturers other than Intel will call their chips 586 chips ('cause Pentium is a trademarked name of the Intel company), but they'll work in a PC about the same.

NERDY
NOTE

There are other "enhancements" built into these new chips, too, that a nerd will gladly bore you forever with explaining. All you need to know is that they're available, and PCs with these chips are unbelievably fast! The first 586- (or Pentium-) powered PCs offered in 1993 are around twice the price of their little 486 brothers and sisters. If you really want CorelDRAW to fly, check out a PC with this new generation of processors in them. Then check out the state-of-affairs with your checkbook!

OK, have you finished choosing, selecting, deciding, pondering, projecting, and evaluating? Are all of your modules and fonts in a neat row? If so, we're ready to move on and actually get CorelDRAW up and running. Life after installation awaits us.

CHAPTER 2

Installing, Finally!

This chapter will hold your hand through
the most unpleasant feature a software
program comes with—the software installation.
Hey, you wouldn't want all the sweat you put into
making backup copies of Corel in Chapter 1 to go to waste now, would you?
We've turned software installation into plain English here, and it will make it
easier to do a required computer-related unpleasantry.

In this chapter, you learn to do the following:

 How to tell CorelDRAW what parts you want to install

 How to install CorelDRAW from a CD or from disks

 How to correct the installation that a nerd performed

 How to sift through the CorelDRAW reference books and decide
which manuals are actually helpful

Let's Get to It

This chapter is mostly a straight walk-through of the installation process. There won't be a horde of special notes and tricks boxes because you don't need to be distracted, and besides there's really only one way to do this. Just pay attention and follow along. So stack those *backup* Corel program disks next to your computer and get prepared to earn the respect of your coworkers.

In the beginning...

You really won't find the installation process any more painful than going to the dentist. Just kidding. The process is really very simple. Just take a deep breath and follow these steps:

1. From the DOS prompt, type **win** and press Enter.

2. From Windows Program Manager, select **R**un from the **F**ile menu.

3. If you are installing CorelDRAW from disks, place Corel Disk #1 in your 3 1/2-inch floppy drive (let's assume that it's drive B). Type **B:\setup** in the dialog box.

   If you are installing CorelDRAW from a CD, substitute the drive letter of your CD-ROM. For example, type **D:\setup**.

    EVERYONE: CorelDRAW will welcome you with a screen when the installation program begins. Click on Continue to continue with the installation (and this chapter).

    Corel then wants you to give it your name and registration number in the appropriate boxes. This box will stop cold anyone that doesn't own a legitimate license for Corel. The installation simply will not continue without entering a name and the registration number found on the front of your owner's manual, or on a sticker tucked between your installation disks.

After we're done with the registration stuff (it's like being in school again, isn't it?), we'll hit that screen we showed back in figure 1.4. We're brave and know that Custom install is the door to choose, so click on the Custom install, and we'll get a screen that offers us an interesting choice, like in figure 2.1.

Figure 2.1

What's your destination?

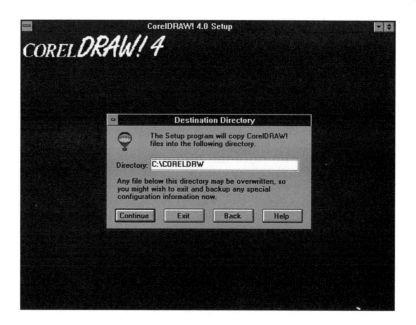

Before you get all the wonderful options to choose or not, which we discussed in the last chapter, Corel now wants to know exactly where you want its payload dropped. Fair enough question. You can either let Corel pick the path it will install itself to, like CD4, or type in a different directory name and drive now. I've typed in CorelDRW in the example because I have trouble finding short names on my directory tree.

If your hard drive's partitioned, you may want to direct Corel's installation to drive D:, or E:, whatever. Don't labor over this one too much. Just allow Corel to install on a drive you know has lots of space. Believe me, your bigtime decision-making is yet to come!

Decisions, decisions

After clicking on Continue, you're presented with the "Grand Menu" I've only alluded to up 'til now. So many choices, so intimidating, right? Not to worry. Instead, seize command of this installation program right now! You know what you want and don't want on your hard drive, right? You read the last chapter thoroughly, right? Well, okay, if you didn't, we'll recap on the really important stuff to choose now, okay? You chose the Custom install like we suggested, and now you've got a screen that looks like figure 2.2.

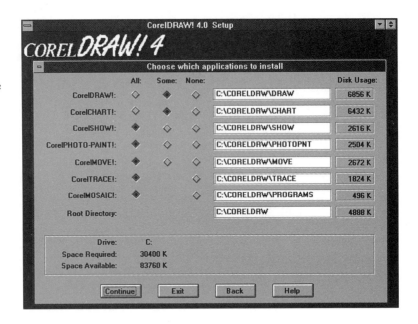

Figure 2.2

Choose Some, one at a time, all the way down the list to see what options the install program gives you.

Goodies vs. Hard Drive Space

All the modules are lined up on the left of the screen, with the options to pick All, Some, or None of them. On the far right is the hard drive space you're going to use when you make the selections. When you select the Some blue diamonds on your screen, Corel gives you an options dialog box where you get to pick and choose what you'd like, as seen in figure 2.3. Notice that CorelMOSAIC and CorelTRACE don't have a Some Options box? It's an all-or-nothing proposition with these modules.

You're never committed to a selection until you click on the **C**ontinue button at the bottom of the screen. Cancel is the "back-out clause" in case you don't want to commit to a choice right now, and would rather ponder all the applications once more. This isn't like a game show or anything, so take your time and mull over the possibilities and their corresponding hard drive toll.

SECRET

If you're the sort of person who selects their meal in a restaurant based on how much cash they know they have on them, this is a really good time for an analogy! On top in the applications choice screen is the "bill," the running tab of the megabytes you intend to install after selecting. On bottom is how much hard drive space you have, your "wallet." Sorry,

MasterCard isn't accepted here, and if the top of your fraction is greater than the bottom, you're gonna get a big "No Can Do" from the installation software.

The real secret to this is that if you have a partitioned hard drive, you can spread stuff out. With enough room on a partition other than where you told Corel to start installing to, you can type in a different location for some of the applications you really need (in the long white windows shown in figure 2.3). It makes for very convoluted and sloppy directory trees on your PC, but who's gonna tell?

Figure 2.3

The CorelDRAW module Options dialog box.

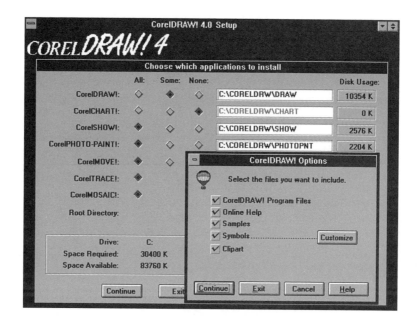

Now you can choose only the items you want. How do you know which items to choose? Read on.

Choosing Your File Options

Choosing file options sounds about as exciting as "choosing furnace filters," but it's actually pretty interesting—you can give yourself a tailor-made setup. I recommend the following installation options for CorelDRAW:

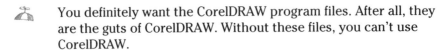

You definitely want the CorelDRAW program files. After all, they are the guts of CorelDRAW. Without these files, you can't use CorelDRAW.

The Online Help is really good to go to when you don't have this book handy to answer your questions.

The Samples are a keeper. They don't take up much space, and it is Corel's intention that you "take them apart" in order to discover some neat ways to do special effects. We'll show you how to unravel these sample Corel drawings and examine them in Chapter 14. And like most toys, after you've taken them apart, you can throw them away.

Keep the Symbols box checked. You'll see it says Customize to the right of it. That's for choosing which Symbols you want, and you want all of them, so leave this button alone.

What about Clip Art?

If you're a CD-ROM user, you don't need to install Clip Art on your hard drive. You can get to your Clip Art from CorelDRAW as simply as picking a drive and a directory. Disk installers have a choice of installing all the Clip Art on the disks, or none. As we mentioned in the last chapter, the Clip Art doesn't take up all that much hard drive space (considering that you'll probably need it), and we'll show you how to selectively delete the stuff you really don't need, so go for it.

Corel's Other Modules

Let's get back to our list of modules options. What to keep, what to let slide? The following information can help you decide.

CorelCHART

If you're not a chartin' kinda person, skip this one entirely, and save yourself the hard drive space. If you need it for work, however, install the whole nine yards: all files, including the Help Line and Samples.

CorelSHOW

This guy is used to create computer "slide shows." You drop in pictures of art from CorelDRAW or some other art source. If you think your business might need a different way to make a presentation, unpack CorelSHOW. Unless you feel it's important, do a "no SHOW" on this one.

CorelPHOTO-PAINT

This is a paint program far superior to Windows Paintbrush. You can re-touch photographs and apply neat effects to them. If you're into photography, and especially if you have access to a scanner, install this one. Um, if you have photos on your hard drive already, you won't need the Samples, so pick Some on PHOTO-PAINT's checklist, and don't select Samples.

CorelMOVE

This module is like CorelSHOW, in that you can make a moving PC screen show with it, and a design program like CorelDRAW. We'll give an example of how to use it in Chapter 11. If your business has no need for presentations, and you need Corel for its wonderful designing powers only, don't make a "MOVE"; leave this one off your hard drive.

CorelTRACE

This program is terrific for turning paint-type art (like photos and other pictures you may already own) into a format that you can work with in CorelDRAW. Definitely install this one, and we'll show you how to do some special things with your "traced" artwork in Chapter 8.

CorelMOSAIC

This is a picture viewer. It lets you see whole collections of computer art on your PC at a glance. If you don't intend to ever pick up the Corel Library Catalog again, it's useful to view the Clip Art categories. But it takes up hard drive space, and you can preview any piece of art in all the Corel modules, so I recommend you select none of CorelMOSAIC.

Filters, Fonts, and Drivers

Once you've made all your selections from the menu, it's time for dessert! Click on Continue, and you'll get a screen that looks like figure 2.4. This is where you get the chance to flex some decision-making power over which and how many fonts (typefaces, everyone calls them the same thing), filters (things that convert CorelDRAW artwork into different formats other Windows programs can understand), and scanner drivers you'll install.

Figure 2.4

Nerd heaven: The
nuts-and-bolts of
installing filters,
fonts, and
scanners.

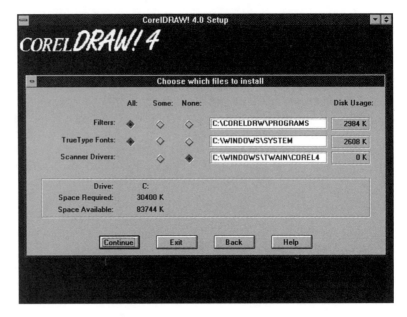

 Filters? Pick All of them. A lot of Windows programs could use your
CorelDRAW artwork, like a spreadsheet, or a word processing
program, but these programs don't "speak Corel." The filters convert
the Corel image into something you can export to these other
programs. We'll talk about exporting in Chapter 7, "Malice Through
the Looking Glass." For now, trust us that you'll want every filter. It'll
make almost any other program you own able to import Corel
graphics.

 Fonts? Click on the Some button (even though All is selected in fig.
2.4) next to TrueType fonts, and this will call up a dialog box like in
figure 2.5. Here we have some decision-making to do. Look at the list
of typefaces Corel provides in the Library Catalog, or a list you may
have made up when we first recommended being selective about
them in the last chapter.

You see in the right column that Corel assumes you want all the
typefaces. To deselect one of these faces, click on the typeface in the
right column, then click on the delete button that will then move the
typeface into the left column. Don't worry that the button says
Delete; you're not really deleting anything. Read the fine print on the
top of the screen—you're picking out typefaces you do not want to
install. They won't be deleted off your backup disks or anything.
They're write-protected, right?

You can reinstall a font you have second thoughts about by clicking on it in the left column (the don't install column), and choosing the Add button.

Figure 2.5

Here you can toss the Harpoon or throw a Bedrock.

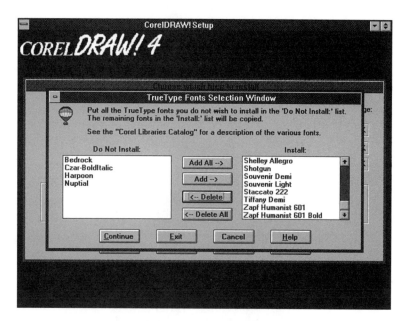

 Scanners? If you don't have a scanner, this one's real easy to choose—None. But if you have a scanner, and you know the model, or if you know your scanner supports TWAIN (a lot of recent scanners do), check this box, then select the driver that matches up with your scanner.

Click on Continue, and we're outta here!

You're Almost Done

Hold your breath and pinch yourself. You're on the home stretch now. Follow the next steps to complete your installation.

 CD installers: Click on Continue on the main Setup dialog box. It's clear sailing to the end of the Installation program. No more buttons to push! It'll take around an hour, so go do something else for a while.

Chapter 2: Installing, Finally!

 Disk installers: Click on Continue on the main Setup dialog box. If you selected only parts of Corel as suggested, the installation should not take too long. Certain disks may not be asked for by the Installation program.

Your patience will be rewarded. Pay attention to which specific backup copy disks the Installation is asking for, and revel in the possibility that the CD-user skipped over the section on formatting disks, and now they might have to pay you for the service if you ever meet.

 In unison: When you've completed the installation, you'll get the screen that looks like the one in figure 2.6.

Simply click on OK, and you return to the Windows Program Manager. You should see a new Group window that looks something like figure 2.7.

Figure 2.6

The very last
Corel Installation
screen.

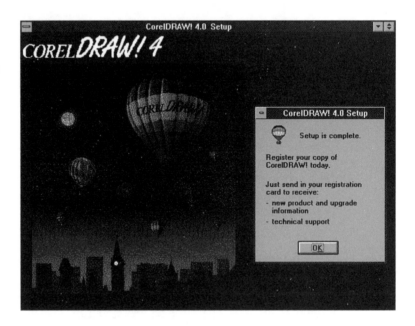

Take a break! You've earned it. I need to talk to the unfortunate souls who had a nerd install CorelDRAW on their computer.

Figure 2.7

A view of the new Corel Graphics Group.

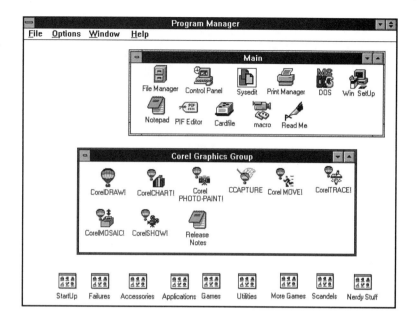

How to Correct a Nerd's Installation

If you thought you'd save yourself some time by allowing someone else to go through the procedures already covered on installing CorelDRAW, it was a good thought. The trouble is, if someone volunteered to do it, that person was probably a nerd.

Now you have over 30M of CorelDRAW on your hard drive (which is a sizable chunk of "real estate," as a nerd would say before you kill him). Don't fret, and don't try to kill the nerd. He'll probably return to Earth as a higher life form, and you don't owe him the favor. Do the following stuff instead.

Whittle those typefaces

The modules (CorelSHOW, CorelMOSAIC, and so on) won't do you much harm installed the way they are. They just take up hard drive space. If you want to do some whittling, though, start with the typefaces.

Go to the Windows Control Panel icon in the Main Windows Group. Double-click on the Fonts icon, and a list of your installed fonts appears, as in figure 2.8. Click on the undesired fonts one by one as you hold down the Ctrl key. This allows you to make multiple selections.

Figure 2.8

You got to know
when to hold 'em,
know when to fold
'em.

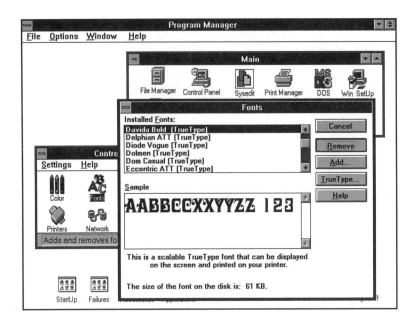

Next, click on the Remove button. A dialog box will appear with a little check box that says Remove Fonts From Disk. You click on this box, and click on the Yes To All button, and these guys are wiped off your disk. Finito. Goneski. If you change your mind, you can always retrieve them from your Corel disks.

Delete, delet, dele, del...

Do you feel confident enough with Windows to use the Delete command from File Manager? If so, the excess Clip Art can be pared down fairly readily. Deleting stuff is risky, however, unless you're absolutely certain you've picked out the right files for deletion. If you make a mistake, you probably won't know it until you really need your now-missing files. Scary, huh? If you want to try, it goes like this:

1. Open the File Manager by double-clicking on the icon in the Main Group.

2. Click on the drive button to get the drive on which Corel was installed.

3. Scroll down the directory tree, until you see a subdirectory that branches off CORELDRW that says CLIPART.

4. Double-clicking on that name should expand that directory branch to the various categories of Clip Art that were installed.

5. If you select, say, the FLAGS category of Clip Art as a category you can live without, click on it, then From File, click on Delete.

6. You will then get a chance to read the directory you're telling File Manager to delete in a Delete dialog box, like in figure 2.9.

Figure 2.9

Weeding out the Clip Art garden.

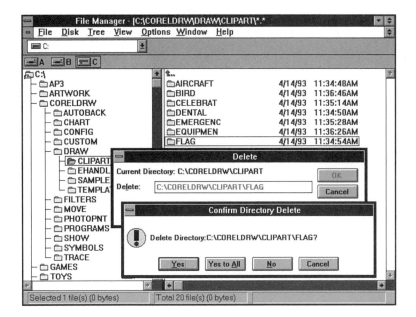

7. When you click on OK, a second box (your last chance to rethink this move) will appear to confirm your decision. Read it carefully! In figure 2.9 we see the Clip Art category of FLAGS at the end of the directory tree, so we're deleting flags. We click on Yes, and...

8. POOF! No more FLAGS Clip Art. You've reclaimed some hard drive space, and if you change your mind later, you'll have to run Corel's installation program again.

UH-OH

Do not try this same stunt with program directories. Program directories are the ones like CORELDRW and PHOTOPNT. These contain files that are interconnected at installation time with various other files that allow programs to work in Windows. To delete these files at this point would mean upsetting the whole system, and delaying the possibility of actually getting to CorelDRAW today!

Aftermath, and Advice on Reference Material

A nerd will take every precaution against PC problems by barricading his or her workspace with charts, guides, and reference manuals. Scientists have discovered that nerds themselves emit powerful magnetic fields that disrupt normal computing, so the books don't really figure in, positively or negatively. Knowing that, an excess of Corel-related guide material isn't gonna weigh us down either. All you really need from Corel's literature are the following manuals:

 The Symbols Library Guide

 The Clip Art Guide

These books are handy for finding that drawing or symbol you want to use. The typefaces you've installed can be viewed and used anywhere in Windows, not just in CorelDRAW. With the guides and this Non-Nerd book, we'll mosey on to the next chapter, a brief guide on how to use Windows and make the most of the Corel Graphics Group.

As to the rest of the paperwork that came along with your new software? Why not keep it in the box your software came in? The Corel box is sturdy, and would look great on your bookshelf, between fiction and nonfiction.

CHAPTER 3

Icon Not Understand All the Corel Icons

C ongratulations are now in order for the second time in this book! If you've followed our steps in Chapter 2 to install Corel, you now are the proud owner of a flock of icons in a spanking new Corel Graphics Group! Behind those icons are terrific software programs that (like anything new that's brought into this world) have certain needs and require a little understanding.

In this chapter, you learn to do the following:

- Get familiar with the icons in the Graphics Group, and pare down those long titles under them

- Get familiar with the CorelDRAW icon, the *really* good module in the Group

- Arrange the groups and icons in Windows' Program Manager in a way that preserves your sanity

- Create a working directory for your Corel artwork

- Understand the **F**ile, **E**dit, and **H**elp menus

The New Icons on the Block

If you turned a deaf ear to the advice in Chapter 2 and "went for broke" while installing CorelDRAW, you'll now have an on-screen box that looks like figure 3.1 when you start Windows.

Figure 3.1

Corel Graphics Group's "window" looks more like a garage door!

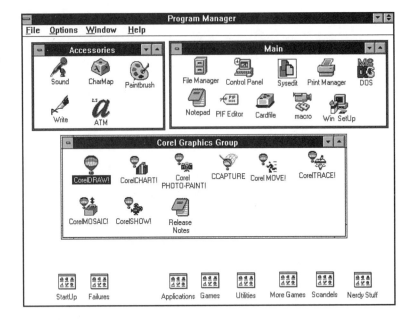

As you can see, the Corel Graphics Group is made up of nine little pictures or *icons*. Each icon represents a program you can use. Icons are supposed to be self-explanatory.

SECRET

If you remember that Corel Corporation is big on balloons, you'll always be able to find a Corel program, even if a nerd comes along and puts your CorelTRACE icon in Windows Main Group or something.

A balloon for everything

The main attraction here is CorelDRAW, represented by a simple icon of a hot-air balloon. CorelCHART is a balloon with a little bar graph, Corel PHOTO-PAINT is a balloon with a little camera. We see a thread of continuity here, right?

Tidy up your desktop

So what's the point? Simple. All those cute little icons take up a fair amount of space on your screen. With the Main window, the Accessories window, and other windows that programs create in the Program Manager, things can overlap and get crowded; your Program Manager window will soon look as cluttered as your desk. The nice thing is, if you want to make the Corel Graphics Group window a lot smaller than it is right now, you can!

If you click once on the CorelDRAW icon, you highlight, choose, or select it—whatever terminology works for you. In order to abbreviate this icon's title, follow these steps:

1. Select the CorelDRAW icon by clicking on it once.

2. From the **F**ile menu selection, select **P**roperties.

    The Program Properties dialog box enables you to specify where a program is found, which icon you'd like to display with a program, and the name Program Manager displays beneath an icon.

3. Windows highlights the description box for you. Type **DRAW!** (or anything else that's shorter than CorelDRAW), then click OK.

See? You've made the title beneath CorelDRAW's icon short enough to fit neatly beneath the icon. And you still know what the icon represents!

SECRET

If you are confident enough that you'll remember what the icons represent, you can eliminate the titles beneath icons altogether. Follow the preceding steps, but instead of typing a descriptive title in the Description box, press the space bar and click OK to make the change and close the dialog box.

Playing hide-and-seek

The truly fun part about screwing around with the icons in Windows is that you can organize your workspace so that everything is within easy reach. For example, let's say you have a group in Program Manager in which you keep your favorite stuff, like a word processor or MineSweeper. You can move the Corel icons you like best into that group's window. Then you can minimize the Corel Graphics Group so that it doesn't take up space on your screen.

Point to the CorelDRAW icon and click with your left mouse button. While holding down the left mouse button, drag the icon into the Main Group. Now release the icon.

Resizing windows

Arrange the icons in this Main Group so they're neat and you can reach them all without *scrolling* (clicking on the down arrow that sometimes appears on the right of a box when you haven't given all the icons enough room). You can resize the Main Group window by moving your pointer to the bottom of the group window and placing it on the border. The pointer turns into a two-headed arrow. By holding down on your left mouse button, you can drag the border of the window up or down.

You then can minimize the Corel Graphics Group to an icon by clicking on the Control Menu button (the little minus sign in a box that's in the upper left corner of every window in Windows), and selecting Mi<u>n</u>imize from the Menu.

Understanding That Directory Stuff

It's important to have an organized workspace on your computer. You have better things to do than play hide-and-seek with computer files. Take the time to do it now instead of later. Why? It's simple—in business, there *is* no later.

By now, you're aware from looking at the File Manager that your hard drive has a structure, with programs and files that branch out all over the place. Most of these items were created for you by installation programs; you didn't have to lift a finger for them to fit into a position where they could work harmoniously with DOS and Windows. These are called *program files* and *program directories*.

When you create a CorelDRAW drawing or a piece of work in any other program, however, you create a different sort of file, which is called a *user file*. You need to store your work in a convenient place. That place is called a *working directory*, because it's the directory you put work in, and will be working from. It's also called a user directory. Same difference, most of the time.

NERDY
NOTE

Whether they belong to a user or a program, files go in directories, sometimes called subdirectories because they branch out from a larger directory. And every one of the directories on a drive belongs to the main or root directory.

Create a working directory

To create a working directory, first think of a name for it. You need to think of something descriptive with less than eight characters, such as "Artwork." Then open the File Manager and open your hard drive directory. Do this by clicking on the little drive icon on the bar that represents your hard drive letter.

If you have two floppy drives (like with most PCs), and your hard drive is not partitioned, the drive icon will be C:. If you have a partitioned hard drive, you may choose D:, E:, or whatever. Just don't click on a floppy drive icon, like A: or B:.

Let's assume in this example that your hard drive is C:. If it's D: or E:, substitute those drive letters. To create a working directory, just follow these steps:

1. Click on the drive letter C: in the left window of the File Manager screen. It's at the top of the directory tree, and will become highlighted when you select it. If you have a long directory tree and can't see all the way to the top of the left window, use the up arrow key on your keyboard to scroll up until you can see it. Then press C: by positioning your cursor on top of it and clicking with the left mouse button.

2. From the File Manager's **F**ile menu, select Cr**e**ate Directory.

    You see the Create Directory dialog box. You should see a line that says that your `Current Directory is C:\`. That's good; that's the root.

3. In **N**ame text box, type an eight-character (or less) name for your working directory. After you type the name click on OK.

Making a path to Corel

The File Manager now has a new directory, one that you and Corel can freely access. But wait! How does Corel know where to find this directory and the subsequent files you create?

1. From the Program Manager window, select the icon that represents CorelDRAW. Click on it once. If you double-click it accidentally, you'll start CorelDRAW and Corel won't be playing with a full deck yet.

2. From the Program Manager's **F**ile menu, select **P**roperties.

3. In the Program Properties dialog box, place the cursor in the **W**orking Directory text box, and type `C:\Artwork`.

4. Click on OK and then look down at this book.

You just created a path to your working directory. When you save artwork, CorelDRAW will automatically save your file to your artwork working directory. Likewise, Corel will instantly offer this working directory up to you when you want to open a file.

NERDY NOTE

There's a nerd term for the stuff we're covering in this chapter: optimizing. There are many kinds of optimizing you can do pertaining to your PC. Memory optimization, defragmenting your hard drive... they're way too nerdy to cover in this book.

Suffice it to say that optimizing means you're making the most of your equipment, hardware, or software. If you didn't "tweak" (optimize) the Windows workspace through the Program Manager and File Manager, you'd be left with the default settings on most stuff, which is neither a nerdy nor smart way to work.

What's New on the Menu Today?

If you've worked with (or even played around with) File Manager, Paint-brush, or some of the other mini-programs that come with Windows, you may have noticed a commonality to their workspaces. One of the most obvious examples of this is the Menu bar, that doober with all the commands with one underlined letter each. The underlined letters are keyboard shortcuts you can use to choose Menu items quickly.

Shortcuts and hotkeys

In figure 3.2, we show all the goodies on the File menu. You can get to a File menu by clicking on it with your cursor, or by using a *keyboard shortcut* (also called *a hotkey* by some users). The shortcut for File is Alt and F. The under-lined letters are the ones you press on the keyboard along with the Alt key. The underlining provides us with a quick visual reference that some people actually memorize after a while.

Figure 3.2

So that's why all this stuff is underlined!

Further keyboard shortcuts within the menu are done by selecting with your cursor and pressing the underlined letter on your keyboard (without the Alt key), or by following the keyboard shortcut commands to the right of an item. Some have 'em, some don't. But there are common menu items on most Windows programs.

The common threads to the Menu bar items throughout Windows programs are the File, Edit, and Help menus. This is for a very good reason. While different programs need special Menu bar items like Font or View, there are a few basic commands that come in handy in virtually every program. The benefits are that you can learn a new program quicker when the workspaces look similar, and more importantly, you can work "between" applications. This means that you can create a drawing in Corel, then put the drawing in a file created in another program, like Microsoft Publisher.

The File Menu

The **F**ile menu is the first menu you see. The name says it all. If you want to do something with a file, select this menu. When you select this menu, you see options like **O**pen and **N**ew.

Open up

A lot of people get hung up because they think **O**pen means to open a fresh, clean file. Nope. **O**pen means to open a file you created yesterday or whenever. To open a brand-new file, you choose **N**ew.

Don't worry about being confused. If you choose **N**ew, and then change your mind and choose **O**pen, most programs ask whether you want to save the work called "Untitled?" Just say no, because you didn't do anything in this new file. You don't want to save a blank page, do you?

Saving stuff for later

The **F**ile menu generally includes the **S**ave and Save **A**s options. These options can be lifesavers sometimes.

UH-OH

Save often! It's a good practice because, well, *stuff* happens. You could have a power failure while working away on your computer, and all your work would be lost. Or small, curious fingers belonging to a five-year-old or a nerd might make their way to your machine while it's unattended. Or your system resources might be low, and it crashes. Is this the first book that has the brass to actually admit that Windows is not 100 percent stable?) You know it's true, we know it's true, and we feel better about having gotten that off our chest. Save often.

Use the Save **A**s option to create versions of a file (drawing, document, or others). Suppose that you draw a red ellipse and you save it. Now you want to draw a blue ellipse. No problem. Once you've saved that red guy, click on the ellipse in Corel to make it blue, then Save **A**s BLUEGUY.CDR. You have two versions of this file. Piece of cake.

This way out

The last menu item that Windows programs share is the E**x**it command. This is the proper way to leave, or shut down, a program in Windows. Double-clicking the Control Menu button (the little minus sign in the upper left corner of a Windows pane) does the same thing. It, too, is proper.

UH-OH

Never turn off the PC to close a program or Windows! You will harm the program directories and files, and this could ulti-mately mean having to reinstall all the program files.

If Windows ever gets "slammed shut" this way, by accident or carelessness, you may be lucky and nothing serious will happen to your program files and directories. But if you start your PC and Windows again and you get warning dialog boxes you don't understand, something's been corrupted. Terms like corrupted, cannot find file, and error are sure signs you've got a problem. If you see something that says Updating Allocation Table *in DOS when you power up your PC, you've got trouble as well.*

If any of this stuff is happening: Call a nerd you trust (it's hard, and don't call them a nerd), call the place where you bought your PC, get your MIS Director at work to come over and help, or as a last resort, call Microsoft Tech Support. The number's in your Windows manual, and they're quite helpful, but it's a long-distance, non-800 number.

The important thing is to get your PC and programs working correctly as soon as possible. Because without your knowing it, you can damage your user files, the ones you work on long and hard to create, if you shut off your PC, restart Windows, and continue to do your work with the program files that are corrupted.

The Edit Menu

This menu is always just to the right of the **F**ile menu. Three Edit menu commands are common in virtually all Windows program Edit menus: the Cu**t**, **C**opy, and **P**aste commands. These three let you move stuff around. Like if you need to write "thank you" a million times in Windows Write, you can copy the phrase and paste it back into your user file as many times as you have the patience to do.

You can also **C**opy and **P**aste between applications, like typing "thank you" in Windows Write, and pasting it into a CorelDRAW design! In figure 3.3, we see the Edit menu for Windows Write. The rest of the Edit menu items vary from program to program. We'll cover Corel's special Edit commands in Chapter 4, "Same Windows; Different Game."

For right now, let's look at Cu**t**, **C**opy, and **P**aste.

Figure 3.3

The Windows Write Edit menu.

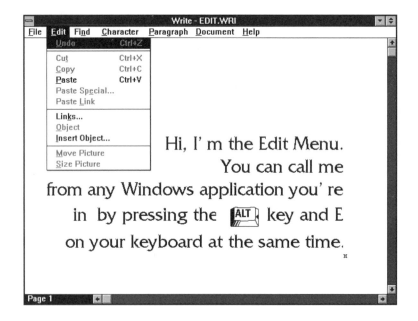

Cutting and copying

To cut a selected item in a program means to take it right off the page you're working on. No fuss, no muss, no sloppy edges. Also, no work! Where does your work go? It goes to the Windows Clipboard, an extremely mysterious utility that even most nerds don't understand.

If you cut an item out of your work, it can be pasted back by using the **P**aste command. But be careful about cutting out parts of your work.

UH-OH

What's to be so careful about? Because the Windows Clipboard is more or less a "one-seat" booth. In other words, you cannot cut a piece out of your work, then cut another piece out, and expect to be able to retrieve that first cut. The Clipboard will only hold onto the most recent (the latest) cut you make. The other ones are trashed. They went to the moon, as data go.

It is much safer to use the **C**opy command when working in Windows. By copying a piece, you've made a duplicate of your selected piece, and it too will wait on the Clipboard for you to use the **P**aste command or until you cut or copy another piece.

SECRET

In Corel, you almost never want to use the Cu**t** command, and you almost always want to use Corel's own **D**uplicate command, which doesn't send copied work to the Clipboard at all, but instead places a copy of a selected piece back into your work.

The only time you want to use the **C**opy command in Corel is to send a finished piece of artwork to the Clipboard. From there it can be pasted into a page belonging to a different program altogether.

Table 3.1 summarizes the Edit menu's main features.

Table 3.1
The Edit Menu

Option	What it does
Cu**t**	Yanks a selected piece out of your work and puts it on the Clipboard.
Copy	Duplicates a selected piece of your work and places it on the Clipboard.

continues

Table 3.1
Continued

Option	What it does
<u>P</u>aste	Reverses the functions of Cu<u>t</u> and <u>C</u>opy. It puts a copy of the cut or copied piece into a program's workspace, regardless of the program the piece was created in.

The Help Menu

Help is available on most software programs in Windows, and you can find general information about Windows itself right there. The <u>H</u>elp menu is always the rightmost menu on the Menu bar.

Getting help requires no explanation in this or any other book, because when you click on Help, one of your options is How to Use Help from the Help menu. Boy, Microsoft's got all their bases covered, huh? But let's do a qualitative analysis of the Help menu item as it relates to this book, all right?

Help with CorelDRAW

Corel's own Help item is excellent when compared to other Help lines in other programs. Corel Help is complete with little pictures to guide you through procedures, and it features a wide range of topics that relate to questions you may have when you begin working with Corel.

A special feature is the Screen/Menu Help. It is the second option down the Help menu list. If you're working in Corel, don't know about what you just did, and don't have this book or Corel's reference guides handy, click on this menu item. You'll get a pointer for your cursor with a big question mark attached, and if you click on any physical area of the workspace (including the Tool buttons), the Help file will immediately fill your screen with detailed information about what you clicked on. Sort of like an air safety bag in a car.

NERDY NOTE

The amazing mode of help just described is called context-sensitive help. It uses a graphical interface to do a hypertext search in Corel's Help files for the information on the area you selected on-screen. Hypertext is the way you can jump around in the Help box to search for key words specific to the problem you're having. To date, though, there is no **H**elp item specifically mentioning why a nerd's only friend is another nerd.

Getting help in all the right places

No **H**elp menu was designed, however, to solve all problems and answer all questions. Even as good a Help line as Corel's is limited because the **H**elp menu takes up space on your hard drive. So test out CorelDRAW's **H**elp menu when you need it, and if you don't get the specific answers you need, there are other options...

 Keep Corel's Technical Support number handy. It's a long-distance call to Canada, so be forewarned on this option.

 Keep Chapters 5 through 12 bookmarked in *CorelDRAW! for Non-Nerds*. These chapters offer the best and shortest explanations of the tools and procedures for doing cool stuff in Corel.

 Don't lose the Corel box in which you stashed all of the product manuals (yeah, we know we told you they generally weren't that great). Because at least once in everyone's lives, we are compelled to actually... gasp... read "the book."

Now I Think Icon Understand

Hopefully, we're arrived at a little understanding of how Windows uses icons, directories, and menu commands, so we can get off on the right foot when we take our first look at CorelDRAW's tools, menu items, and options in the next chapter. You'll see more of the same, and a whole lot of stuff you'd never see in Windows Write and Paintbrush!

Relax, we'll be your tour guide on this exciting, mysterious adventure. CorelDRAW obeys all the rules in the Windows world (like offering **F**ile, **E**dit, and **H**elp menus), but it's a whole new world within Windows' world!

CHAPTER 4

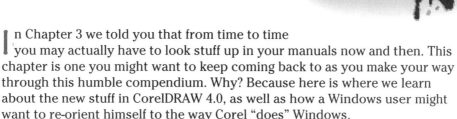

Same Windows; Different Game

In Chapter 3 we told you that from time to time
you may actually have to look stuff up in your manuals now and then. This
chapter is one you might want to keep coming back to as you make your way
through this humble compendium. Why? Because here is where we learn
about the new stuff in CorelDRAW 4.0, as well as how a Windows user might
want to re-orient himself to the way Corel "does" Windows.

In this chapter, you get a chance to do the following:

- Push almost every Tool button and menu item just to see what they do

- Set up the CorelDRAW workspace to minimize confusion and maximize productivity, and play around with more controls

- Learn which options will be of the most use to a beginner, and the ones that'll mess you up royally

Orienting and Organizing

Up to this point, you have played around with menu options that looked pretty familiar to most Windows users. Now it's time to look at the new options that CorelDRAW 4.0 has to offer. Don't worry. Although some of the options have pretty weird sounding names, soon you will be able to recite their names and uses.

Double-click on the CorelDRAW icon in the Windows Program Manager, if you aren't in CorelDRAW now. After the start-up screen appears, you'll see Corel's workspace.

SECRET

After you open Corel a few times, you will notice that the title CorelDRAW! on the start-up screen changes color every time you open the program. And every once in a while, CorelDRAW! will appear in a rainbow of colors! The official explanation from Corel Corp. is that the software developers were getting a little punchy in the wee hours before shipping Corel, and did something reminiscent of their hippie days.

CorelDRAW's main workspace has an outline of an ordinary piece of 8 1/2-inch-by-11-inch "video paper" on it. The whole scene may look unfamiliar and intimidating, but go ahead and click on the old, familiar **F**ile menu (see fig. 4.1). See? Your old familiar friends the **N**ew, **S**ave, Save **A**s, and the all-important E**x**it commands appear here just as in all Windows programs.

CorelDRAW's File menu does contain a new option. The Inser**t** Object command is for Windows' Object Linking and Embedding (OLE). By using OLE, you can put text or a drawing from another program into a Corel drawing.

SECRET

When you link or embed an object, you can update it in Corel by double-clicking on it. The program in which you created the object pops up so that you can do the editing. It's kind of spooky to double-click on something and have an entirely different program appear on your screen; therefore, unless you're really familiar with how Windows works with OLE, leave this option alone.

If you want to know more about OLE, pick up a copy of Windows for Non-Nerds, from New Riders Publishing, for an explanation humans can understand.

Figure 4.1

The drawing space, with the File menu activated.

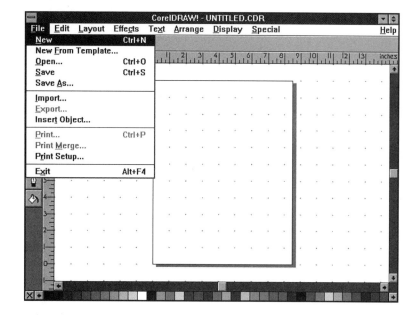

Let's Customize

What you have been looking at is CorelDRAW's default workspace. *Default* is just a nerdy word that means the way a program, such as CorelDRAW, works unless you tell it otherwise. Just as you probably set up your office workspace to suit your needs, you can set up CorelDRAW's workspace to work more like you work. When you set up a program to suit your needs, you are *customizing* the settings.

Displayin' Around

You will find quite a few customizing options on the **D**isplay menu. Each option lets you choose what you see on-screen. You can turn these options on and off. If you select an item, a checkmark appears next to the option name. If you decide you don't want to use an option, you just select the option again.

The activity of *selecting* and *deselecting* menu items from *drop-down menus* is called *toggling* because checking and unchecking the options seems like flipping a toggle switch.

SECRET

In CorelDRAW and other Windows programs, menu selections stay checked or unchecked after the menu item zips back up. In Corel, the settings you check or uncheck *remain* that way even after you close the program and open it hours, days, or weeks later. No one has satisfactorily explained, however, why you can't make more than one selection without the menu zipping back up. Wouldn't it be nice if you could set *all* the options, and then have the menu box zip up? We think it has something to do with Bill Gates' tribute to the *Macintosh* Menu Bar system. Or maybe it's sunspot activity.

Fooling with rulers

Unless you plan on creating only 8 1/2-inch-by-11-inch drawings, you may want to add some rulers to your page. You simply select the Show **R**ulers option from the **D**isplay menu. The rulers appear at the top and left sides of the screen (see fig. 4.2).

Figure 4.2

Rulers, and a few other useful tidbits.

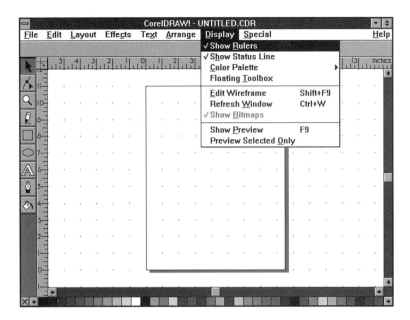

Aha! Why rulers aren't located on the Layout menu is left to better minds than ours to figure out. Before you click on Show **R**ulers, let's browse for a second.

What's the status?

Beneath Show **R**ulers is an item called S**h**ow Status Line. This is a terrific helper while you're working. It displays all the teensiest details of what you're doing on the fat gray bar directly beneath the Menu Bar. This option tells you the following details:

- Where the relative position of your cursor is (good for zeroing in on *precisely* 3.17", for example)

- What the current fill color and outline width is of the shape that you've clicked on (*selected*)

- What size and typeface you are using

- Whether you've got a nasty Snap-To command accidentally activated

The Status Bar will *not* tell you what you accidentally deleted, what time it is, who's presently in the bathroom, or when the ice cream truck is outside. Still, it's a good item to have around, so if there's no check mark next to it, click on it after we've finished snooping around.

Your pal, the palette

CorelDRAW's color palette appears at the bottom of the screen. It doesn't look like the typical artist's palette; it looks like a TV test pattern created by munchkins. It's the quick way to choose colors to fill in the shapes you draw in Corel. You already have a perfectly adequate default color palette, so there's not much sense in exploring other palettes when you haven't used the one you've got; but now you know where to go to change it.

Go where you want to go

Next, it's the amazing Floating **T**oolbox! You can detach the tools (those symbols on the far left of your workspace) so you can move the whole strip any place you want on top of your workspace. My advice at this point is to leave this one unchecked. Why? Because where else do you want to put them? Again, it's there when you need it.

Wire we all here?

The **E**dit Wireframe option is an important option to remember. This option turns everything you draw into a *wireframe*, which is an outline-only view of what you've drawn. You can even fool nerds sometimes who have never seen Corel by clicking on this option. They'll ask what you're doing, and you tell them, "Oh, another CAD drawing in AutoCAD 12." They'll walk away impressed.

Working in the Wireframe mode has a number of advantages:

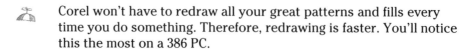 Corel won't have to redraw all your great patterns and fills every time you do something. Therefore, redrawing is faster. You'll notice this the most on a 386 PC.

In Wireframe mode, you can select and move shapes you've drawn that have been hidden behind other shapes much easier than if you work in Preview mode.

If you draw a shape that's white with no outline, there's almost no way to *find* the thing on a white background. If you activate Wireframe mode, you can always see the shape.

Of course, Wireframe mode does have its disadvantages. They include:

You have no real artist's eye as to the color composition of your drawing.

Shapes are harder to select; you must click *exactly* on their outline. They have *no fill* in the Wireframe view to click on, see?

You may experience some visual fatigue, which can lead to faintness, dizzy spells, and the desire to operate heavy machinery. The boss will send you home sick. Maybe this isn't such a disadvantage after all.

Corel's installation default is the Preview mode, so don't sweat any decision-making for the moment.

No bitmaps like show bitmaps

Show **B**itmaps is yet another option you can set. It lets you import bitmaps into Corel. Clear now? Actually, one of Corel's powers as a design tool is that although it's a vector design program, it can have bitmap (paint-type) art co-existing within a design. It's pretty useful.

NERDY
NOTE

Let's say you wanted to draw a frame around a bitmap of the Mona Lisa, for example. Corel gives you the option of turning the bitmap on or off because bitmaps take a really long time to redraw themselves in Corel (or anywhere else, for that matter). When we go moving around the workplace screen later, you'll appreciate the advice. If you uncheck, or *deselect*, this item, when we get around to importing stuff, all that will show of your bitmap will be an empty frame indicating the position of the bitmap.

Preview

The last two items, Show **P**review, and Preview Selected **O**nly, are variations on a theme. Choose Preview Selected **O**nly, and when you go to a full-screen preview (the Show **P**review option), only the item or items you've selected with your cursor appear. Sounds stupid, right? Not at all. If you've got a large, complicated design, and you only want to see if one little piece is drawn or colored right, you can save redraw time.

Show **P**review clears the screen of everything except your work. It's a nice way to show off your work. To get back to the menu list you just wiped off the screen, click your right mouse button. See? You *do* actually use the right mouse button in life!

Select the Show **R**ulers and S**h**ow Status Line options for now, and let's explore the *next* menu box.

A Special Place

Again, some items on the **S**pecial menu would make more sense if they were located in a different place, but then again, Canadians drive with their headlights on in the daytime, so go figure. You will use some of the options on this menu extensively; others not at all (see fig. 4.3).

You will never use **C**reate Pattern in this book and maybe not in your *life*. It makes a pattern out of a Corel drawing you've created. You then can fill a shape you've created with this pattern. I understand this was used extensively in Mayan textile manufacturing eons ago.

Figure 4.3

The Box next
door...

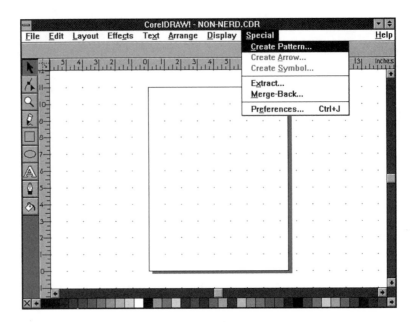

The Create **A**rrow and Create **S**ymbol options are only available if you have
a shape already drawn on the workspace. They allow you to add your own
arrowheads and symbols to the collection CorelDRAW ships with. Frankly,
Corel has installed a spectacular collection on your PC, so unless you have
a specialized need in your company to be able to draw a line with a custom
arrowhead, or you constantly need to use the same custom symbol all the
time, forget these options.

E**x**tract is an advanced function that allows a designer to make big-time
revisions to the text in a Corel drawing. If you have a massive paragraph or
something in a page layout, you click on this option, one or two dialog boxes
pop up, and then Corel exports the text into a .TXT file, where you can do
your editing.

Merge Back is the opposite of the E**x**tract command. Use it when you want to
put the edited text back into your design.

Moving right along to the real reason you opened the **S**pecial menu, there is
indeed something special. And a little confusing. And you'd better get used
to it, because this happens a lot in Corel...

Future Preference Reference

If you select the Preferences option, a series of dialog boxes branches out. On the surface, you have a few boxes in which you enter values and others whose little blue diamonds you can click on. You can change certain options and defaults here.

On the right side in figure 4.4, you see buttons whose comments end in *ellipses* (those three dots after a word that suggest a thought is to be continued elsewhere). Think of those Chinese boxes that had boxes inside of boxes inside of boxes. Same theory with some of Corel's special options. Fortunately, you only have to dig really deep through options once to set them.

Figure 4.4

The door that opens many doors.

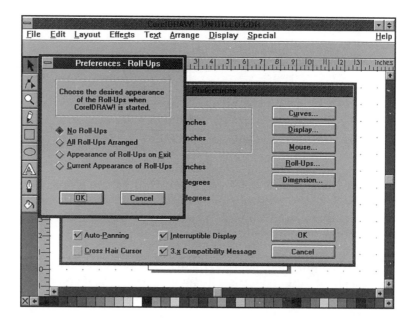

NERDY
NOTE

The author is referring to a feature in Windows known as *hierarchical nesting*. In order to make more options accessible from one main window, Corel's programmers put the most valuable options in a *menu nest*. Meaning that to get to an option that is nested deeply, the user clicks an option, then a second, and a third to reveal a cascade of sub-menu boxes. To return to the main screen, the user clicks on OK after making a selection in the last box, then the previous one, and so on. It helps to leave a trail of bread crumbs along the path to find your way back.

The Place Duplicate options enable you to duplicate any shape you design in Corel. The default setting places duplicates +.25" on the vertical axis and +.25" on the horizontal axis. In English, this means that duplicates appear slightly to the right and up from your original. Chapter 6 explains this option in more detail.

By setting the Duplicate coordinates to a "0" value, you place the duplicate directly on top of the original. Corel's default settings make it easy for users to spot where their duplicate landed on their workspace. That's true. But there are also some exceptionally neat things you can do, design-wise, with a duplicate sitting exactly on top of the original.

PROFOUND
REALIZATION

Suppose that you draw a square. If you duplicate it, then rotate it 45 degrees *directly on top of the first*, you have a star. Other examples abound, but you get the point.

Don't worry. We're going to screw around with the next option so you won't have to worry about finding the original beneath duplicates.

The Nudge option is a terrific *tool*, even though it only seems like an option. The default setting when you installed Corel is set at .10". Let's change this by typing `0.008"`. Wow! You mean Corel can measure stuff in thousandths of inches??! But that's not the point.

You'll notice that, next to all the boxes you just changed, are the measurements of these numerical items in increments. If you need to do work in picas, or centimeters, you can make the changes here. I recommend you keep to the English rule of inches because all the references in this book are in inches.

Hopping across the border

Beneath the Duplicate and Nudge boxes are four diamond-studded buttons. Auto-<u>P</u>anning is set to be on. What is auto-panning? It's when Siskel and Ebert immediately dislike a movie. Only kidding. Auto-panning means that the workspace frame in Corel tracks along with you when you're using the cursor to draw a line.

That means you can draw right off the page border and keep on moving. This feature separates Corel from many other programs; you're not locked into a page dimension when you're designing. This is important to know. You can use the page borders that Corel installed as a default (8 1/2 inches by 11 inches), work outside of them, and place stuff outside the border (of course, they won't *print* if you do, because your printer's generally set up for 8 1/2 by 11 inches). Auto-panning will always keep you in the center of things. Even if you colored outside the lines as a kid.

Turn Auto-panning off, and the next time you want to draw clear to the right, right outside of your monitor almost, you'll be stopped cold. Then you'll have to use the Windows scroll bars to access that region. Listen to me: Leave Auto-**P**anning on, and save yourself a future headache.

Nothing but interruptions

By default, the **I**nterruptible Display is turned on. Leave it that way. When you work in Preview mode, Corel redraws the page every time you add something new to it. It's a hassle trying to see what you're doing, and this interrupts your work. The **I**nterruptible Display feature turns the tables and makes Corel wait to redraw the display every time you add something.

The fine points of pointing

The **C**ross Hair Cursor default is off, and for a pretty good reason, too. This option turns your cursor into a large "+" sign all the time. This option adds precision to your designmanship, according to Corel's reference manual. If you ever get bored sometime and want to try it out, fine. But my experience, as a designer *and* as a human being, is that this option will drive you up the wall and push you over the edge. Leave it *off*, please.

Backward compatibility and stuff

The 3.**x** Compatibility Message option should be on. It flashes a warning on your screen when an owner of Corel version 4.0 tries to open a drawing done by someone in Corel 3.0A, 3.0B, or 3.01BA. The messages usually pertain to little things, such as that version 4.0 can't find the typeface used in a version 3.0 drawing. If you have a bunch of people in your office using Corel, and you're the only one with this latest version, remember two things:

Drawings from a previous version may not always read correctly.

 Someone using version 3.0 to read your 4.0 drawings is going to have a real tough time. In other words, leave the message option on, and don't mix files with different software versions.

Now that we've goofed around with all the options on this level of nests, let's get to the really fun (and necessary) preferences that we started this whole exercise for. Let's break away from convention, because we're *artists* at heart, and not start from the top down. Let's choose the Mouse... nest.

The Power of the Right Button

You ever notice that this book dwells on left-mouse-button commands? And we never get around to the *right* ones? If you're like most people, your mouse has a left and a right button. And you may be wondering *why* it has two buttons.

If you or your systems administrator have done any cruising around the Windows Program Manager and opened the Mouse icon from the Control Panel icon, you know that you can set the mouse so that the right button does all the fancy selecting. This is a good feature for left-handed people. They can choose to use the right mouse button so that they don't need to do any more awkward adapting than they already have to. But what else is the right mouse button good for?

When you choose **M**ouse, you see a second box of preferences. For the Mouse option, this is the *bottom* nest. Lot of confusing options, huh?

Let's pick a simple one, like assigning the **F**ull screen preview to the right mouse button (see fig. 4.5). Why not? It's a lot less complicated than clicking on the **D**isplay menu bar every time you want to preview something. And a second click on the right mouse button brings you back to the familiar workspace. As time goes by, you may want to assign your right mouse button to a different function, but for now, click on OK.

Rolling along

If you're beginning to get the hang of this nesting concept, you're going to love Corel's **R**oll-Ups feature. Directly beneath the **M**ouse button is **R**oll-Ups (see fig. 4.6). What is a roll-up? A fruit snack made out crushed apricots wrapped in cellophane? An alternate exercise to push-ups? Nooooo. Click on the **R**oll-Ups button while I explain.

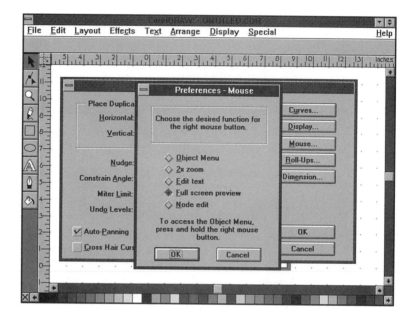

Figure 4.5

Where you set your mouse preferences.

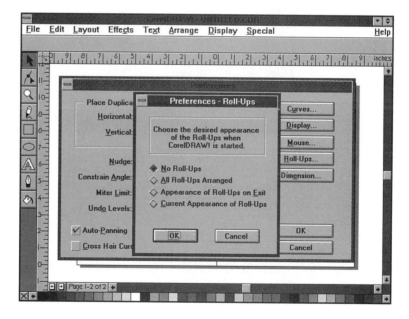

Figure 4.6

The Roll-Ups menu.

Roll-ups are a program invention unique to Corel. You won't find this feature in any other program. There are a number of Menu Bar and Toolbox items that you can modify as you draw in the Corel workspace.

In figure 4.7, we've clicked on a button nested beneath a button in Corel's Toolbox to call up an example of a roll-up menu. They look kind of like regular menus, with one important difference. Once you call one up, they *stay* on your workspace until you do one of two things:

   You click on the top left Menu Command button to close it.

   You click on the top right arrow button to make it *roll up*!

Figure 4.7

An example of a
roll-up menu.

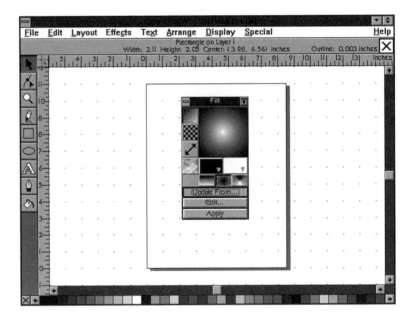

Roll-ups are designed to take up very little space when they aren't in use. They roll up to a tiny size and you may comfortably get five or so of them going in their retracted position during a work session. You'll find it helpful to have these Menus-That-Don't-Zip-Up-Until-I-Want-Them-To next to your cursor for quickly modifying your work.

But to have them *all* automatically displayed when you start up CorelDRAW is a little overkill, no? I suggest you leave this option unchecked, and just call the roll-ups when you need them.

Working completely out of order, next click on the **D**isplay button.

The options in this dialog box refer to your monitor's *behavior*, rather than the **D**isplay menu command, which refers to what's *shown* on your monitor. Clear as mud, right?

Displaying Fountain Fills and other stuff

Anyhow, you have the option to set Preview **F**ountain Stripes at a certain frequency (see fig. 4.8). By default, Corel sets this with a value of 20. I suggest you leave it that way. Why? Because Fountain Stripes are a special sort of fill we can apply to shapes, which we'll talk about later.

Figure 4.8

The Display preferences dialog box.

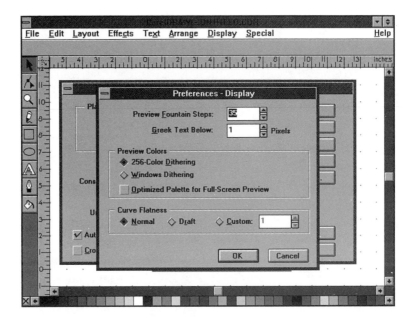

Basically, Fountain Stripes are a wonderful shaded fill that will make your work look more dimensional. And the frequency of Fountain Stripes means how much "banding" Corel tells your monitor to display when creating a picture of Fountain Fills in a drawing.

NERDY
NOTE

Banding is the term used to describe an effect seen on-screen that simulates a continuous tone, like from black to white. If you squint real hard, you'll imagine that the colors' fade from one color to another is continuous. But it's not. It's actually little narrow bands of color that successively make a transition from the first color to the last.

A value of 20 in the frequency range usually gives you a pretty good idea of how a fill is going to print, when we eventually get around to printing pieces in Corel. By setting the value to a high frequency (like 120), you achieve glorious fills, with almost no detectable banding, and your screen redraws will take half an hour to finish. So let's leave the Fountain Fills menu item alone.

Corel handles the Greek tragedy

The **G**reek Text Below option doesn't mean that your text in Corel will turn into fraternity letter gibberish. It's another option to help noticeably speed up your work.

NERDY
NOTE

Greeking is a typographer's term for faking a long block of body text. You get lines where all the characters in the text should be, giving you an idea of how much or how wide a text block is.

You can't actually *read* greeking, but that's okay. Greeking saves Corel screen time. And Corel wants to know at what point the Greeking option should take over. The default is set at nine pixels. A pixel is *really* small. And nine is a good number. But if you feel the need to change it, make it a larger number, not a smaller one.

Working with the "Big" box of crayons

Now, the Preview Colors option is a good one. One of the first pleasures you'll discover when working in Corel is that it supports more than a handful of colors. If you've ever played around with Windows Paintbrush, you've noticed that its palette is fairly limited. To be exact, it's limited to 16 pure colors.

NERDY NOTE

Monitors and monitor cards are capable of showing up to 16 million colors these days. Unfortunately, most software programs don't take advantage of this nicety. Unlike Corel, what they do is *dither* the 16 pure colors. Dithering means to display an in-between shade of two of the 16 pure colors.

The programs put two different colors every other pixel to approximate that color. It's as hard on your eyes as the roughly screened photos you find in newspapers. The 256 pure colors Corel can show is a much more natural way of viewing your designs. Nerds like 16 dithered colors because it makes their work look like a comic book.

Usually, Corel's installation program finds information on your PC system that tells whether you have a monitor (and a monitor card) that supports a number of colors greater than the basic 16, and installs Corel with the 256-Color **D**ithering box checked. The box beneath it, **W**indows Dithering, refers to the aforementioned 16 color dithering.

The **O**ptimized Palette for Full-Screen Preview button is good for showing pure colors in the Preview mode, but makes Fountain Fills look "banded" and will throw you off if you think it will print that way. So leave this button unchecked for now.

Don't touch the Curve Flatness controls. This was set by Corel's installation program to simulate the best vector curves on your screen when you draw them. Just click on OK now, and let's move on.

Don't touch the C**u**rves button on the main Preferences dialog box either. Rocket scientists and nerds alike can't figure out the nested menu behind this button. So we won't try, either.

A dimension of time, and of space

Click on the Dim**e**nsions button and the screen shown in figure 4.9 appears. Dimension lines are useful features in Corel if you're doing mapping or technical charting. We'll see the buttons you select them with in the next section about the Toolbox.

Dimension lines are drawn to encompass a drawing of a gear or map that you've already done. They have little draftsperson's numerical values attached to them, like *3"* or *20mm*. And when you change the size of your gear or map, the Dimension lines change their values along with the drawing. So after making your drawing, say, twice as big, the numerical values in the corner of the Dimension lines will read *6"* or *40mm*. It's highly technical stuff. But this is a *non*-technical book, so let's leave the Dim**e**nsions box checked on **G**eneral, and dig our way back to the main Preferences menu.

Figure 4.9

The two nests behind the Dim**e**nsions button.

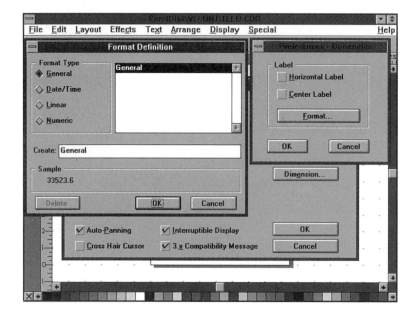

You've done about all the customizing you need to from the Preferences sub-menu, so click on OK. You're on your way to the last stop on our guided tour of Corel's menu settings.

Laying It All Out

The only other truly inspired menu left to explore is the **L**ayout menu. In figure 4.10, you see that you have the means to insert a page, delete a page, and go to a different page. The **P**age Setup option is used to change the page border on your workspace to something other that 8 1/2 by 11 inches, which is the CorelDRAW default upon installation. Let's not fuss with the Page Setup, because when it's time to print your first masterpiece, it'll most likely be to a laser printer full of 8 1/2-by-11-inch sheets of paper.

Figure 4.10

The only inspired
menu left to
explore.

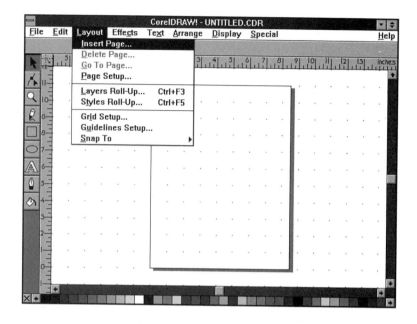

**PROFOUND
REALIZATION**

CorelDRAW version 4.0 is a *multi-document* design program.
Unlike a lot of other drawing and painting programs, you can
actually do *desktop publishing* with Corel. That means words
and graphics on one or several pages. So you can do the one-
page flyer for the company Bake Sale, or a four-page newsletter for them with a headline about how the company Bake Sale
lost money. And you can thumb through a multipage document
with a control box that appears on the bottom left of the
screen when you have more than one page in your Corel
document defined.

Unless you're really pressed to get a multipage brochure out right now, we'll
breeze past these options. One page at a time, okay?

The **L**ayers Roll-Up and St**y**les Roll-up are exactly the kind of roll-ups I was
discussing earlier. If you click on either of these options, you get a roll-up
specific to a Layers or Styles option very similar to figure 4.7 in its construction. But without actually clicking on these options, let's talk for a moment
about what layers and styles are.

CorelDRAW is capable of creating several levels on one particular design space. They call them *layers*. They start with Layer 1, and as you add them by using the <u>L</u>ayers Roll-Up menu, you'll find you can hide, lock, and even stack individual layers in different order, from top to bottom. This is useful when you've drawn a map of something, and spent four hours on it.

If you lock that layer, you can't mess it up or work on it, which means you have to get a *Layer 2* going. If this map is meant to show directions to a party, you'd leave Layer 1 locked and alone, and put the address of the party on Layer 2. When Chip calls and says the party's been moved across the street, no problem. Without futzing with your four-hour long map, you simply move the address text box on Layer 2.

There are plenty of other uses you'll find for the Layers option in Corel. I just like parties.

The S<u>ty</u>les Roll-Up gives you access to a handy resource for laying out standardized pages, or for repeating complex designs that you've given a style to. This S<u>ty</u>les Roll-Up looks a lot like something you'd find in a desktop publishing program.

PROFOUND
REALIZATION

The author has referenced the term "desktop publishing" about three times in this chapter without a trace of an adequate definition of the term. *Desktop publishing* means the compiling of a newsletter, report, or magazine from one's desktop computer. This sort of stuff can really be done these days. In fact, many of the same software programs that you can buy in a store are used by big publishers like Prentice Hall and Ziff-Davis daily. Although Corel probably wouldn't be your first choice for designing a 400-page book, it nonetheless has the features and tools required to excel at desktop publishing.

You need blocks of text arranged so they're justified. That means the sentences in a paragraph are aligned to the left (flush left justified), right (flush right justified), or fully (neat blocks of text with no "raggy" edges on a column). Corel has the means to justify blocks of text, and the S<u>ty</u>les Roll-Up gives you the means to save a particular combination of text justification, typeface, size of typeface, and graphics placement within the confines of a page layout you're happy with. But let's save the dreams of becoming a desktop publisher until we have the basics of designing in Corel down first, okay?

The next grouping of menu options under **L**ayout pertain to CorelDRAW's *guidelines* properties. In real life, you may use a hard-edge tool or a ruler to draw a straight line that's perfectly parallel to your 8 1/2-by-11-inch page. You can do this with Corel, as well, by accessing two things:

 The G**u**idelines Setup

 The **S**nap To option

Forget about the G**u**idelines Setup for the moment. This only tells you how to orient your page, like you'll call the upper left of your page border *0*", and work your way across and down numerically. The default that Corel installed is just fine, it makes sense, and life with a PC is confusing enough. If you go to the **S**nap To option and click on Guidelines, every guideline you pull out will become *sticky*, and a shape you move close enough to the guideline will "snap to" it. A very useful feature. *So* useful, in fact, we're going to break with all this exploring to try this out. Check the Guidelines in the **S**nap To options, the **L**ayout menu will zip up, and we are ready to try a little experiment.

Figure 4.11 is an artist's depiction of getting a guideline out of the ruler. The three "speed lines" are there to indicate motion. Although you'll experience the feeling of speed when dragging out a guideline, the three "speed lines" are fictitious and you won't get them on your screen unless your PC has been doing drugs.

We place our first guideline by following these three steps:

1. Place the arrow-shaped cursor in the center of the up and down ruler. By center, I mean the *width* of the ruler, not at 5 1/2 inches.

2. *Click and drag* by holding down on your left mouse button, and pull something *you essentially can't see* to the right onto your page border.

3. Release your left mouse button within the page border.

Now while you were moving the invisible *I-Don't-See-What* to the right, an interesting phenomenon appeared: a light blue dotted line. That is the guideline. And the same thing will happen if you repeat the procedure with the top-across ruler, to get what technical experts call a horizontal guideline. And you can keep doing this until your page is hopelessly littered with these guys, or until Corel pops up a warning that the limit to guidelines on-screen is 40 or something.

Figure 4.11

Dragging a
guideline out
of the ruler.

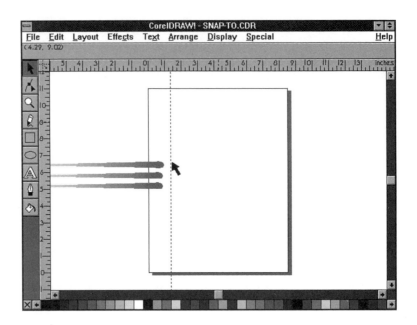

When you want to get rid of a guideline, you just put it back where it came from. Guidelines and grids (which we'll get to shortly) do not print when you go to print your artwork, so it's up to you whether you leave them on the workspace. And they go away completely when you open a new file.

SECRET

Light blue lines, like the guidelines in this section, are a throwback to the days of designing on drafting tables, when designers would use a non-repro pen or pencil to do rough sketches. These lines didn't need to be erased before printing the design, because although faintly visible to the human eye, the camera wouldn't pick them up to reproduce. Hence the name Non-Repro Blue. These pens and pencils are still available in art stores for around three bucks apiece. I still own a collection of them that I'd be willing to sell to you if you're interested.

Tools for Thought

Since we're basically done with setting the defaults on the Menu Bar, let's take a whack at one of the tool buttons to see how we can test our new-found guideline.

1. First, pick the tool shaped like a box. This is called the Rectangle tool. When you click on it, it depresses and turns a darker shade so you know which tool you're using. Also notice that on your new Status Bar, it should say Rectangle on Layer 1—because you haven't added any Layer other than the one you're beginning with. Rectangles are cool because they're simple and business people use them a lot. Sort of "cause and effect," if you catch my drift.

2. Move your cursor over to the workspace, inside the page border, and away from the **S**nap-To guideline. The cursor should now look like a crosshair.

3. Following another one of the fake "speed lines" you won't actually *see* when you perform this maneuver, make a downward-and-to-the-right motion with your mouse while you're holding down on the left mouse button, like we've dramatized in figure 4.12.

Figure 4.12

Drawing a
rectangle.
What else?

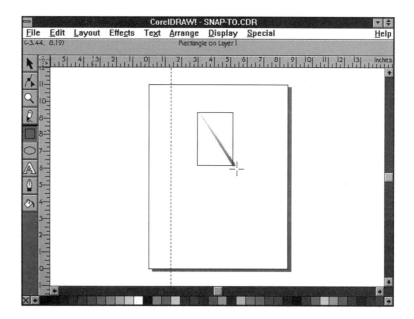

4. Release the mouse button. You now have a rectangle. You now also have a cursor that is free to roam about without creating further rectangles, as long as you don't click and drag with the left mouse button.

Now since we are working in the Preview mode of Corel, it's far easier and lazier to select this new rectangle if there's a Fill inside of it. As we mentioned earlier, you can only select a shape you've drawn by clicking on part of it.

Let's deselect the rectangle tool by going over and clicking on the Pick tool. It's called a Pick tool because you *pick* things with it. Remember that shapes remain selected after being drawn, so you're in luck that the rectangle is still selected after clicking on the Pick tool. Go down to your color palette.

Let's select a color to fill our rectangle that will be easy for us to understand in this black-and-white book, like a 50-percent gray, as shown in figure 4.13. It's okay if you screw up and pick 40 percent or 60 percent because they're not labeled, and this is only a test run. In time, you'll be able to spot the shades of gray by eye. Also, you'll notice that the right corner of the Status Bar shows what color and outline the rectangle now has.

Figure 4.13

Going to the
color palette.

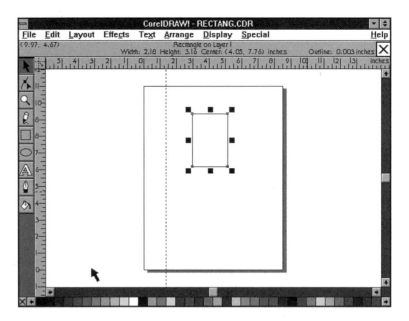

The rectangle will be easy to select and deselect. Try clicking outside of the rectangle's border. The eight little black boxes disappear and the Status Bar shows you nothing is selected, right? Try clicking on the gray rectangle again, and the black boxes and Status Bar come alive. Good.

Move the selected rectangle toward the guideline using your Pick tool cursor. Slowly, slowly. When you get close to the guideline, what happens? There's some sort of weird magnetic attraction! The rectangle gets bolted to the guideline, and it resists your moving it away, until you forcibly jerk the thing free (see fig. 4.14).

Figure 4.14

The darn thing won't come loose!!!

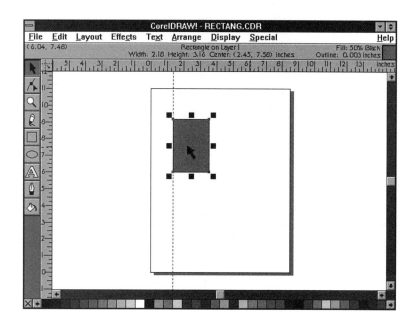

This is the way guidelines work. You will think of many useful ways to get your drawings precise in their alignments and measurements in the future.

Snap-To it

The **Sn**ap-To options extend far beyond working with guidelines. If we go back to the **L**ayout menu item, and check out the Gri**d** Setup option, we see a lot of superfluous nonsense like **G**lobal Units, and so on. All we really want to do is to show the grid, and have stuff *snap to* it.

So check these boxes, go down again to the S**n**ap To Grid box and deselect the Guidelines option we selected earlier. We want to get the full effect of the grid and its stickiness.

Figure 4.15

The Grid nest.

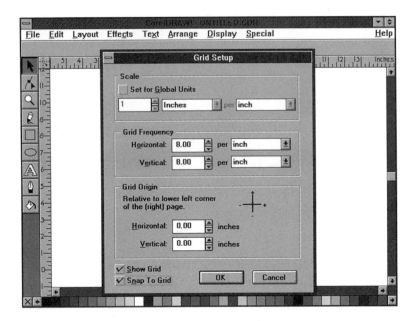

Figure 4.16

The grid on your workspace.

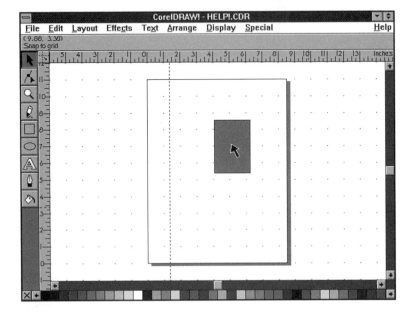

Now try moving the rectangle around. It's hard, right? The rectangle is moving around like you've shifted into the wrong gear! Actually, there's a positive, non-annoying purpose for the snap-to grid. That is that the grid is aligning the rectangle to precise, 1/8-inch increments all over your workspace. If you ever need to align stuff in a very professional, draftsperson-like fashion, these are the options to choose. If you're like most of us, however, leave the snapping grid turned off, as well as the guidelines.

The last item we'll skim over before taking a break from this epic chapter is the Snap-To Object option. Now I know that we've been calling this rectangle a *shape*, but Corel refers to it as an *object*, and they'll use the term frequently throughout roll-ups and menu options. Let's let a nerd elaborate on this distinction, shall we?

NERDY NOTE

The nature of designing in Corel is called many things, besides confusing. Corel basically is a vector drawing program, which translates out to non-nerds as a precise program that delivers sharp designs with no "stairsteppy" outlines. Corel is also called an *object-oriented* drawing program, because you can draw discreet objects, open or filled in, that can be moved around independent of each other.

Unlike a *bitmap* or paint-type program like CorelPHOTO-PAINT, CorelDRAW doesn't take every pen stroke and lock it into the background, where it's nearly impossible to move around ever again. So, object-oriented programs give you the freedom to move individual objects you create around. Corel is also called a *resolution-independent* drawing program; all three of the terms are correct when describing a program such as Corel.

If we were to draw another rectangle, as shown in figure 4.17, by following our steps for drawing the first rectangle, and coloring it in so it's easy to select, we can precisely align the two boxes merely by moving one into proximity to the other.

The Snap-To feature seeks out node points (we'll talk about this one later) on the rectangles and will snap to any of the four located on the rectangles' corners. Neat, huh? Now you can draw a checkerboard if anyone asks you to.

In our next episode...

Finally, now that you have two rectangles you could care less about on your screen, you want to close. Corel will always ask you if you want to save "Untitled?" You could say no. But if you do this one simple thing, Corel will close without a peep. Put your cursor on a rectangle and select it. Now, press the Delete key on your keyboard. Poof! Do it again, and you've got an empty workspace (guidelines don't count). You can exit Corel as if you never worked on anything! There is a Delete command in the **E**dit menu options, but why ever bother when you can trash stuff you don't want with one little keystroke?

Figure 4.17

A new object in town.

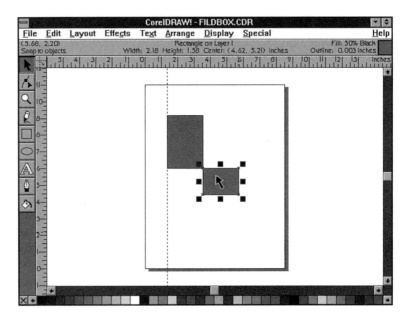

This concludes the section on setting your defaults to be a more productive designer. We've managed to cover a lot of ground so far, and we're almost ready to explore some of the neat tools we can use to create shapes. I think we've earned a well-deserved break at this point, so get up and stretch, be sure to visit our concession stand for your favorite refreshment, and curtain call for the second act is in ten minutes. Put your coat over your chair to save it in case you're getting up now.

Tooling through Corel

Glad to have you back! In this section, we'll examine the tools in the Toolbox that we haven't peeked at already.

Getting a scope on your workspace

As we look at figure 4.18, we see the Zoom tool flying out to reveal other little buttons. What is the Zoom tool? How did you do that? What do these other symbols mean? Can Pee-Wee Herman *actually* be classified as an "entertainer"?

The answer to these questions are:

1. The Zoom tool is Corel's name for a magnification/demagnification tool. That's why there's a little magnifying glass icon there to represent it. You can zoom in on stuff, zoom out on stuff, and return to your original position with the Zoom tool.

Figure 4.18

The Zoom tool in its flyout position.

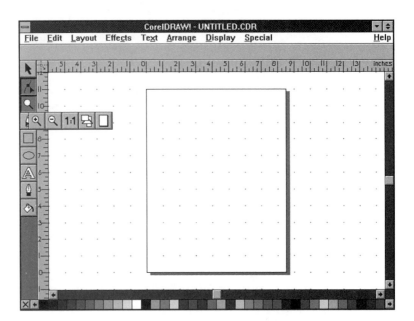

2. To access all of the Zoom tools, you click on the Zoom tool button. There are other tools on the Toolbox that do the same thing. They offer you different options, so when you look at these nine tool buttons, they actually represent about 30 different options.

3. From left to right:

    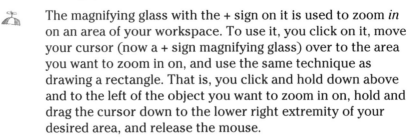

    The magnifying glass with the + sign on it is used to zoom *in* on an area of your workspace. To use it, you click on it, move your cursor (now a + sign magnifying glass) over to the area you want to zoom in on, and use the same technique as drawing a rectangle. That is, you click and hold down above and to the left of the object you want to zoom in on, hold and drag the cursor down to the lower right extremity of your desired area, and release the mouse.

    The magnifying glass with the minus sign is the demagnifying tool, which will zoom you *out* to the position of your workspace before you zoomed in. No fancy mouse moves; just click it and you're popped back out.

    The third symbol, **1:1**, means a one-to-one view of your workspace, where an inch is represented by an inch on the screen. It's useful to get an idea of the size of things before you print.

The fourth symbol is a very oblique one. This is the Include All Zoom View. You will zoom in to include everything you've drawn on your workspace. So if you have only one rectangle drawn, it'll zoom in to fill your screen!

The last Zoom tool is the Page View, which returns all your zooming around to the view setting when you first opened CorelDRAW.

Oh, yes. About that last question we brought up concerning Pee-Wee:

4.   No comment.

Drawing the line somewhere

The most important design tool in Corel is the picture of the pencil. This is the Line Draw tool, and it's used to draw both lines and shapes. "So what's the diff' between lines and shapes?" I can almost hear you asking.

A line, or series of connected lines, can go all over the place and still not form a closed shape. This is important to know, because a lot of new users don't understand why they draw something resembling a *shape*, and can't fill it with color from the color palette. A *closed shape ends where it begins* and you can fill it. Like the rectangle we drew earlier.

To draw a line or series of connected lines is a no-brainer. You take out the Line Draw tool and put the crosshair-shaped cursor on your workspace. Click once to begin a line, click a second time to end it.

Now, there's a technique you can use to create *connected line segments*, and ultimately, a closed, irregular shape that you can color in. First, you start your line with a click. But when you're ready to end the line, don't click a second time. Instead, double-click the left mouse button. What this does is finish a line segment and begin a new one on the same pinpoint, so the lines are connected. Try the following dance steps in figure 4.19.

By clicking once at the beginning point, double-clicking every time you change a direction, then clicking once to stop with this crazy line, you may now have a shape similar, and hopefully more interesting than, figure 4.18. But it's not a *closed* shape, so you can't fill it in. It's considered a line, or an outline. To make a shape you can fill out of it, do this:

1. The connected line segments are still connected, and you still have the crosshair cursor on the screen. Go up to the Zoom tool and click on it to fly out the other icons.

2. Select the Includes All Zoom View button. Your screen will zoom in to a point where you can see the beginning and end of the shape more clearly. Notice how on the far corner of the Status Bar, it says Open Path, with an "X" marked inside the box. This reaffirms our suspicion that this is not a closed shape. In figure 4.20, you'll see a destination route to closing this path.

Figure 4.19

Creating an irregular shape.

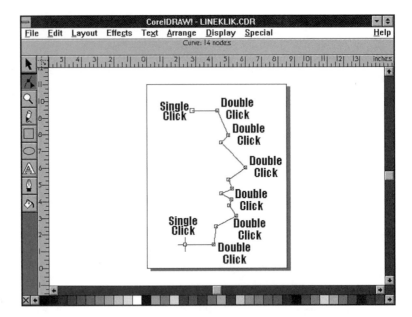

3. Click once on the beginning node (the little box between line segments) with your crosshair cursor, then move to the last node, and click once.

4. You're done! The little box on the Status Bar says there's no fill with the "X" still there, but the Open Path comment is gone. You now can go down to the color palette and choose a fill for this irregular shape, like in figure 4.21.

Figure 4.20

Connecting the dots.

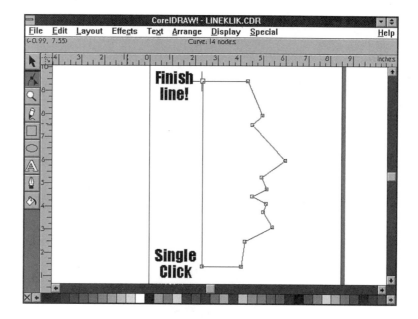

Figure 4.21

Looks like one of those Easter Island statues or something.

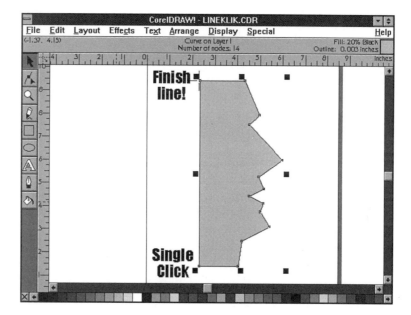

The Line goes on and on

Like the Zoom tool, the Line Draw tool has several buttons hiding behind it. But in order to access these, you have to click and hold down on the Line Draw tool. I recommend against it: it'll slow you down in learning the essence of CorelDRAW. But we'll list what the other Line Draw options are, to satisfy the terminally curious.

 The second tool from the left is the Bezier Line tool. This tool creates curved lines everywhere you double-click. It's an entirely different method of drawing than the straight Line Draw tool. That's why Corel keeps it hidden, I think. It's frustrating to use, and very few budding graphic designers will want to learn to use it, because this Bezier tool will turn them into *cranky old* graphic designers in the process. Turning all your straight lines into curves in a drawing is simple; you don't need a Bezier Line tool to do it, and we'll talk about curves in Chapter 5.

 The next three tools are Dimension lines that we went over in the first section of this chapter. They have nothing to do with drawing a line or shape *per se*, but of *measuring* lines and shapes. So let's go back to the Line Draw tool we started with, and our connected line/ filled drawing.

So what happens if you now want to change the direction of one of these connected line segments without wrecking anything else?

An ode to nodes

One of the most incomprehensible tools in Corel is the Shape tool. Most people call it the *Node Edit* tool. It's the tool between the Pick tool and the Zoom tool. And what it does is change certain properties of nodes that are in your objects. *It edits nodes.* So why is it called the Shape tool? Because by editing nodes, you're changing the shape of objects.

A node is not something Stevie Nicks gets on her vocal chords regularly. At least not in CorelDRAW. A node is a "joint" between two line segments in a shape. The drawing in figure 4.21 has 14 nodes, because we changed direction 14 times, and because it says so on the Status Bar when the shape is selected. When we were Snapping To the rectangles earlier, the snap-to points on the rectangles were their *nodes*.

To move a node within a shapes, select the Shape tool, and move it onto your drawing. We'll continue on our Easter Island Guy in figure 4.22. The Shape tool should turn the cursor into a boomerang-y sort of cursor.

Figure 4.22

Easter Island
Guy gets a
facelift.

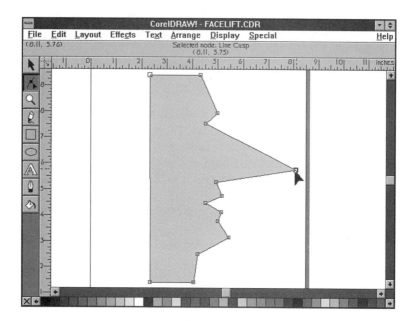

See? By pulling on a single node, we can alter the length and direction of the node and the two connecting line segments! Consider the possibilities.

The Shape tool works differently according to what shape you're trying to alter. Text shapes (which we will cover in Chapter 8) don't change at all with the Shape tool. Rectangles and ellipses cannot be turned into irregular shapes by doing what we've just done, either. But you should have a basic understanding now of how you work with the Shape tool, and remember that it only *edits nodes*. And we will create wonderful, rounded shapes with magnificent curves with it, in one of the Non-Tutorials in the next chapter.

The round and square drawing tools

The Rectangle tool, we've been through. By the end of this book, you'll be an old hand at drawing things that are rectangular.

The Ellipse tool is the tool button to select when you want to draw circles and ellipses. And by using the Shape tool, you also can create a "pie slice" out of an ellipse. But that's in the next chapter, too.

All we really need to know about these two shape-creating tools in this, our exploratory chapter, is that these tools always draw objects *that can be filled in.*

Fill 'er up

The last two boxes we'll go through on Corel's Toolbox are very similar. These are the Line tool and the Fill tool, shown in figure 4.22 as the bottom two boxes (the pen picture, and the bucket of paint picture, respectively). We're going to devote Chapter 8 to the Text tool (the little box with the "A" in it), rather than skimping on it in this chapter.

In figure 4.23, we've clicked our cursor on the picture of the paint bucket to reveal a lot of other little pictures. Basically, these are options for filling a closed shape that reach way beyond the default color palette you see on the bottom of the screen.

Figure 4.23

The Fill tool flyout box. Try saying that twice quickly.

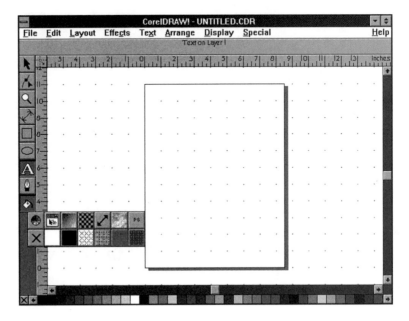

The bottom row is a set of percentages of black, and you fill an object on-screen the same way as you do by touching the color palette on the screen's bottom. But the upper row of pictures do really weird, funky stuff, as fills go. The calmest of the bunch is the top, left "color wheel."

In figure 4.24, we see the Uniform Fill options. You may pick any color your heart desires here to fill a shape. Click on Cancel and we'll return to the other, more exotic shape fills, seen in figure 4.23.

Figure 4.24

Ooooh, the colors.

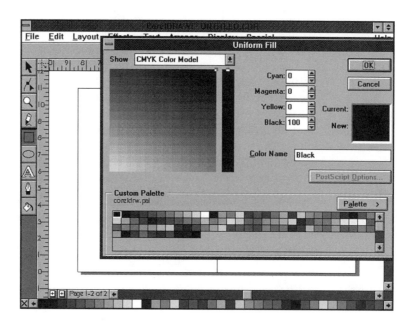

In order, across the top, we have:

 The little box that looks like a menu. This is the Fill Tool Roll-Up. When you click on it, a limited version of all the possible fill options appears. This is great when you have minor modifications to do on your work, and don't feel like entering into a lengthy dialog with one of the full-featured Fill tool boxes.

 Next, it's the Fountain Fill tool. Fountain fills are also called *ramp fills* and *graduated fills*, according to which artist or nerd you're talking to. What they do is fill in a shape with two colors, one fading into the other. Sort of like a shading effect, if you use it correctly. Fountain fills come in three flavors: *Linear, Radial,* and *Conic.* We'll try some out later, but don't be afraid to experiment on your own.

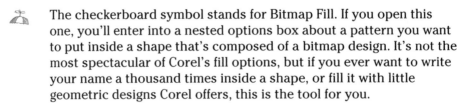

The checkerboard symbol stands for Bitmap Fill. If you open this one, you'll enter into a nested options box about a pattern you want to put inside a shape that's composed of a bitmap design. It's not the most spectacular of Corel's fill options, but if you ever want to write your name a thousand times inside a shape, or fill it with little geometric designs Corel offers, this is the tool for you.

The twin-headed arrow symbol represents the Vector Fill tool. Since Corel is a *vector* art drawing program, this means you can do a drawing in Corel, then use the drawing as a pattern-type fill inside a shape you've just drawn.

The cloudy sky box is the Texture Fill tool. This is a really exciting way to add photo-realistic textures, or fills, to your shapes. Corel has outdone itself here, and without getting too nerdy, the program actually builds a high-quality bitmap (*tons* more sophisticated than the Bitmap Fill tool) of fire, clouds, fabric, and minerals you can fill your shapes in with. Also, be aware that the larger your shape, the longer the process will take. If you want to fill in a 4-by-5-inch shape with one of these wonderful Textures, expect your PC to sit and think and not let you do anything else for a good 20 minutes or so.

The last Fill tool on the right is the PostScript Fill box. It covers a lot of the same fills as the Bitmap and the Vector Fill tools, and unless you have a PostScript printer, it won't work, so let's concentrate on the other fills through this book, okay?

Now, the button above the Paint Bucket Fill tool is the Line tool. This is where you set all the line thickness options that you want to specify. Also, what color, whether the line is dotted, and if the line has arrows on the end of it (and the shape of the arrowheads). Also, if you were to click on this button, a flyout, similar to the Fill tool's, would present you with a very similar scene.

On the bottom row are preset percentages of black. When you have a shape, closed or not, selected on screen, and press the flyout Line tool, you can give your line a light gray or a dark one, by selecting from the bottom row. There's a little color wheel box on the far left that acts the same way as the color wheel box in the Fills tool, except these offer you a complete range of colors for only *outlines* of shapes, *not* fills. The top row is a little different.

Here is where you can customize a line you've already drawn. You can change the color, thickness, and shape of the "pen" you're drawing with, and have a wide selection of dotted lines you can turn your lines into. Click on Cancel, and let's take stock of the remaining buttons.

Next to the pen nib, we have a box that looks quite like the little menu drawing from the Fill tool menu. This is, you guessed it, the Line Tool Roll-Up, and it's even handier than the Fill Tool Roll-Up, when you want to access 90 percent of your line options without entering into an off-screen options box.

The rest of the tools on this flyout button are preset widths for lines. These cannot be changed, but they're pretty common widths, ranging from a Hairline to Awfully Fat. The "X" box means *no line*.

SECRET

Although you can't change the pen shape directly from your workspace, you *can* change the color of it, or even select to have *no* outline to your shape! The color palette at the bottom of the screen is generally thought of as the way to get colors to fill in shapes you've drawn. And as we've discussed, you *do* this by selecting a shape, and clicking on the color palette with your left mouse button. But, if you do the same thing with your right mouse button, you'll change the color of lines, or outlines, you've drawn.

Furthermore, if you click on the "X" on the farthest left of your color palette, you'll have a shape with no outline. Of course, if you have only a line and not a closed shape on the workspace, and click on the "X," you'll have a line with no color, which is ridiculous, because then it sort of doesn't exist!

Graduation Kudos

I believe some congratulations are due at this point. If your mind is like a sponge, you've just absorbed the sum total of all the options and tools Corel has to offer. And that's quite a lot. If your mind is like a strainer, at least *some* of these gems have become lodged between the mesh, and you know that this chapter is always here to go back to for reference.

If your mind is non-nerdy, active, impatient, and inquisitive, you're like most of us. And we want to get to actually *doing* neat stuff with Corel, and leave our now well-organized, fully explored workspace alone. You may want to dust once a week, check the oil, and put a new primer coat on every other year from here on in, though.

From graduation cap to thinking cap

Chapter 6 has a few tutorials to help get you through some interesting design work using the tools we've described in this section. But don't be put off by the term *tutorial*. Normally, a tutorial is a boring, stupid exercise. But this is not a normal book.

CHAPTER 5

I Can't Believe It's A Tutorial!

T utorials are like leftovers in your freezer: you dig past a lot of unpleasant stuff until you finally find something palatable in the back. They're a fact of life, and as Mrs. Grimble said to you in 3rd grade while you were handed your first tutorial, "If you cheat on this, you're only cheating yourself." Pretty lame, right?

In this book, we try to discourage any cheating we don't personally sanction by simply putting all the good stuff out in plain sight. And this is good stuff. You won't want to duck out of class, because in this chapter, we will:

   Throw traditional concepts of tutorials out the window

   Refine our skills in box- and circle-making so they stand a chance of being relevant to your work

   Use the Shape tool to do some serious modifying of shapes

   Pull down one or two heretofore unexplored menu items that'll add pizazz to your shape-drawing

This non-nerdy approach to tutorials you're staring at right now will teach you to design stuff in Corel that you'll actually use in your daily designing routines. This works subliminally to teach you the principles behind the drawings, so you'll be able to invent and create variations once you put this book down. Our first stop is to take an ellipse and play with it so severely that its own mama won't recognize it...

The Tutorial that Will Come Full Circle

There are a lot of things you can do with an ellipse in the world of CorelDRAW. Most of those things have to do with changing the ellipse into something else. But before you can follow along, you have to create the ellipse we'll change around. So do this:

1. Click on the Ellipse tool from the Toolbox and create an ellipse using the click, hold, downward-and-to-the-right motion, then release the left mouse button.

2. Let's go for the gusto in this tutorial: get a little wild, and fill this ellipse with red. It'll show up as a dark gray in this book, 'cause we don't have the budget for color plates, but you can still follow along. You fill the shape by going down to the color palette and clicking on the color while the shape is still selected, remember?

Now this next step may come as a shock to you, but you can actually create an entirely different shape out of this ellipse with one deft stroke of the Shape tool!

3. By clicking on (selecting) the ellipse with the Shape tool, a node is revealed. The hard and fast rule is that ellipses have only one node. Click on that one node on the ellipse, hold down on your left mouse button, and drag the Shape tool down while keeping the tool inside of the red ellipse, like in figure 5.1.

If you kept your Shape cursor inside of the ellipse while you were pulling down on the ellipse node, you should have a pie wedge, like in figure 5.2. If not, out of accident or spite, you now have a curved line with no visible fill. And yet, if you make this accident, the ellipse's properties have not been changed, at least in Corel's eyes.

Figure 5.1

Reshaping an
ellipse, part 1.

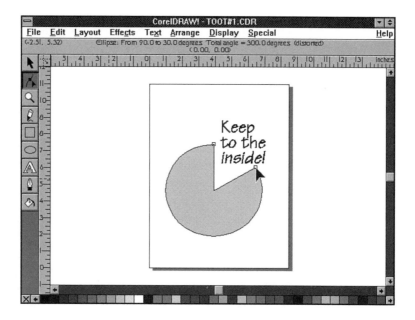

To prove this, click on the Pick tool for a second to display the properties of this selected object on the Status Bar. In figure 5.3, it says it's an ellipse, and on the far right the Status Bar tells us it has a red fill! This means we have to get used to the way this program paraphrases things sometimes. You only have to understand that you haven't changed the math behind the ellipse shape, only its appearance, and the ellipse stands a good chance of being whole and filled with color the moment we correct this mistake.

If your figure looks more like figure 5.3 than 5.2 at this point, this book and Corel have a solution.

With the Shape tool, click on the lower of the two nodes on your curved line, hold the button, and pull directly to your left. Let go of the left mouse button.

Your curved line should now look more like figure 5.2.

Figure 5.2

If you stayed on
the inside.

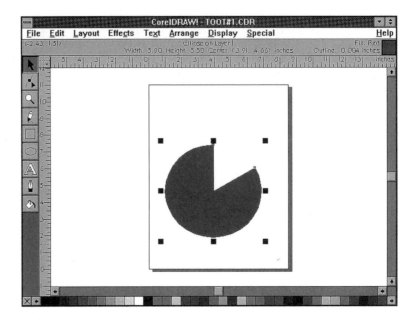

Figure 5.3

If you didn't.

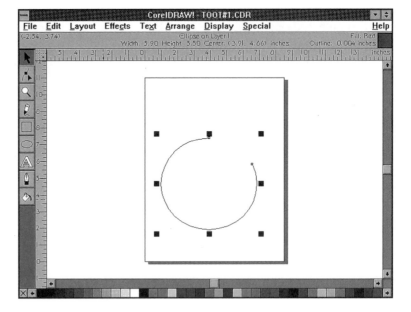

SECRET

This was a "fix" relating to a specific problem in this tutorial. If you should ever get yourself in deeper with a drawing, Corel features an <u>U</u>ndo option by default, which will back up to a point four moves ago in your designing. You can change this default to up to 99 <u>U</u>ndo steps by selecting <u>S</u>pecial, then Pr<u>e</u>ferences on CorelDRAW's Menu bar. But that's pretty paranoid. We're here to instill confidence, not to offer you "quick outs" at every turn, and besides, you'll put a strain on your PC's memory if you set your <u>U</u>ndo to 99.

To access the <u>U</u>ndo function the next time you make a mistake (or series of mistakes), go up to the <u>E</u>dit Menu item and click on <u>U</u>ndo. Ridiculously simple, right? The only time this won't work is when you save a piece, exit Corel, then start Corel up again.

I will leave to your own imagination all the uses for a pie shape we've just created. Let's keep mutating our ellipse, okay?

As ellipses in Corel go, they're pretty limited in terms of modifying them. You can make pie shapes into curved outlines if you do modification wrong, and the shape always retains its ellipse properties. You can make the ellipse—in its pie shape, curved outline shape, or plain circular shape—bigger, wider, or smooshier with the Pick tool. Let's try this:

1. Use the Pick tool, and select your ellipse pie shape.

2. Pull on one of the corner selection handles (one of the four black squares) around your shape. Never expect to move an object with these handles. They're only good for resizing something. You move objects by clicking and dragging on the fill (or outline, tough as that may be) of an object. You distort the shape of an object using handles.

3. Pull either toward the center of the ellipse pie shape or away. The dotted line on the ellipse in figure 5.4 shows we're about to get real small.

Depending on which way you moved the selection handle with the Pick tool, you now have an ellipse pie shape that's child-size, or will serve 12. Notice that this cursor changes into a lot of stuff? The four-headed arrow cursor tells you that when you're pulling on a corner handle, proportional changes are made to an object. Corel does this two-dimensionally (height and width), operating on all four sides of the object. Wanna just goof with one dimension?

Figure 5.4

Honey, I shrunk the ellipse.

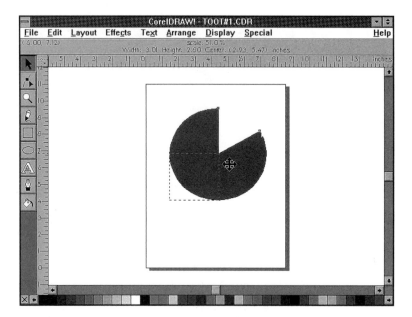

To disproportionately reshape an object (or *smoosh*, as non-nerds would call it), you use the side handles of a selected object.

1. Take hold of the ellipse pie shape by the right side, middle handle. Click and hold.

2. Pull either toward the object, or away from it.

3. Release your left mouse button. Give yourself some applause.

Corel calls this process *scaling*, and we should, too. When you pull or push on a selection handle, the Status Bar will display the scaling percentage, as shown in figure 5.4. Hmmm, we've scaled this ellipse pie wedge 51 percent, it says. It's hard to scale something precisely using the selection handles. I was actually shooting for 50 percent—half-size, you know? Fortunately, there's a second way to scale an object, proportionately, or not, without futzing with the side or corner selection handles at all.

1. Let's get the ellipse pie more normally shaped. Choose the **U**ndo command from the **E**dit menu item two or three times.

2. From the Effe**c**ts menu item, choose **S**tretch & Mirror. You'll get a box like in figure 5.5.

Figure 5.5

The Stretch & Mirror option.

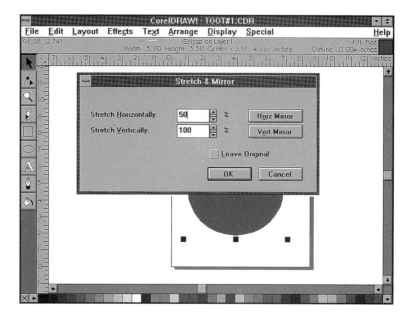

3. Type a 50 percent value in the box that says Stretch **H**orizontally. This translates out to shrinking the width, if truth be known, but technically you're stretching something to a value of less than 100 percent of its original dimension. Notice you also have options here to flop a design. Corel calls this H**o**rizontal and V**e**rtical mirroring. There's also an option to perform all this distorting stuff on a duplicate of your ellipse pie piece, by selecting the **L**eave Original box.

4. Click on OK. Your ellipse pie shape is looking pretty slim now, huh? Kind of like figure 5.6?

Let's backtrack for a second. We started this tutorial with a simple ellipse. We turned it into a pie slice, made it bigger, and then narrower. Yet after all this, the Status Bar tells us it's still an ellipse; evidently we haven't truly changed the properties of the ellipse. I believe, though, that this misshapen ellipse has served about all it's going to in this tutorial, and it's time to maim a different shape! So do one of three things now:

Figure 5.6

Why, yes. My
ellipse pie shape
does indeed look
pretty slim!

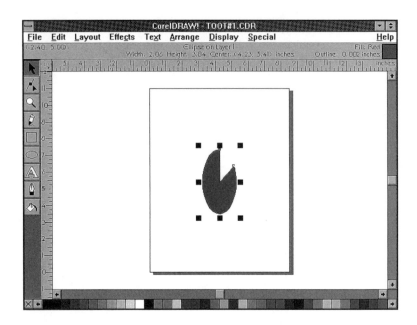

 Select the misshapen ellipse pie shape and press Delete on your
keyboard to clear our work space for Twotorial #2.

 Open a new file from the File menu item. Corel will ask you if you
want to Save the Untitled misshapen Ellipse Pie Shape (Untitled)? If
you're a kind-hearted soul with plenty of hard drive space for
garbage like this, click on Yes, and the Artwork working directory we
set up in Chapter 2 will appear. Name this file Fred (every file has to
have a name, but make it eight characters or less... besides, "Sir
Frederick Withermore the III" is a stupid name for a misshapen
shape).

If for some reason your Artwork directory is not the directory Corel
has offered to save your design in, select the proper drive and
directory for Artwork by clicking on the arrow next to Drives (if you
have a partitioned hard drive). Next, select the Artwork working
directory.

If your drive is not partitioned, click on the C:\ , the root of your
drive, and the working directory we've set up should appear. Click
on this working directory to select it, as seen in figure 5.7. Always try
to keep your artwork in a directory of its own, so you don't have to
go hunting for it when you need it.

Figure 5.7

Here's where you can name a file and select a directory to put it in.

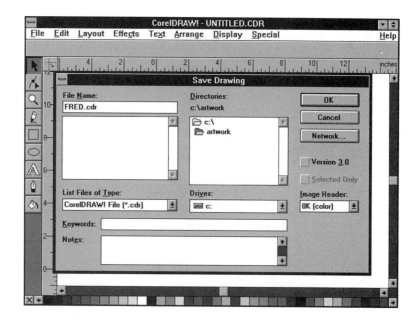

Start a New File, and answer No to Corel's box that asks you if you want to save this file. It's quicker, but you've lost the misshapen shape forever.

One Square, Two Square, Green Square, Blue Square: Twotorial 2

We've created rectangles and ellipses so far, but have gone out of our way to make them imperfect. Let's make a perfect rectangle right now, okay?

NERDY NOTE

There is no such thing as a "perfect rectangle." What the author means is that you're going to create a square. A square has four sides equal in length, joined by 90-degree angles at the corners. Sort of like a nerd's head.

We need to do something special after selecting the Rectangle tool. That something special is to perch this book where you can read it next to your PC, because this is a two-handed exercise.

1. At the same time as you're clicking, holding, and dragging-down-and-to-the-right with the Rectangle tool using the left mouse button, press and hold down on the Ctrl key on your keyboard.

2. Release both the mouse button and the Ctrl key, and entertain the idea you might just be ambidextrous. And check out figure 5.8.

3. Pick this book back up again, and while your perfect rectangle is still selected, let's go crazy and choose a blue color from the color palette.

Figure 5.8

The blue square.
The Red Square
is in Moscow.

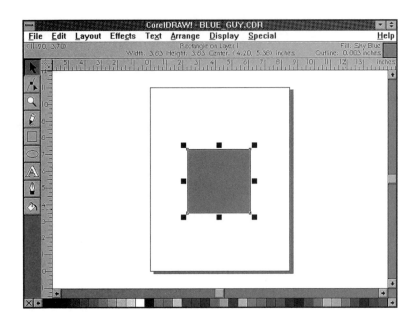

Beats a misshapen red ellipse pie slice for looks, huh? If you were to pull on a corner handle of this square, it would still be equal on all four sides. And if you pull disproportionately on a side handle of the blue square, it'll stop being so perfect.

Let's see what happens if we use the Shape tool on this guy.

We select the blue rectangle with the Shape tool, and four nodes appear on the rectangle. Unlike the ellipse's construction, the rectangle is made up of four nodes. Until we change that. Select a node on the rectangle, hold down on the left mouse button, then move the node toward another node, as seen in figure 5.9.

Figure 5.9

The blue square turns into an airplane window.

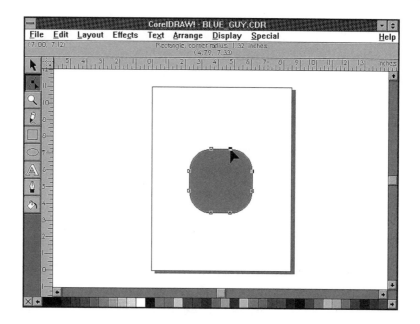

We can see in figure 5.9 that the Shape tool affects objects with different properties differently. The blue square did not turn into a pie shape, and I'm sorry if any of you are disappointed. In fact, if you drag one of the corner nodes on a rectangle toward the shape, it softens the corners of it, until you meet up with an adjacent node. At that point, the rectangle looks like an ellipse, and I think we've had enough of ellipses for the while.

PROFOUND
REALIZATION

The Shape tool...

 Turns ellipses into pie sections, unless you do it wrong.

 Turns rectangles into soft-cornered shapes.

 Turns back into a pumpkin unless the mice get Cinderella back home by the last stroke of midnight. Sorry.

Of course, we can regain our sharp-edged, blue square by using the Undo command from the Edit menu. We can also "eyeball" the thing back by using the opposite motion with our Shape tool. Do one or the other right now. In case you're wondering, the way to create a "perfect" ellipse (nerds call them equilateral circles) is to use the Ellipse tool in combination with the Ctrl key, a very similar concept to Perfect Rectangle-making.

Still, we've mentioned the properties of rectangles and ellipses without getting much into how to change them. For circles and squares alike, the easiest way is to use the Con**v**ert to Curves option under the **A**rrange menu item. This changes the way the Shape tool reacts to the nodes in a rectangle or ellipse.

1. Make a duplicate of the blue square, because we'll want a spare around for later. Click, hold, and drag the blue square three or four inches away from its original position. Before you release the left mouse button, click on the right mouse button, then release both buttons. If you find this stunt amazing, you didn't read Chapter 0.

2. With one or the other of the blue squares selected, go up to the **A**rrange menu, and click on the Con**v**ert to Curves option.

3. With the Shape tool, click on one of those four corner nodes and tug on it in any direction. Aha! It doesn't behave like our original square now, does it? Go to the color palette and select a nice green for this wacky square so that we'll be able to tell the difference between the two shapes when things get complicated later. When you convert a rectangle to curves, there's no end to the amount of odd-angles you can create between two adjacent line segments in the shape, as seen in figure 5.10.

Figure 5.10

A rectangle with an attitude.

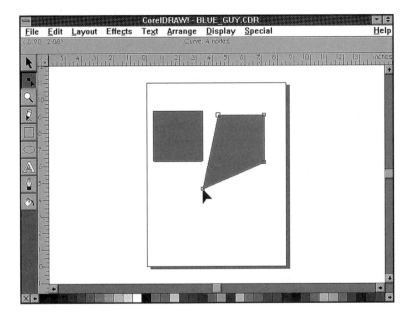

What we've just done is change the property of a rectangle, as our suspicions are confirmed by the Status Bar. But our creation isn't called a rectangle at all; it's called a curve.

NERDY NOTE

As far as "converted" rectangles go, Corel defines a curve as a shape whose lines meet at a node at more, or less, but not equal to, 90 degrees. And this can only be done by converting a rectangle to curves. They look like a bunch of straight lines, and not curvy as we think of them, but I think the author will explain how to make them curvy using the Shape tool, as well.

Now this is only one way Corel and you have to demolish a perfect rectangle. We can also do this by combining and welding rectangles together. Are you game?

1. Make yet another copy of the Perfect Blue Rectangle with the drag-and-click-both-mouse-buttons maneuver, as we did before.

2. Delete the green guy. He's outlived his usefulness to us.

3. Make the duplicate of the original Blue Rectangle about half the size of the original. Do this by either tugging inward on a corner handle, or by using the **S**tretch & Mirror menu option. (Hint: set both the Stretch H**o**rizontally and Stretch V**e**rtically boxes to 50 percent.)

4. Select both rectangles, large and small. How? The easiest way is to "scoop" them both up by using a mouse routine you've already learned. Place the Pick tool above and to the left of both boxes, hold down on your left mouse button, and drag down and to the lower right of both the rectangles. This is called *marquee-selecting*, because the blue dotted line that appears when you do this sort of looks like a movie marquee surrounding your work. The Status Bar should now say 2 Objects Selected on Layer 1.

5. From the **A**rrange menu box, select **A**lign, and you will get your choices of how you want the two guys aligned. Pick C**e**nter for both horizontal and vertical values, like in the example in figure 5.11. Click on OK.

Figure 5.11

Both guys
selected, and
ready to get
aligned.

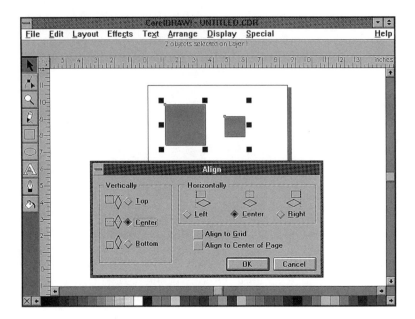

Now that we've got these two guys lined up, let's not only destroy their properties as rectangles, but create a new, closed shape out of them! We could choose **C**ombine or **W**eld from the **A**rrange menu. Let's choose Combine and see what happens. If you don't like it, choose the **U**ndo command. Does your design look like figure 5.12?

Without getting into a lot of nerdy details, you've created a shape by drilling the smaller square into the larger one. In figure 5.12 the resulting shape has no rectangle characteristics, although it looks sort of like one. Further, if you click on this shape with the Shape tool, you'll find it has eight nodes—one for each of the square's corners that you just mutated.

The opposite command of **C**ombine is Brea**k** Apart. The only problem with breaking apart something you don't like is that the two combined shapes won't reform rectangles or circles; they become broken-up, separate shapes, each with the fill and outline of when they were combined. Always use the **U**ndo command if you want to retrace steps.

The **W**eld command is a variation on the **C**ombine command, but an extremely useful one. Try this one out...

Figure 5.12

A square, blue donut.

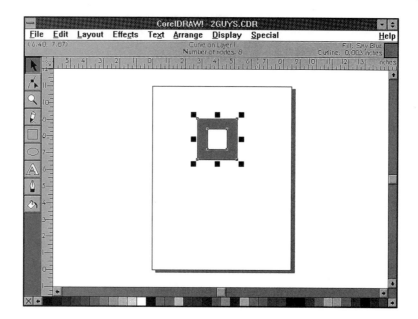

1. Open a **N**ew file. **S**ave, or don't save, the square donut. Select the Ellipse tool and create a perfect circle (use the Ctrl key in combination with the click-and-drag mouse technique).

2. Fill the circle with a color, then duplicate it.

3. Move the second circle so it overlaps the first one like in figure 5.13.

4. Marquee-select the two overlapping ellipses, or go to **E**dit and choose Select **A**ll. There is almost always more than one way to do things in Corel!

5. Choose the **W**eld command from the **A**rrange menu, and you should get one shape, not two, like in figure 5.14.

The **W**eld command has removed the overlapping sections of both ellipses. You now have a drawing of the view through a pair of binoculars on a smoggy day. (Los Angeles residents: You now have a view through a pair of binoculars on a normal day.)

There are tons of uses for the **W**eld command, and it will make your life a lot easier when you have a collection of objects that you want only an outline of that you can fill in.

Figure 5.13

A partial ellipse eclipse.

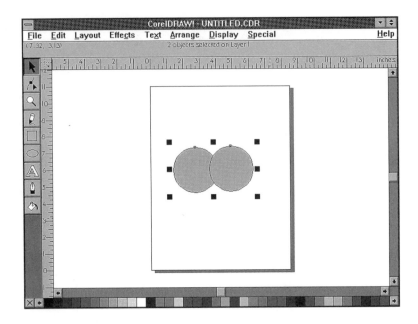

Figure 5.14

Binoculars!

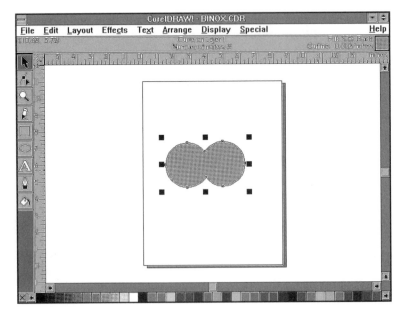

It would have been a poor move to try to combine the two circles while they were overlapping. Why? Because the <u>C</u>ombine command would have included the overlapping piece in its path, and you'd have an object that looks a little like the MasterCard logo.

PROFOUND REALIZATION

<u>C</u>ombining two shapes "drills" the second one into the first one. And if you have overlapping segments, it gets sloppy; you can't fill the path segment where the two shapes overlapped.

<u>W</u>elding two shapes shears off their overlapping segments to create one blobby outline. This outline can then be filled in. You can <u>U</u>ndo this command, but you can't break the new design apart.

So <u>C</u>ombining and <u>W</u>elding have their unique qualities. As you become more experienced with CorelDRAW, you may be comfortable drawing designs without the <u>W</u>eld command. You'll simply pick up the Line Draw tool and draw the binoculars by hand. But the <u>C</u>ombining option is the only way to create a "donut hole" effect in Corel. If you want sunlight peeking through a closed shape, use the <u>C</u>ombine command.

Changing Your Path

The last tutorial in this chapter has to do with paths. A *path* is the route connected line segments take to produce a closed or open shape. Think of it as the directions you'd mark on a map—you start at this point, go here, go there, and you're finished. A path has connected line segments between nodes (points), and it has a direction, even though the path may weave around a lot.

NERDY NOTE

The paths we've created with the Rectangle and Ellipse tools go in a clockwise direction starting from the upper left corner. Why? Because we've used the upper-left-to-lower-right of the screen mouse click and drag technique. If you were to click on the lower right of your screen, hold, and drag the cursor up to the upper left of the screen, the rectangle's path would start on its lower right node and travel clockwise. But the rectangle would appear the same shape, and it's a silly way to draw.

The simplest way to sum up all this stuff about paths, properties, and modifying them is to start with a closed shape you drew yourself on the workspace. Get out the Line Draw tool, start a path with a single click, and double-click three other points so that you have three sides of a box-type shape, like in figure 5.15. It doesn't matter if the lines are not parallel. If you wanted parallel lines, you would've used the Rectangle tool.

Figure 5.15

Three-quarters of a box.

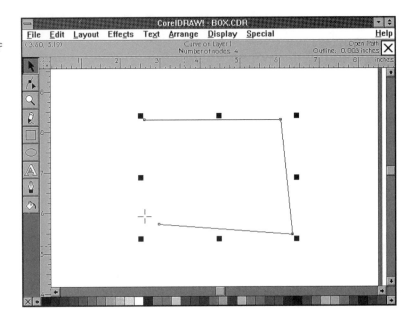

1. Use your Zoom In tool (the button with the "+" sign on it) to marquee-zoom in on your three-quarters box, like in figure 5.15. We've zoomed in for the incredible event of turning this open path (as it says on the Status Bar now) into a closed shape.

2. Click once directly on top of the last place you clicked, then finish up the path by clicking once on your beginning point.

3. Now the fun begins. Select the Shape tool and double-click, on either a line segment or a node, on your closed, box-like object.

4. Surprise! You've activated the Node Edit menu for the Shape tool!!! Now we can screw around with all sorts of properties relating to the path of your box-like object's shape!

This is where we can turn straight curves into wavy ones and all sorts of stuff, as long as your screen looks like figure 5.16. If it doesn't look like figure 5.16, take time now to make this so. If you have a fill in the closed shape now, you can get rid of it by clicking the "X" on the far left of the color palette. Also, you might consider checking Chapter 0 on how to fix Corel's Fill and Outline defaults.

Figure 5.16

The Node Edit
Roll-Up.

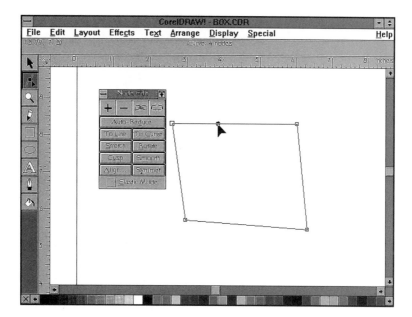

5.   You have only the menu options on the Node Edit Roll-Up that are in darker type, but that's okay. Let's click on the To **C**urve command. This will turn the top line segment in our box-like shape into a line that can be made wavy.

6.   You'll get two Control Handles on the top line, if you clicked on the top line segment (one for each of the nodes surrounding the top line segment). They kind of lay flush with the line, until you take, let's say, the left one and pull down, and the right one and pull up, until you get something like figure 5.17.

Figure 5.17

Makin' a wave.

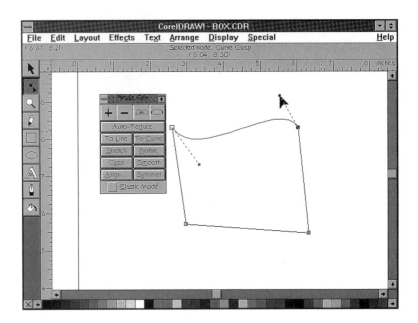

The first time anyone discovers the Control Handles on curves in Corel, the immediate reaction is to play with them for a while. I think you should indulge yourself for at least three or four days, nonstop, doing exactly this. *Not.*

But do experiment with the other options in the Node Edit Roll-Up. Briefly, this is the run-down on this roll-up...

 The + sign adds a smooth node to the line segment you click on.

 The – sign deletes a node you've clicked on.

 The next two buttons join and break apart a line segment along a path. You cannot draw two different lines (they contain two different paths) and use the command to join them.

 Auto-Reduce reduces the amount of nodes in a shape that has redundant, unnecessary nodes along its path. We haven't created any superfluously noded line paths, though. So when do you use this button? When you use CorelTRACE to convert a bitmap to a vector drawing (like these in CorelDRAW). No, you haven't slept through any chapters; we'll be getting to the features of CorelTRACE later in this book. And then the usefulness of Auto-Reduce will become obvious.

To **L**ine converts a wavy line segment we've created into a straight line, with no Control Handles on the nodes. It's the opposite function of To **C**urve that we've just used.

 Stretch and **R**otate are commands that only affect the nodes in your object if you have more than one node selected at a time. How do you select more than one node at a time?

SECRET

There's yet another way of selecting multiple "things" in Corel. The first is to marquee-select some stuff. The second is to use the Select **A**ll option from the **E**dit menu, except you're selecting everything on your workspace, regardless of whether this is your deepest wish or not. The third is to click on the thing you want, then, with the Shift key on your keyboard depressed, click on the second thing you want, the third, and so on.

This process of "additive selection" can be used on nodes when using the Shape tool, or on shapes when using the Pick tool. And deselecting stuff in your herd of objects is the reverse process: start with many things, and with the Shift key depressed, deselect items. The Shift key is used a lot in combination with mouse movements in Corel. Stay tuned!

When you select two or more nodes in your drawing, you can stretch only those nodes away from the unselected ones in a proportionate, smooth manner. Rotate works the same way. By rotating several nodes around a connected, stationary node, you can get some amazing effects. Again, experiment, please.

 Cusp and **Sm**ooth are characteristics of nodes. Think of cusps as sharp turns in a path, and smooth ones as... well, smooth! Smooth nodes have Control Handles that operate like the handlebars on a bike: the one you're not pulling on pushes. Cusp nodes have control handles that operate independently of one another. One can be at a steep angle off the line segment, and the other can be a very gentle angle.

 Align is a command that will allow you to align two or more nodes horizontally or vertically. This helps when you want to straighten out a shape you've been playing with.

S̲ymmet(rical) takes the idea of a Smooth line even farther. The beginning node of a symmetrical line has Control Handles that behave like weird magnets; you pull on one, the other goes the same way at a 180-degree angle. You pull one handle farther from the node, the opposite one moves out farther as well. You have to play with it in order to see the advantages Symmetrical nodes will give to your line segment.

 E̲lastic Mode creates a very strange and wonderful behavior among your nodes. They will work in concert, sort of. When this feature is checked, if you pull on a node, the node handles on the nodes next to the one you're pulling will move to make a smoother transition toward the node's new location. This eliminates any "spikey" effects you don't want when modifying a curve made out of connected line segments.

Back to Node One

The cynical at heart will say at this point that they haven't learned anything "special" while doing these tutorials. I'd say creating mutant pie slices, square donuts, and binoculars full of smog is indeed special, but then again, I think staying in on a Saturday night is special.

And on to the next level

Be that as it may, the next chapter is packed so full of Gee-Whiz, How-Did-You-Do-That stuff, you'll be doing your own science fiction movie by the end of it. Or actually half-believing you could. You gotta be careful about promises you write in a book, you know.

The material we'll tackle next involves using some of techniques we've gone over in this chapter, as well as blending, contouring, extruding, and rotating into new unparalleled heights of professional, precision designing.

So check your nerdometer at this point to make sure none of this technical stuff is getting to you while you learn, and press on!

CHAPTER 6

Enough Tutorials... Show Me Some Cool Things

If you've made it through this book to this chapter, you've been asked to click, drag, hunt, peck, and be patient while we taught some basic stuff you need to know in CorelDRAW. We understand that patience is a precious commodity these days. Nonetheless, you're getting to the point of asking, "Hey, where's all the cool stuff, like in ads and magazines, with things leaping out at you and lasers going all over the place?"

Your patience is about to be rewarded. Like in school, we aren't done with all the basics, but hey, it's Friday night—let's party!

In this chapter, we will:

 Turn a duck into a man

 Produce legal fireworks

 Create a 3-D ball with shading and everything

 Make an international "No Dinosaurs" symbol

In this chapter, you'll be using Corel's Symbols Library. The libraries we told you to go ahead and install in Chapter 2 contain mini-drawings. They're not as detailed as the Clip Art drawings we'll look at in Chapter 9, but they're very useful in your everyday work.

We're going to pick a few subjects from the Symbols Library for our experiments in this chapter, but first we have to turn the page on its side. Don't stop reading! We mean the page border on Corel's workspace! We need a wide page, not the tall one that's Corel's default page border. If you turned this book's page on its side, all the words and letters would fall off and spill in your lap! (Okay, they won't, but work with me here.)

Shaping Up for the Cool Stuff

In order to do the truly spectacular things this chapter overpromised, we'd like to readjust our view of Corel slightly. We need a wide page, instead of a tall one. So go to the **L**ayout menu item, click on Page Setup, and in the upper right corner of the Page Setup box, click on Landscape, instead of Portrait. You've now got a wide page border in Corel. But we're going to be doing neither landscape paintings nor portraits, if anyone asks.

What we want to do now is access CorelDRAW's Symbol Library. There's a variety of predrawn shapes covering many categories just waiting at your fingertips (if you know which button to push). If you click on the button that has the capital "A" on it (the Text tool) and hold it for a moment, two other buttons will fly out. They look like a sheet of paper and a star. The sheet of paper is for applying styles, which we aren't going to do here. The button with the star on it, the Symbol Library Roll-Up, is the guy we'll be using as the "star" of our cool stuff in this chapter, so click on it!

Figure 6.1

*Got your Library
Card handy?*

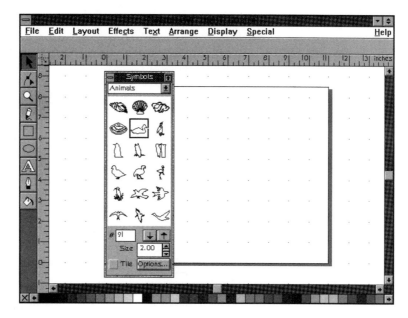

If you installed all the symbols with Corel (as I suggested in Chapter 2), the
first category of symbols will be Animals, as seen in figure 6.1. It's a handsome roll-up isn't it? Wanna know how to select one of these symbols? Well,
read on!

Making the Incredible Duck Man

In this section, we turn a duck into a man. You do this every day, right? You
don't have to have a magic wand or a degree in bioengineering to do this
feat, but if you don't own CorelDRAW, the other two options might help.

Using Corel's Symbols, and our first special effect, the Blend command, we'll
not only play Dr. Frankenstein for a day, but use our experiment as a spring-
board for even cooler stuff that comes later. Let's go! Lightning is flashing
over the castle, and we got all the parts we need waiting in the lab!

Let's go duck hunting

We'll need a drawing of a duck to start. So find the down arrow beneath the
frame of symbols on the roll-up, and click it three times. As the roll-up
scrolls down, you'll notice a lot of great symbols you can use any time you

feel incapable of doing a drawing entirely by your lonesome. Now that the Animals symbols have revealed birdlike objects in its box, follow these steps to get a duck:

1. Click on the drawing as shown in the box in figure 6.1. You'll know it's a duck when #91 appears in the little box below the main roll-up window.

2. Hold down on the left mouse button and drag the duck symbol onto the workspace.

3. Release the symbol, and it should appear to be 2" big because that's what Corel's factory default is for symbols. Which is okay, because you already know how to proportionately scale stuff (use the Pick tool on an object's corner handles) from reading the last chapter.

You now have a predrawn shape of a duck on your workspace! This duck, with regards to Corel drawings, is every bit as real as shapes you'll be designing yourself. It's just that a duck might be a little hard for you to draw at this stage of the game, and Corel knows this. They've graciously included simple little drawings, covering topics such as Animals, Weather, Arrows, and other categories relating to business. The clip art library Corel comes with contains designs that are much finer in detail, but let's not stunt our creative growth by relying on that right now.

NERDY
NOTE

Remembering that closed shapes in Corel have a path whose starting point is the same as its end point is helpful at this point. This is because we're almost ready to Blend this aquatic fowl on our workspace into a human. As a simple little experiment, take the Shape tool and click on your duck. The Status Bar says the curve has 17 nodes, right? This reassures us that the duck is a legitimate Corel design that we can modify, because we know from the last chapter that if something has nodes on it, we can mess around with it. Okay, let's add a nice 40 percent black fill to our unmodified mallard, and move on to the operating room.

Now let's go human hunting

By following the same steps as plucking the duck from the Animal Symbols Roll-Up, we need a human for this experiment as well. Do this:

1. Click on the up arrow on the bottom of the Animals Symbols window, until you've reached the top. The first symbol is a man. Which proves my mother was right when she told my sister she wouldn't find a good man in a bar. A good man is actually symbol #33 in Corel, who, like my sister, thinks all men are a subset of Animals.

2. Pull symbol #33 onto the workspace, give the guy a 10 percent gray fill, and position the duck and the man so that they look sort of like figure 6.2.

3. Double-click on the Control button (the little left-corner "minus" sign) on the Symbol Roll-Up, because we're through with it for the moment and you'll want an uncluttered screen for the Big Event.

Figure 6.2

How does a man get down from a duck?

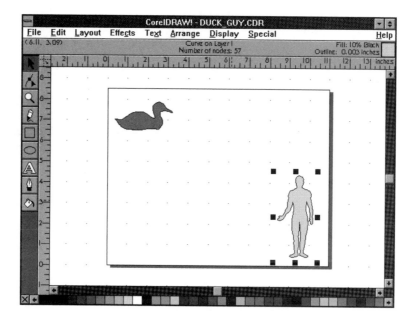

Putting a duck in the blender

Follow the next steps carefully in order to disprove any Darwinian theories that man descended from the ape:

1. Select both the duck and the man. You can use the Select **A**ll command from the **E**dit menu, or pick each one up separately by using the Shift key and clicking on both with the cursor, or by marquee-selecting, as described in the last chapter.

2. From the Effects menu, select Blend Roll-Ups.

3. The default view of the Blend Roll-Up is the three little pages in the upper left corner, the main Blend command. Here you specify the number of steps things blend into one another. The default number is 20. We'd like a smaller number, because we've just begun our Blend adventure, so move your cursor into the box and type 3.

4. Click on the bottom of the three upper left pictures, the one that looks like a meter, as shown in figure 6.3. This is the box where, among other things, Node mapping is performed. In the last chapter, there was an emphasis on the paths that shapes are drawn in, like clockwise from the left, and so on. Chances are pretty good that the professional artists who drew the duck and the man symbols didn't start at the same places along the paths that form these two outline drawings. In fact, the duck and the man don't even contain the same number of nodes. But the Map Nodes command takes care of this. Select this option now.

Figure 6.3

The Blend
Roll-Up.

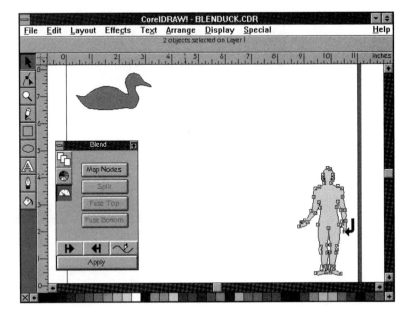

NERDY NOTE

A Blend is made by taking the orientation and angles of the nodes in one shape, and in a sequence of steps, gradually moving toward the characteristics of a second shape. But sometimes the two shapes don't share a beginning node in the same place, like on the top, or on the side, or something.

You change this with the Map Nodes command. This forces the shapes to start at the same beginning node and travel in a path that's in the same direction. You can create some interesting effects if you don't map nodes in dissimilar shapes, but most of the time the resulting blend would look like the transporter room on the *Enterprise* was having a bad day.

5.   What you should do now is to take the "bent arrow" your cursor turned into and click on the man's middle finger on his left hand. Then, the arrow will turn upside-down, and it's time to click on the very point of the nose of the duck. Don't you feel silly? Why are we doing this? Because, in order for the transformation from the duck to the man to happen so it looks like anything vaguely profound or humorous, we need to map the nodes on both shapes so they have a common beginning, like the middle-right of the symbols. You could have clicked somewhere on the left of both, but the explanation would have been just as long.

6.   We now have to apply the Blend effect, so click on the button labelled Apply.

7.   Push your seat back in awe. A five-step transmogrification just like in figure 6.4 should appear. You can say, "Oh, wow!" as well, if it's considered cool this week to say that.

Well, gosh. Aside from creating the main attraction at the midway of a carnival, we've also applied our first Effect. Of special note here is that these two objects are now "linked." If you click on the duck, your Status Bar will say it's a Control Curve. This means you can control all the intermediate blend steps by moving, resizing, rotating, or otherwise changing the duck. Or the man. They're both Control Curves now. If you want to make the duck green and the guy purple, hey, go for it. Or if you want to make 30 intermediate blend steps, to create a "strobe" effect, specify 30 Steps in the roll-up box window, and let 'er rip. It'll be duck soup.

Figure 6.4

I like the part where he loses his beak and grows hands.

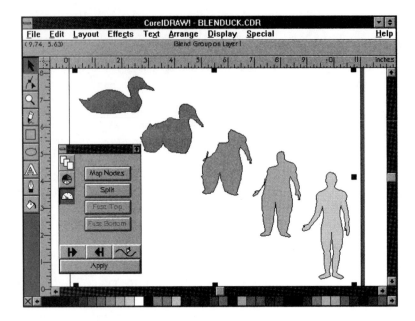

Making Fireworks (Legally)

A different use for blends is to create a soft fuzzy transition in color tone, and shape properties by using the same shape twice. The fireworks on this chapter title page were created this way.

1.   First, a fireworks display of this magnitude was worthy of a dark night to show it off against. A big rectangle was drawn to fill the page. A black fill was added by clicking black on the color palette with the left mouse button, and no outline by clicking on the "X" with the right mouse button.

     I then drew a small, firework-y shape and filled it with white. I gave the shape no outline, by selecting it and clicking on the "X" of the color palette with the right mouse button.

2.   Then I duplicated the shape right on top of the other, by using the **D**uplicate command from the **E**dit menu.

3.   This second firework-y shape is both on top of the first and white. And we wanted it to be neither. We wanted to send this duplicate back one step in our sequential fireworks construction, so we chose **A**rrange, **O**rder, Back One from Corel's Menu. A good keyboard

shortcut for this maneuver is Ctrl+Page Down. If we had pressed Shift+Page Down, we'd have sent the duplicate all the way to the back of our design, behind the black rectangle sky.

And that would have been wrong.

SECRET

When you draw shapes, or pull in symbols or anything else, within Corel's workspace, the order they are in, the "in front of" or "in back of" qualities, are determined by which one drew first. This is why we need to use the Arrange, Order command.

4. So the second firework-y shape is behind our original, and if we click on a black fill for it, we're well on our way to this special sort of blend. We then take the Shape tool and pull the nodes away from the first shape, until the black firework-y shape is slightly larger than the original white one.

5. By selecting both shapes and setting the Blend steps to about 20, we get a smooth, airbrush-type edge to the piece of firework. Or anything else you want to add a soft edge to.

So as we can see, we can create intermediate steps between two dissimilar shapes, or smooth transitions between similar shapes. We just use the Blend effect, with a little messing around with the Shape tool here and there.

UH-OH

The only word of caution in using the Blend effect is that if you go overboard with one on a drawing, the file size (measured in bytes, or kilobytes) of your finished piece may be bigger than you expect. That's because when you do a 20-step transition between 2 shapes, you might see only the effect, but you've actually got two control curves, plus 20 extra shapes sitting on your workspace! So don't specify a 3,000-step Blend on 2 shapes, unless you're working on someone else's PC that you want to bring to its knees.

There are other Blend options you can see on the roll-up menu, but essentially, they're further modifications you can apply to the same principle. So if you've got the principle down, we'll move on to Graduating. No, this doesn't mean you've finished this book and get a diploma. We're talking about fills that graduate from one color to another.

Have A Ball

We looked at the little Fountain Fill button on the Fill tool fly-out when we checked out the tools. We also noted that the Fountain Fill default of steps is 20, in the **S**pecial, Pr**e**ferences menu items when we cruised around Corel's workspace. So it seems like a more than overdue time to actually fool around with this sucker now! It'll be a rounding-out of your education.

Fountain Fill is not some guy

One of the first neat discoveries new Corel users roll around in is the Fountain Fill, or Graduated Fill, or Ramp Fill option, depending on which nerd is describing it to you. They all mean the same thing, which is to go smoothly from one color to another within a closed shape. We've already shown you how to do a smooth blend from one color and/or shape to another using the Blend effect. If you're not transforming a shape, and just need to go from one color to another within a shape, the Fountain Fill option is much less fuss.

In order to use the Fountain Fill option, you need to have an object drawn first, so let's open a clean workspace and draw a perfect circle by using the Ellipse tool, our famous click and drag routine, and by holding down on the Ctrl key, while reciting all the U.S. presidents' middle names in reverse order. Almost did that last one, didn't you?

We're going to select the Fountain Fill button by clicking on the fadey-looking button on the Fill flyout. Why not try this yourself right now?

Taking fill to the ball

We've got a lot of options here. But only one or two if we want to create a 3-dimensional ball.

1. The default Fountain Fill type is a linear fill. We don't want that. By its name, Linear Fill suggests a straight line-type fill, good for shading in boxes and stuff. We want a Radial Fill, 'cause our shape has a radius, like most good ellipses. Choose the **R**adial-type Fill.

2. The little box on the right in figure 6.5 looks like a Radial Fill, with the shading going from light to dark starting from the center going out. This is good. But if we left this box alone, we'd wind up with a Fountain Fill in our perfect circle that looks boring.

Fountain Fills are used to create lighting effects, so do this: Place your cursor inside the Radial Fountain Fill example box. You should have a crosshair-shaped cursor now. Click, hold, and drag your cursor up and to the left, and release it. If all has gone well, the two Center Offset boxes directly to the left of the example box just went nuts, and they've changed their values. That's good also. Basically, if your screen looks like figure 6.5, we're in excellent shape.

Figure 6.5

Fountain Fills galore!

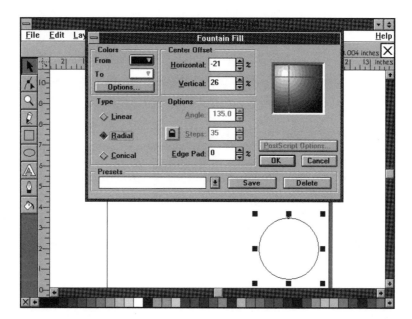

3. Click on the OK button, and we're outta here. Take a look at our new creation in figure 6.6.

Figure 6.6

Just LOOK at that thing, would ya?!!

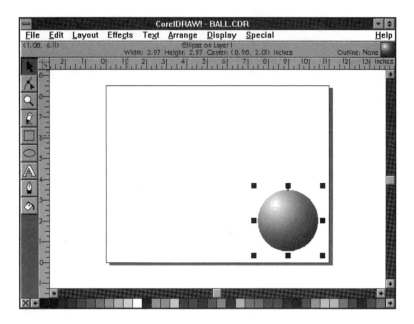

Getting the ball rolling

First things first. Get rid of the black outline by clicking on the "X" on the color palette with your right mouse button. It ruins the "effect."

Half of the reason why we now have a beautifully lit, 3-dimensional ball on our workspace is because we picked a Fountain Fill that was identical to the shape we filled. You might get some interesting effects if you filled in the duck with the Radial Fill, but something wouldn't look quite right about it. Which is due to the other half of the reason the ball looks so good: we gave the ball realistic lighting. All we did was to move the center of the Radial Fill up and to the left. To achieve good lighting on everything you do in Corel takes time, practice, and greater understanding than what's described in this section. I suggest that you play with lighting effects in your off-hours to see what looks good and what looks like a mistake. Let's get back on track, and back to having a ball!

Shadow play

It might be good to give our 3-D ball a little "ground" so that it's not simply sitting in space. The Blend effect is ideal here for creating a realistic shadow next to our 3-D ball so that it's not just floating in space.

First, we need to understand that our 3-D ball is lit from the top left of our workspace. So a realistic shadow will be placed to the lower right (always the opposite of the light source) of the ball. And shadows are always more intense at the base of the object responsible for the shadow, and they sort of fade off into nothingness. A Radial Fill, although it got us this neat 3-D ball, is not the best tool for creating a shadow, because you have no control over the shape and the fade at the same time. So try this:

1. Using the Ellipse tool, create an imperfect circle (no Ctrl key) that sort of meets with the bottom of the 3-D ball like in the following figure. Use the Zoom tool to move in on this piece for precision's sake, if not to avoid eyestrain.

Figure 6.7

The beginning of a shadow.

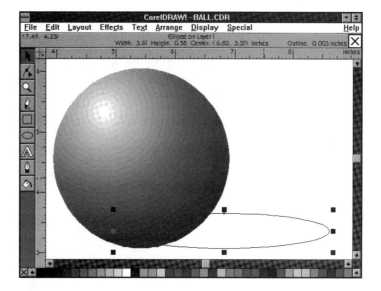

2. Since the shadow we're building should go behind the ball, put this new ellipse to the back of the ball by using the **A**rrange, **O**rder, To Back menu options, or press Ctrl+Page Down on your keyboard.

3. Select a nice, light, 30 percent black fill from the color palette, and while you're down there, get rid of the outline by clicking on the "X" with the right mouse button.

4.   Duplicate the 10 percent gray ellipse. Here's the easiest way to do this (I've been holding back on this trick until now in order to better govern the flow of wisdom you're soaking in).

SECRET

When you open a Menu item, there are stupid little key combinations written to the right of most of the commands. Although they look like aliens might've left them here eons ago, these key combinations free you from the drudgery of leaving your work with your cursor and having a big, fat menu box come down and momentarily obliterate your design. We'll provide a list of the most helpful ones in Chapter 8, but for now, remember that pressing Ctrl and D simultaneously will duplicate an object.

5.   After pressing Ctrl+D, make this second, identical ellipse a darker color. Then drag the ellipse up and to the left with the upper right corner handle surrounding the selected, darker ellipse. Make it smaller, and stop when you can barely see it peeking out from behind the 3-D ball, like in figure 6.8.

Figure 6.8

Building a shadow, part 2.

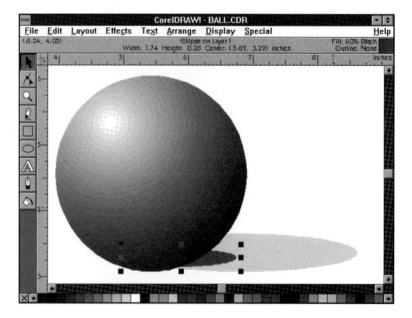

6. Select both ellipses, then use the Blend command in the Blend Roll-Up. Set it for 20 steps, and press Apply. Now check out figure 6.9

Figure 6.9

How can a good thing possibly get better?

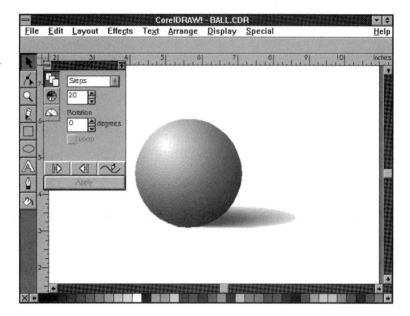

Oh, and FYI, the Rotation box won't help you create a shadow, but it will screw up your blend. When you specify the number of degrees you want in a blend, Corel takes the second shape in your blend and pretends the second shape was rotated to this angle. Your second shape remains stationary and unchanged, but the blend tracks a path as though it was rotated a certain number of degrees. It's a good effect if you do blends with two shapes outside each other, like the duck and the man. If you have one shape inside another, and specify rotate the blend, the result looks like someone came by and bumped you while you were working.

Fun-filled Fountain Fill facts

In this section, we've seen that the Blend effect can provide intermediate steps of transformation between two dissimilar objects, and is useful for creating graduated fills that are not limited by the Fountain Fill preset options. We've also seen what a no-brainer it is to create a realistic ball with a Fountain Fill.

Fountain Fills also come in Linear and Conic flavors. Linear is good when shading a wall or other surface that's supposed to look flat. The Conic Fountain Fill is neat when you want to create an aerial view of a silo, or the shading of a nautilus (... the sea shell, not the personal fitness machine).

The nice thing about Fountain Fills in general is that you can make a drawing more interesting with them, regardless of whether they are appropriately applied or not. Show a bunch of people an ordinary rectangle, and four out of five will yawn. The fifth is a nerd who will marvel at the right angles.

But give the rectangle a Conic Fill, and people will "ooh" and "ahh" and usually never get around to asking what the drawing is supposed to represent. Corel is a simple tool to create effects, but it's also a powerful tool when you've got an idea and the working knowledge of the program to make things happen.

Now that you've graduated from graduated fills, let's keep going...

A Sign of the Times

Although we've played with shapes from the Symbol Library, we haven't tried combining these simple drawings into something that is uniquely ours. What's true of Clip Art (which we talk about in Chapter 9) is also true of the Corel symbols: they usually won't do you much good in a specific assignment unless you can "customize" them.

We know now how to create a closed path, how to fill that closed path with color, and how to eliminate the outline around the closed, filled path. This, combined with our knowledge of the Symbols Library, is going to take us into a realm of highly customized, very commercial designing—sign-making! If you follow these steps, you might get promoted (or demoted) at work to the position of Most-Revered Chief Sign-Maker!

You Can't Park Your Dinosaur Here

International symbols are a big thing. They communicate beyond the language barrier and provide important advice to the viewer at a moment's glance. A skull and crossbones on a bottle usually means the contents won't be good to ingest. Or that the bottle belongs to a pirate.

In any case, the Red-Circle-With-a-Slash-Through-It, accompanied by a black silhouette of something inside is universally recognized as meaning, "Whatever's inside the circle, don't mess with it."

Besides being extinct, dinosaurs are large. And probably would be a nuisance if someone were to park his outside your building. So we will use Corel's Symbol Library to create a custom sign that will get a lot of attention, and it will communicate effectively. In fact, we guarantee you will see no dinosaurs outside your building after we do this exercise.

Ten steps to curb those 'saurs

1. There is a blank international Do Not... symbol in Corel's Signs category within the Symbol Library. Pick it and pull it onto your workspace like you did the duck and the man.

Figure 6.10

You'll be drawing stuff like this all by yourself some day.

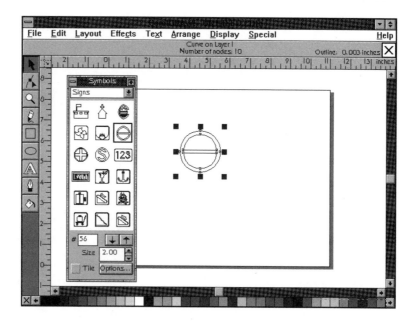

2. Fill this shape with a red color, and get rid of the outline.

3. Go to the Animals section of Symbols, and pull out a dinosaur. We'll be using #54, so why don't you, too?

4. Color the dinosaur black, and this time we'll take advantage of the Outline default Corel has. Our Status Bar tells us that the dinosaur has a .003" black outline. Let's change this to a .003" white outline by clicking on white on the color palette with our right mouse button.

5. Our red "No" sign doesn't look so swift. The slash across it is going straight across, and we want it angled so the dinosaur's head can peek over it. Zoom in using the Select All button on the Zoom flyout. Click twice on the red "No" sign to get Rotate and Skew Handles around the sign's border, and take the upper right corner handle and pull up on it so it angles like in figure 6.11.

Figure 6.11

The easy, yet imprecise way to rotate an object.

6. Precise rotation of the No Sign would've required going up to the Effects menu and calling the Rotate and Skew box, which would've asked how many degrees we want to rotate the sign clockwise or counterclockwise. We're shooting for "art," not precision this time out, but it's a good thing to know nevertheless.

7. Place the dinosaur in the center of the No Sign. The dinosaur is a little too small in proportion to the No Sign. Fun Fact #37: Dinosaurs are large. So select the dinosaur symbol, click on a corner selection handle, and pull away from the page ever so slightly. It doesn't take a lot to turn a puny dinosaur into a Thunder Lizard.

We can see now that the white outline on the dinosaur is separating the shape from the No Sign. Which is good if you're going to try printing this piece on a black-and-white printer; the shades of gray you'd get without a white separating outline would make this No Dinosaurs sign look like a blobby waste of toner cartridge and laser paper. Still, there's something missing from this sign.

I think the slash should go over the dinosaur. But the circle part of the No Sign should still go behind the dinosaur. But the slash and the circle are all one piece. What do we do? We cheat.

8. Go to the Wireframe Mode of CorelDRAW's workspace, because we need to do some precision cheating. Press Shift+F9 simultaneously to get the Wireframe Mode, if you don't feel like pulling down the Display menu. Take your Line Draw tool and draw a closed shape that overlaps the slash part of the No Sign. Use the wireframe of the slash as your guide. You're doing it right when the lines in the shape you're building are directly on top of the wireframe of the slash. What we're doing here is creating a shape that'll paste over the offending parts of the dinosaur. (See fig. 6.12.)

9. Go back to the Preview Mode in Corel by pressing Shift+F9 again. Your shape should look similar to figure 6.13.

Figure 6.12

This dinosaur is on the verge of extinction.

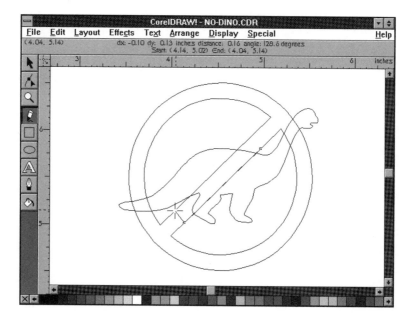

Figure 6.13

Almost there!

10.   The shape you've drawn is the most "recent" shape on Corel's workspace, so it will, by default, go on top of the whole No Dinosaurs sign. Give it a red fill and no outline, and for all intents and purposes, your No Dinosaur sign will appear to have the dinosaur in front of part of the No Sign, yet behind another part.

SECRET

You can use this technique any time you need to hide part of a drawing. It's not really cheating (we'll get to *really* cheating in Chapter 10), and it's a useful technique when you want to make part of an object look as though it's on top of another and a different part of the same object appear on the bottom.

How This Stuff Helps You

Soon you'll be at the point where you'll be designing stuff that will eventually be used in software programs other than CorelDRAW. You know, like the guy down the hall needs a pie chart in his spreadsheet, and this loser has his compass, pencil, scissors, and paste all set to go.

Figure 6.14

Violators will be towed by King Kong at their own expense.

Part of the wonder of CorelDRAW is that it's a Windows program, and by its nature, it obeys a lot of Windows conventions, like Copying and Pasting. And if you want to put a Corel design in a non-Windows program file, like WordPerfect for DOS, Corel has Import and Export filters to let Corel transform your work into a format that the other program understands.

More cool things to come...

The next chapter will introduce you to the process of sending a Corel drawing to a program that's limited to word processing, presentations, or whatever. We do this by using filters, a little sweating, a lot of swearing, and the Windows Clipboard. We probably won't even lose much data in the process, either.

"I beg your pardon, but did you notice whether I was coming or going?*,"*
she asked.

"That depends upon whether you are importing or exporting,*"*
said the Clipboard. And with that, he vanished behind another window.

CHAPTER 7

Malice Through the Looking Glass: Using the Clipboard

In the last chapter, you graduated from doing nutty geometric shapes to honest-to-goodness graphics. If you follow the advice in this book, you'll continue topping yourself in fairly short order, because Corel belongs to a world of intuitive, very powerful design programs.

But what about other worlds? Like your graphically starved word processor? And how about that label-maker program you can't design your company logo in? Can they benefit from Corel's world of graphics, too?

They can, and will, if you simply read on. The corridor between worlds in Windows is a crazy funhouse mirror called the Clipboard. Assisted by its cronies, the import and export filters, you're empowered to send and recieve copies of text and graphics from almost any point to any other point in Windows. And like the little lass in the storybook, things can get a little unpredictable if you don't take directions from a reliable source.

In this chapter, we will:

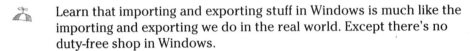 Learn that importing and exporting stuff in Windows is much like the importing and exporting we do in the real world. Except there's no duty-free shop in Windows.

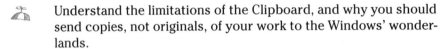 Understand the limitations of the Clipboard, and why you should send copies, not originals, of your work to the Windows' wonder-lands.

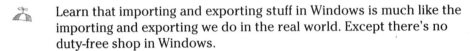 Take a look at work that's been translated, transformed, and taken for a ride through a "looking glass" that even Lewis Caroll would've thought was far-fetched.

Importing/Exporting Business

One of Windows' standard features is the ability to work across, or between, Windows programs. And there is anything but a standard explanation as to how all this clipping, copying, importing, exporting, and pasting works! Windows has a "home-brew" import/export filter, called the *Clipboard*, which was designed to supply programs with a means of sharing whatever that program produced (text, pictures) with other Windows programs. CorelDRAW comes fortified with import/export filters of its own, thank you, but it's still good to know about the Clipboard. It's the easiest, if a somewhat unpredictable, way to move your stuff from and to places. Sort of like public transportation.

We'll show you a list of types of filters CorelDRAW features shortly, but first we'd like to offer a little explanation of what an *import/export filter* is. Folks get nervous when they hear about information (data, your design) being "filtered," because that typically means something's been filtered out. Not to worry. In this chapter, we'll show you how to get your work to other programs that only wished they had Corel's design capabilities! And we'll do it through a filter, not the wringer.

It's Not All Greek to Filters

At least once in your life, you've overheard a nerd. And they might've been talking about import and export filters. This is probably because they haven't the know-how to talk about sports or sex. And although those filters are really important when using CorelDRAW, you probably thought an import filter was something you bought for a Volvo.

Import and export filters, as they relate to your work and fooling around with Windows and Corel, are *translation programs*. They actually convert a copy of your Corel design and make it digestible to other programs. Corel itself contains import/export filters for Windows, and some that will allow your design to travel to DOS applications and even to the Macintosh.

Fee-fi-fo-file... the name game

It's important to know how to save a file (the piece of work you want to import or export) because these converted copies of your work will have extensions that are different than Corel's own .CDR. But this one is easy. When you save a drawing of a ball in Corel, you save it by naming it something that's eight characters or less, then adding a period (.), followed by the extension, which with Corel is CDR.

The whole saved file name, for example, could be BALL.CDR. An exported copy of the BALL.CDR file of your work would still be named BALL followed by a period, but the extension will be different according to the type of file you're converting the work to.

Selecting the right file extension, which means the right filter for what you want to import or export with, can be tricky. Corel has provided a brief descriptor next to the file extensions available when you choose one of its filters. We think we can shed additional light in this book, though, with a chart of extension names and the programs that will be able to use the imported or exported piece. Remember that an exported piece cannot be modified unless the program you're exporting to has design tools. For example, a paint-type program has editing tools; a word processor usually doesn't.

Table 7.1
Import/Export Filters

You export a ball as:	You can use it in:
BALL.CDR	CorelDRAW.
BALL.PCX	CorelPHOTO-PAINT, Windows Paintbrush, most paint-type bitmap programs, a lot of DOS and Windows spreadsheet, word processor, desktop publishing, and presentation programs, and Macintosh paint-type programs.
BALL.BMP	CorelPHOTO-PAINT, Windows Paintbrush, most paint-type bitmap programs, and a lot of Windows spreadsheet, word processor, desktop publishing, and presentation programs.
BALL.EPS	Any program that supports output to a PostScript printer. If you or your company owns an HP laser printer, you most likely won't be using this file format. Also, typeface-creating programs like Fontographer and FontMonger use .EPS files to do their work.
BALL.GIF	A lot of DOS-based programs, like screen slide shows. If you want to share your masterpiece with the world via CompuServe, this format produces a high-quality, compressed file that can be read by almost anyone with a PC.
BALL.CGM	A fairly universal file format. Most older DOS and Windows programs support .CGM graphics.

You export a ball as:	You can use it in:
BALL.JPG	Photographic retouching programs like PHOTO-PAINT, Adobe PhotoShop, and others that understand JPEG compressed photo files.
BALL.PCT	Macintosh computers. .PCX files work with Macs, too, but the .PCT file format is the best for Corel designs. Macs are different than IBM-based personal computers, but if you save a file with a .PCT extension, any Macintosh owner will be able to use your file.
BALL.TIF	Most imaging programs that come with a scanner. Also the retouching programs, like PHOTO-PAINT, Adobe PhotoShop, and Aldus Photo Styler. TIF-file formats are most widely accepted by desktop publishing and presentation programs.
BALL.WPG	The WordPerfect family of products, and programs that will accept the WordPerfect graphic file format.
BALL.TTF	Windows! This format is the formula for TrueType. You can create a typeface in CorelDRAW and export your typeface so all the Windows programs that support text can use it.

The list goes on, but this should give you a good place to start. The surest way to ensure that an exported file will arrive safely at its destination is to check out the other program's import filters.

The simplest method of importing and exporting a file doesn't require this file naming stuff at all! There's a Windows program that's technically an import/export filter even though most users wouldn't think of it that way. Because it's not called a filter. It's called...

The Windows Clipboard

The concept of the Windows Clipboard is incredibly easy. And yet it's hard to explain. Which makes it perfect for a nerd to do the talking for a moment.

NERDY NOTE

When you cut or copy something in a Windows program, you are actually sending information to Windows Clipboard. This Clipboard is able to understand information in three different formats: text, bitmaps, and vector art. The Clipboard acts like a universal import filter when it does this. The Clipboard then holds onto this information until it is called for, or this information is replaced by another piece of information you've cut or copied to it. The Clipboard only hangs onto one piece of work at a time, so beware.

When it comes time to paste this information into another program, the Clipboard acts like a big export filter. The Clipboard turns the text or graphic into a metafile. This file can be interpreted about seven different ways by Windows. Chances are good that another Windows program will understand at least one of the seven Clipboard descriptions of the information.

After that nerdy note you probably realize why it is a hundred times more important to know how to use the Clipboard than to understand how the Clipboard actually works.

Follow the bouncing ball

We're going to send the 3-D ball we designed in the last chapter bouncing through Windows' wonderland via the Clipboard. Our trip through this looking glass begins by opening the BALL.CDR file in CorelDRAW. We select the shadow and ball by marquee-selecting them with the Pick tool. From the **E**dit menu, we choose **C**opy (not Cu**t**), as seen in figure 7.1. We don't want to experiment with the original masterpiece, only with a copy of it.

Figure 7.1

*One small step
for Corel...*

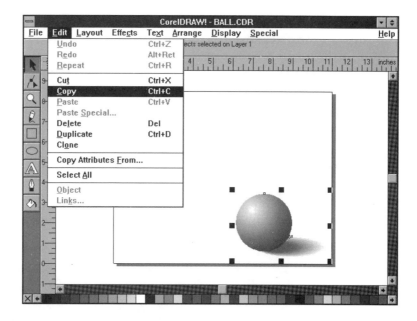

Corel will then reply to this command by showing us a dialog box that says Corel is copying.

PROFOUND REALIZATION

An interesting note is that when we selected to copy the ball and shadow, Corel copied every object that makes up the masterpiece. We used 20 blend steps and two control curves for the shadow, and an ellipse for the ball itself. So Corel obliges and will show you a "running tab" of its progress, like `Copying...Object 10 of 23`, and so forth. When it gets to the Clipboard, though, the Clipboard treats all the objects as one piece.

We want to close Corel now after copying. Why? Because we'll be going to the Clipboard, and then to another software program, and it's a drain on Windows' resources to keep several programs open at the same time. *Resources* means the memory it takes for your PC to keep Windows running. So exit Corel by selecting File, then Exit, or by pressing **ALT+F4** on your keyboard. Or by double-clicking on the Windows Control Menu box. It's the little minus sign on the far upper left of your screen. Bet you didn't know there were so many ways to get out of a window, did you?

Now that we're back in Windows Program Manager, click on the Clipboard icon. It's located in the Main group, unless a nerd's been playing with your PC. In figure 7.2, we see our copy of the ball through the "looking glass," and it looks like we've had a practical gag played on us!

Figure 7.2

Who sat on my ball?

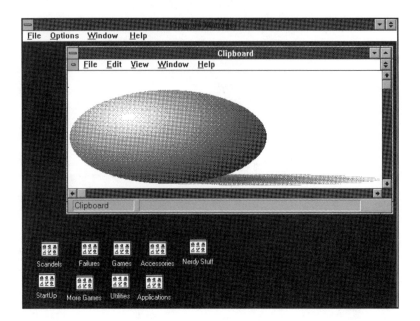

Our ball visits limbo (the Clipboard)

Figure 7.2 is the view of your ball through something called the Clipboard Viewer. Funny-looking view, right? A lot of people consider the Clipboard Viewer the same thing as the Clipboard, probably because it's easier to think of it that way. Just trust the fact that the 3-D ball is safe and undistorted, and the Clipboard Viewer displays graphical information in sort of a "draft mode," rather than an *accurate* one.

If you would like to save the 3-D ball as a Clipboard file, you can do that now by clicking on **F**ile, and then choosing Save **A**s. But the real fun of having copied the ball to the Windows Clipboard is the ability now to paste it into another Windows program. Why don't you open the Windows Write program now, go up to its **E**dit menu item, and select **P**aste?

Our ball lands in a faraway program

In figure 7.3, we just happened to come by a Windows Write file that needed a little artistic flair...

Figure 7.3

Ball and Chain letter.

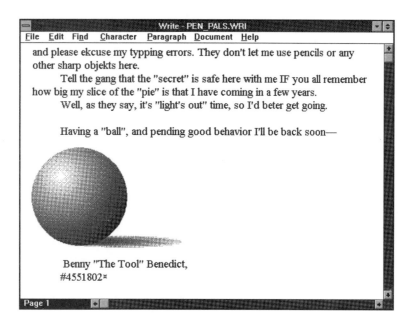

You see? Windows can store graphics (or text) on the Clipboard and put it in other programs. Windows Write can't create artwork, but it can use artwork created in some other Windows program (um, like Corel). This is the main reason for importing and exporting information: to supplement programs that lack features you need to complete an assignment, or to reuse something you created elsewhere.

Malice doesn't live here anymore

So what are the drawbacks?

 Windows 3.1's programs, like Write, can handle a Corel drawing going through the Clipboard easily. In fact, if you wanted to copy the ball from Write and place it in a new Corel file, you could. But some programs, older programs especially, are "ignorant" of today's version of Corel and Windows 3.1. You may not be able to paste a Corel graphic from the Clipboard into a Windows program that was designed before 1991.

PROFOUND REALIZATION

If you do paste a graphic into an older program and later try to copy it out of the older program onto the Clipboard and into a newer program, it might not copy successfully. That's why you should save your Corel files and copy from them, instead of cutting things out. Cutting removes an object from the original once and for all. As an overall rule, copy—don't cut.

 There is a limit to how "large" a graphic stored on the Clipboard can be—in terms of complexity of the graphic, not its physical dimensions. A Radial fill, for instance, is a hefty piece of change for the Clipboard to handle, because the fill is mathematically complex. The 3-D ball had only one Radial fill, though, and because you're seeing it now, it obviously worked. But if you were to try sending three or four objects at once that have Fountain fills, and those in turn are made up of 200 connecting line segments each... you might get only part of the design onto the Clipboard. This would definitely not be useful.

 A simple truth we all have to live with is that Windows' resources diminish during the workday. Windows resources are a chunk of your PC's RAM (Random-Access Memory), which Windows uses to help programs to run. The only problem is that most programs don't put back all the memory when they're finished, so the Windows resource pool gets smaller as you open, close, clip, paste, and do the normal things you do in Windows.

The Windows Clipboard takes a dip in this resource pool like every other program. And programs simply don't work like they should when there are not enough resources to tap into. So if you've been active in Windows all morning, and then you try to export a math-ematically complex graphic to the Clipboard, you could get a "No Go," a partial "Go," or your PC could actually crash due to this attempt. Closing all of your programs, exiting Windows, and then restarting Windows "recharges" your resources, so it is a good habit to restart Windows at least once a workday.

UH-OH

If your programs start acting a little flakey—the Clipboard won't clip properly, or you get error messages (`Cannot Write to Drive`, `Cannot Complete Operation`)—try restarting Windows to recharge the resource pool. If the flakiness continues, you'll have to call a nerd (sorry).

The Clipboard is a Windows utility, so unless you're a nerd, or have read New Riders Publishing's *Windows for Non-Nerds*, pasting a Corel graphic into a DOS-based program is a little tricky.

 Depending on which program you paste the Corel Clipboard image into, you may get different, sometimes unexpected (or unwanted) results. If you paste the 3-D ball into the Windows Paintbrush program, it'll look unrefined because this program converts the image into the only type of image Paintbrush has the ability to understand: simple, unsophisticated bitmaps.

Whenever you export an image, whether it is with the Clipboard or Corel's own bunch of filters, you are bound to lose something. This is because the image is translated into a format the receiving end can handle. The phrase "Something was lost in the translation" is an applicable one with import and export filters.

Some data loss is unavoidable, but it doesn't outweigh the benefit of being able to put a CorelDRAW graphic in a presentation or spreadsheet that needs livening up. The real trick, then, is to select the best filter to use. That is, the filter that does the least amount of translating. The Clipboard does Corel graphics beautifully. So does a .CGM export. The .PCX and .BMP filters are necessary to convert a Corel drawing to a format paint-type programs can understand.

Ultimately, the best judge of which filter to use is your own eye. Look at the monitor, and look at a printed sample of your exported work. If it's not everything you expected, try exporting again using a different filter. Time and experience will help you decide on the best filters for each job.

Clipboard at a backward glance

Before we explore the other ways of getting Corel drawings into other programs, let's recap. **The Clipboard:**

 ... will hold one copy of something. The next time you copy or cut something to the Clipboard, it erases the previous thing you had on it.

 ... will save an item as a .CLP file in its own format if you choose **F**ile, Save **A**s while working with the Clipboard Viewer. For example, you can save the 3-D ball as BALL.CLP by typing in an eight-characters-or- less name in the Save box. You can paste a .CLP file (that's a copy of a Corel drawing) back into Corel, and it will be unchanged, for reasons best explained by a nerd.

 ... works better with more recent programs, especially those designed after 1991.

 ... is safer to work with if you always work with copies; if you remember to copy instead of cut; and if, in general, you practice learning the ins and outs of importing and exporting.

Exporting Bananas

Let's suppose you work for the Dayo Banana Distributors, and your boss, Mr. Vellaconte, has a Microsoft PowerPoint presentation all set to go, but he wants a picture of some bananas in it. PowerPoint is a good presentation program, but it lacks Corel's sophisticated drawing tools to create graphical bananas. You are therefore given two tasks: to create the drawing of the bananas, then to export the bananas to a file format PowerPoint will understand.

If we look back to table 7.1, we see that presentation programs generally accept .TIF images. Again, it's a good practice to check out a program's import filters before exporting a Corel design, but PowerPoint does indeed accept .TIF images. Do you think we staged this, or what?

So let's move to the task of creating the drawing.

1. In the Symbol Library, there's a section with pictures of food, as shown in figure 7.4. Pull the banana shape onto the workspace, then zoom in using the Select All button (the second one from the far right with all the rectangles on it) from the Zoom tool flyout, because we've got some tinkering to do with the bunch.

2. The banana symbol is composed of four shapes that the artist combined to create one path. We'd rather the bananas were individual paths so that we can color them in separately. Choose Break Apart from the **A**rrange Menu. We now should have an outline of the bunch, and separate outlines for the individual bananas.

Figure 7.4

Picking some bananas.

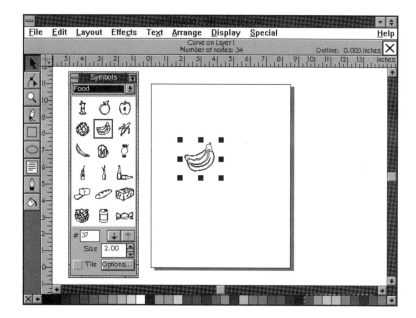

3. Select a banana and fill it with yellow from the color palette. Then select the outline of the whole bunch and fill it with brown. The brown will cover all the shapes, because the outline shape was positioned on the top of all the shapes when we broke apart the symbol. Send the banana outline To Back of everything by using the **A**rrange, **O**rder command, or by pressing Shift+Page Down. Finish filling the other two shapes with yellow. Your picture should look like figure 7.5.

4. Select all the shapes, remove the outline by clicking on the "X" on the color palette with the right mouse button, then choose **G**roup from the **A**rrange Menu item. And we'll have bananas that will never fall apart.

5. With the **G**roup selected, go up to the **F**ile menu item and choose **E**xport. You'll get a menu that looks like figure 7.6.

Figure 7.5

Not too green,
not too ripe.
Actually, rather
gray.

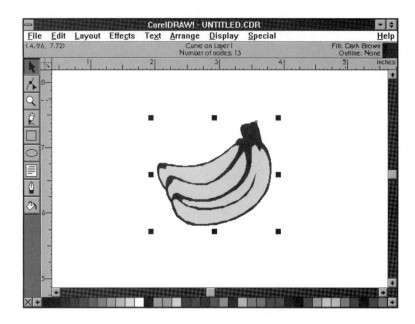

Figure 7.6

Exporting
bananas.

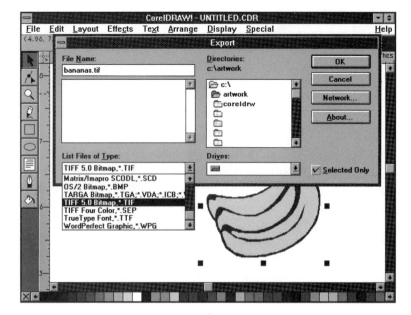

6. First, we see that there are several different kinds of file formats you can export with Corel. Corel's designers packed a small fortune into this program! But we only need the TIFF extension file format, so scroll down the box where all the formats are listed until you find the TIFF 5.0 Bitmap, *.TIF, like in figure 7.6.

7. We need to name the copy of your file, so bananas.tif seems like a simple, obvious moniker.

8. In the **D**irectories box, we see the working directory we created in Chapter 3. This is where your new, exported file will wind up.

9. Click on the **S**elected Only checkbox. You should do this as a standard practice because you've selected only the bunch of bananas on your workspace for export. This helps keep your file sizes small, because it leaves out everything else on your workspace, like a page border, an item you forgot about and is laying around, and so on. Click on OK, and we're off to the next menu box.

10. According to the information in figure 7.7, the Export Bitmap box, by default, is ready to export our bananas in 16 million colors! No way! This is going to create a file size bigger than the national debt! We used only brown and yellow in our design!

Figure 7.7

Decisions, decisions.

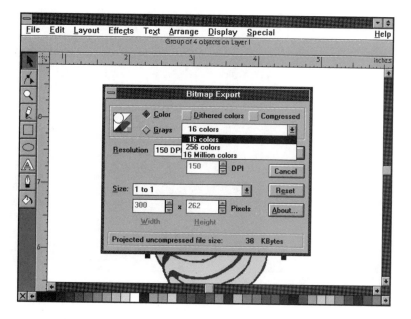

A palette of 16 million colors will indeed have our brown and yellow colors. But so will a 256-color palette. As well as a 16-color palette. For simple designs, the smaller the palette you can work from, the smaller the export file size will be. As a rule of thumb, the smaller the file size, the easier it will be to export a file.

SECRET

11.   Choose 16 colors, leave the resolution alone because 150dpi is fine for our purposes, notice that the file size is a comfortable 38 kilobytes, and click on OK.

Whew! The bananas are now exported. But to where?

They weren't exported to the PowerPoint presentation, because the PowerPoint presentation isn't open, and computers are stupid that way. The bananas.tif file is sitting patiently in the artwork working directory, waiting for someone to import it. Figure 7.8 shows what it will look like.

Figure 7.8

The PowerPoint program you probably don't own.

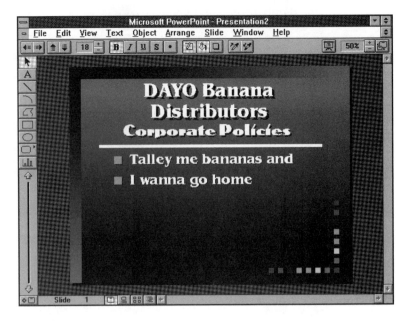

Importing Bananas

This is the end of the road for most of our readers here, in terms of actually having to do any PC work—partially because you deserve a break, and mostly because you probably don't own Microsoft PowerPoint. But you may own another program that could stand to have a snappy graphic imported to it, and this is a good example to follow.

1. We open the graphically starved file in PowerPoint, as in figure 7.8.

2. We choose to **I**nsert (import is the *technical* term) a **P**icture, as shown in figure 7.9.

Figure 7.9

Bringin' home the bananas.

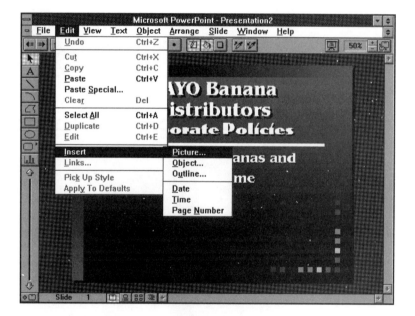

3. We select bananas.tif from our working directory, as shown in figure 7.10.

4. We select the bananas.tif file to import, and click on OK. See figure 7.11 for the final banana-rama.

Figure 7.10

Picked from your
working directory.

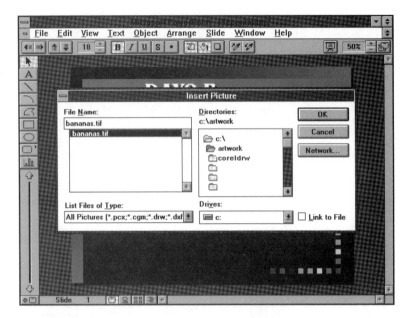

Figure 7.11

Didn't you know
you could get
bananas at the
7.11?

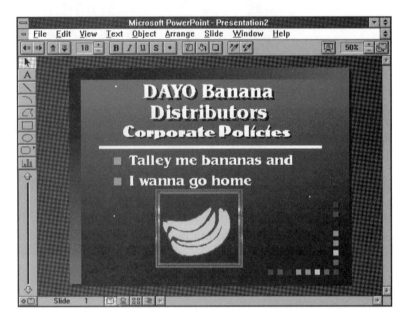

5.   We now have our exported bananas ready. We now can dress up an application that had no drawing tools but was in desperate need of tropical fruit. Figure 7.11 is a PowerPoint file, and yet it contains a CorelDRAW graphic!

Final Thoughts on the Clip Trip

The example in this section on using Corel's import/export filters is about as complicated as it gets. You may find variations on this theme when you want to export a different type of file to a different program, but the theory remains the same, and so does the procedure. As with everything else in CorelDRAW and Life, you've got to practice and play around to really get to know it.

Corel does just about everything when it comes to the easy, non-nerd approach to creating graphics. That's why being able to export your work to lesser, graphically impoverished programs is good to know. But Corel only gets a B-plus when it comes to word processing. By that, I mean that it's the wrong tool to use. It's much quicker and easier to write a paragraph in Windows Write, for example, than in Corel.

From Clipboard to keyboard...what's next

This is where importing with Corel comes in, and working with type and the keyboard on your expensive PC should be addressed. And it's so important, it gets a chapter of its own—the very next one in this book, in fact!

CHAPTER 8

The "Keys" to CorelDRAW!

So far, we've focused our attention on using the mouse as an input device to work in Corel. Which is good, because design programs sort of rely on your ability to move stuff naturalistically all over the PC screen. But you also have another input device, the PC keyboard, as an invaluable hardware-type tool for designing stuff.

The keyboard is where the text that accompanies your pictures hangs out (as well as coffee spills, paper clips, and eraser stubble, if your keyboard is like mine). You can take shortcuts, access special typographical characters, and select Menu items all on these same glorious keys. Don't let your creativity stop at clicking and dragging! Let's explore the power that's at your fingertips in CorelDRAW!

In this chapter, we will:

   Get some text going to accompany your drawings

   Do more special effects using text

   Learn a few keyboard commands that will speed up working in CorelDRAW

   Learn why the keyboard is better than a typewriter

Yes! This is IT! This is the chapter where we finally get around to experimenting with the alphabet, which forms words, and then sentences, and paragraphs, and whole bookshelves of best-selling novels, and we'll never use Corel again to do ducks, and...

Getting the Word Out

Let's do a reality check here. CorelDRAW is a business graphics bundle, and Corel packed about every conceivable tool into this package to help the designs you think up do one thing: communicate. And ideally, communication, in a professional, businesslike sense, involves the creative use of graphics and text *combined*.

We've segregated text from Corel's drawing tools up until this point because it's simply too much to throw a beginner new drawing tools and text tools at the same time. Corel can actually treat text two different ways: as a graphic, and as typeset body copy.

We'll save the spectacular graphics we can do with text for later in this chapter. First, let's see how to get normal text onto Corel's workspace...

Another (Type)Face in the Crowd

CorelDRAW comes with 152 different typefaces on its installation disks, and 600 more bonus typefaces you can use if you have a CD-ROM drive hooked up to your PC. Corel has packed two CDs with a wealth of clip art images, and high-quality Type 1 and TrueType typefaces, in the hopes that you'll be motivated to run out and buy a CD-ROM drive. (You see, Corel's president owns stock in a CD-ROM drive manufacturer... only kidding!) The practical reason for jamming all these goodies on two CDs is because Corel wants to give you your money's worth when it comes to the total design package they advertise Corel to be. And all the typefaces and clip art would require around about 45 billion disks otherwise.

Hopefully, you followed my advice in Chapter 1 about looking at Corel's printout of all 750 typefaces before you installed, and wisely chose to install only the ones that would serve you best. Corel uses the TrueType or Type 1 face that's installed at the top of an alphabetical list on your PC as a default typeface. If you installed the Amelia or Avant Garde Book typeface, you'll get one of these each time you start typing in Corel. Corel's default size for the typeface is 24 points. For the examples in this section, we'll be using Toronto, which is very similar to Times Roman, which virtually everyone on earth owns. If you'd like to use Toronto, or Times Roman instead, we'll show you how...

NERDY
NOTE

One point equals ¹⁄₇₂ of an inch and twelve eggs equals a dozen eggs. So 24-point text is about one-third of an inch high, or like this

24.

1. First, select the Zoom In button on the Zoom tool flyout to marquee-select an area around four inches wide on your workspace. This gives us a better view of what we'll be doing.

2. Select the Text tool from the Toolbox. It's the one with an "A" on it, not the rectangle, and not the star (the Symbol Library).

3. Move your cursor, which should look like a crosshair now, onto the workspace. Click once with your left mouse button, and the crosshair should turn into a blinking vertical line.

4. Start typing! Corel is behaving like a word processing program now, except you can make an "insertion point" (where the blinking vertical line marks the beginning of your text) anywhere on your workspace! Figure 8.1 shows that we're off to a good start. Now, you don't have to type "I have...," but try to use quote marks, because you'll be playing with them later.

Unlike a word processing program, you can continue typing clear off your field of view in Corel! You don't want that, but you do want to finish your thought, so if you need more room to finish your first thought here, press the Enter key when you get near the right side of your screen view.

You'll notice that when you press the Enter key, the lines of type in Corel are, by default, flush left. Complete your "thought," select the Pick tool with your cursor, and let's see what else you can glean from your first experience with text, Corel-style. The text in figure 8.2 has been selected, you've got selection handles going around it, and the literary world is abuzz with excitement.

Figure 8.1

A good beginning
of a thought.

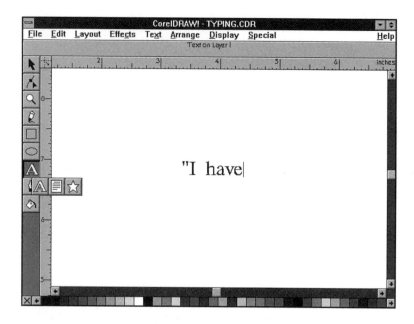

Figure 8.2

A completed
"thought." Also
known as a
sentence.

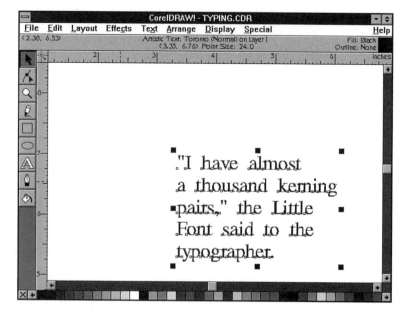

The Status Bar tells you that your typing is in Toronto (or whichever type-face you've used), at a 24-point size, as Artistic Text, and is selected on your workspace. It also tells you that the sentence you typed has no outline, and a black fill.

Once you've stopped typing and selected the Pick tool you can go back to using the Text tool in the same place as you left off by pressing the space bar on your keyboard. So if you made a typing error, you can go back and correct it without switching tools. This is only one of many Corel keyboard shortcuts!

SECRET

By default, text in Corel has no outline. Do not confuse Corel's term for "outline," which is the border of a shape, with a word processor or presentation program's use of the term. Their "outlines" are the kind used in English class, whereas Corel's outlines are graphical, thick, thin, absent, purple, and so on. The reason why text in Corel has no outline is because you'd probably never use an outline around the characters in text—it makes them clunky. The drawings that you create using the Line Draw, Ellipse, and Rectangle tools have a default of 0.003", because it's easier to select them. Imagine a shape with no outline and no fill. Kinda hard to select, huh?

Anyway, your 24-point, left-justified, Toronto Artistic Text is, well, interesting, but you may have a few reasons to be unhappy with it. For example, the spacing between the words is too much, the space between lines is too little, you detest left-justified text, and you may be using Amelia instead of Toronto and it's painful to look at. Other than that, everything's OK. So let's make some changes to your thought, OK?

1. Click on the Te**x**t Menu item, and select Edit Te**x**t.

2. Click on the Spacing button to bring up a nested menu. Your screen should look more or less like figure 8.3.

3. The first item on the Spacing Menu is **C**haracter spacing. Leave this alone. Although if you ever were to use a really wide typeface, you'd adjust the character spacing here. The next one is the **W**ord spacing item. By default, Corel sets this to 100 percent, which is usually too wide. So set it to a moderate 70 percent. **L**ine spacing is an artistic call, but most of the stuff you read in the papers is set at 120 percent between lines, so follow this example. Click on OK, and let's play with your thought some more.

4. From the main Artistic Text box, you have control over point size, typeface, and justification, which Corel calls Alignment, so you will too, from now on. Additionally, if you have any text on Windows Clipboard, you can click on the **P**aste button, and the text will flow

into the top viewing window. For the moment, set the Alignment to Center. Your thought just realigned itself to the center of the viewing window, didn't it?

Figure 8.3

Where the words hang out.

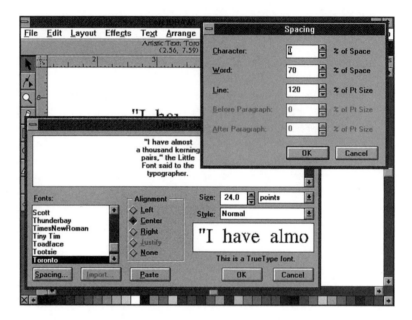

5.   For those out there who are using a typeface other than Toronto or Times Roman, here's your big chance to make the switch. Scroll up or down in the Fonts window until you find Toronto. If you're already using Toronto, or don't have Toronto installed, pick a different typeface. It's only an exercise. You don't win or lose points in this book.

6.   Leave the point Size alone. It's fine the way it is. Click on OK, and you're back to your Corel workspace.

You've used quote marks in your thought so you can *modify* the quote marks. Corel is all about changing and modifying, and text elements are not exempt. The text changes in this example are made from, you guessed it, the keyboard! You've probably noticed by now that your keyboard isn't exactly like a typewriter. It's got more keys and pilot lights, and it jams if you try to stick a sheet of paper in it. All because it's not a typewriter. You can do strange and wonderful things with a keyboard if you move on to the next section.

Typesetting, Not Typewriting

To begin with, there are 92 characters you can use on both the PC keyboard and on a typewriter. Here the similarity between the two ends, because TrueType and Type 1 typefaces have a character set in them comprised of 256 possible characters. Not all typefaces take full advantage of that number. In fact, a face like Playwright contains only 100 characters. But that's because it's a decorative, or headline, typeface, and you almost never need the special characters in a headline.

These special characters in a typeface character set consist of accent marks above vowels (for foreign languages), copyright marks, trademarks, fractions, British pound and Japanese yen symbols, and things called typesetter's quotes.

If you look back to figure 8.2, the quote marks you used in your thought look like they came fresh off a typewriter. In fact, you could use them to denote inches, as well as the beginning and end of a quote. But the text in this book uses typesetter's quotes for single and double quotes, and for apostrophes, as well. It looks more professional, and it's easier to read.

Getting a good quote on paper

There's a trick we're going to do now with the quote marks on our thought, and afterwards we'll provide a small list of "special character" codes for everyday use, providing you use CorelDRAW every day. Try this next example:

1. Either use the spacebar on your keyboard, or click on the Text tool to get the blinking vertical line back. You're going to edit your thought.

2. Place the insertion point before the first quote mark, like at the beginning of your thought in figure 8.4. Highlight the first quote mark by dragging the cursor backwards over it while clicking and holding the left mouse button. Your insertion point cursor will turn into an I-Beam if you're doing this right, as shown in figure 8.4.

3. Now that you have the quote mark highlighted, leave the mouse alone, and let's concentrate on some power keyboarding.

4. Ever wonder what good the number keypad is on your keyboard? While holding down the ALT key on your keyboard, type **0147**, then release the ALT key. Presto! Check out figure 8.5.

Figure 8.4

Highlighting the
first quote mark.

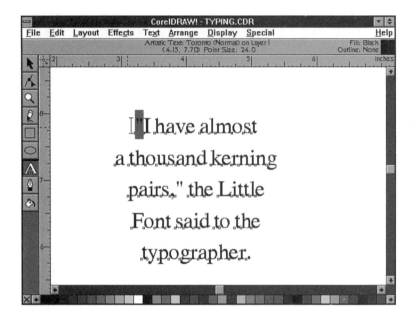

Figure 8.5

You can quote
me on this.

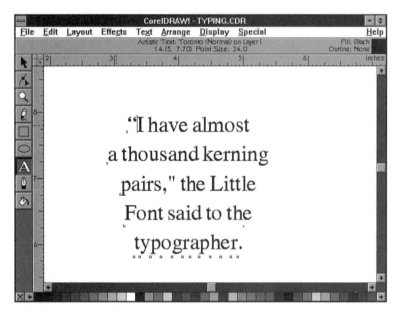

What we have here is one of Toronto's special characters, the typesetter's open quote! In order to create a perfect typesetter's close quote, you'll do the same thing with the second quote mark, except hold down on the ALT key and type **0148**. This is the way you can access special characters.

Using ALTernate characters

Windows has a Character Map utility in version 3.1 that'll show you the complete character set to any typeface. You can select and copy the character from there, but you'd have to leave Corel to do it, and that's a hassle. Instead, here's a table (table 8.1) of common special characters that most TrueType and Type 1 typefaces contain.

Table 8.1
Special Characters You'll Wanna Use Lots

You Want	You Need	You Call It
'	ALT+0145	(Single quote)
'	ALT+0146	(Apostrophe)
"	ALT+0147	(Open quote)
"	ALT+0148	(Close quote)
•	ALT+0149	(Bullet)
¢	ALT+0162	(Cent sign)
©	ALT+0169	(Copyright symbol)
—	ALT+0151	(Em dash)
™	ALT+0153	(Trademark symbol)
®	ALT+0174	(Registered mark)
°	ALT+0186	(Degree sign)
¼	ALT+0188	(One-quarter)
½	ALT+0189	(One-half)
¾	ALT+0190	(Three-Quarters)
`	ALT+0232	(Grave accented 'e')
´	ALT+0233	(Acute accented 'e')

Again, there are plenty more characters to play around with, and you should open Windows Character Map if you're hunting for a special character not listed here.

Another Face in the Crowd

If you've played with Corel's typefaces before reading this book, you're probably aware of another distinction the PC has versus the typewriter: bold and italic typefaces. Yep, these are what nerds and type foundries alike call families of typefaces.

There are usually at least four variations on the basic design in a typeface family. For Toronto, you have Toronto Normal, Italic, Bold, and Bold-Italic. Without applying any special sort of effects to the Toronto family, you can express yourself typographically, in a way a typewriter flunks out on. Italic lettering within a sentence usually emphasizes something. Let's emphasize a word in your thought.

1. Get out the Shape tool, and select your Artistic Text thought. A whole bunch of little boxes appear in front of each character. These are selection boxes. They help "select" the character immediately following each box, for editing purposes. You only want to italicize the word *almost* in your thought, so select each box by either marquee-selecting the six characters, or by selecting each one with the Shape tool, while holding down the SHIFT key.

2. You need the Text **R**oll-Up for these next steps. The Text **R**oll-Up gives you a lot of options for modifying text, without the hassle of digging through menu boxes. There's even a keyboard shortcut to get it—press CTRL+F2. Or if you're missing the mouse in this chapter, select Te**x**t, then Text Roll-Up. In the example in figure 8.6, you see the Text Roll-up ready for action, and it's already done its home-work. It's telling you that the Artistic Text is Centered, and that Toronto is your featured typeface.

3. Change this by clicking the little down arrow to the right of the word Normal. You are only changing the six characters that make up the word *almost*, because these are the only ones you've selected with the Shape tool. A preview of the change to italic flies out of the Text Roll-Up. Corel obviously had a lot of fun designing this program, huh?

4. As with all Roll-Ups, you must click on Apply in order for the change to be applied, so do this now. And check the results in figure 8.7.

Figure 8.6

The Text Roll-Up.

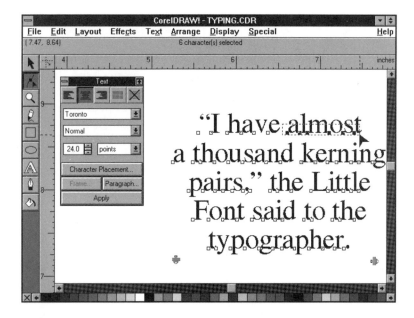

Figure 8.7

Almost looks
perfect, right?

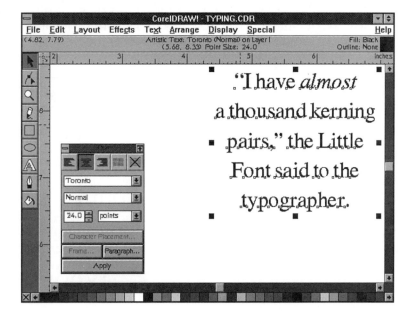

Twistin' and Kernin'

You've used the Shape tool to change part of a sentence here. But there are other changes you may apply to the sentence with the same tool. Notice the little honey dipper-shaped guys that appear on the right and to the bottom of your thought in figure 8.6? These only appear when you have text selected using the Shape tool. If you pull down on the lower left one, this will create more space between the lines of type. This space is called leading, incidentally. By tugging on the lower right honey dipper, you can change the space between the characters of your thought on all the lines of type.

You can also use the Shape tool to rotate, resize, and even pull characters out of the rest of the text.

By clicking on the Character Placement button on the Text **R**oll-Up, you get a menu box to pop up, and the option to select an angle of rotation. You can apply this to one, or several characters, as long as you've remembered to select them first. In figure 8.8, the 17-degree angle value we entered will send the "F" in a counterclockwise direction. A negative value would have rotated it clockwise. I'm certain you can find a constructive design use for this feature, but for now, you're simply ruining professional typography. But wait! Let's make a bad thing worse...

Figure 8.8

The Character Placement menu.

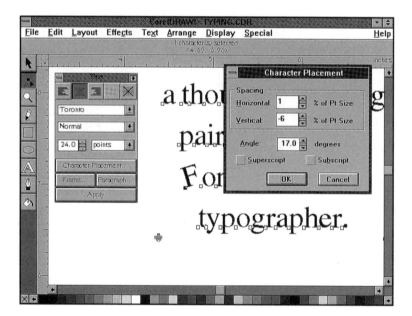

In figure 8.9, we've pulled one character away from the rest. You can do this too, and if you'd like to constrain the movement to either up and down or horizontal, pull in one direction while holding down on your keyboard's CTRL key. With the Shape tool and the Edit Te*x*t menu, there's an almost limitless variety of customizing you can do to a block of text. My personal favorite is the "Ransom Note" effect, as follows in figure 8.10.

Figure 8.9

A runaway F.

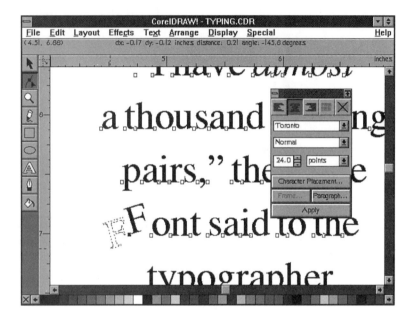

What I did here is to select each individual character with the Shape tool and reassign its typeface, type family, size, and angle of rotation. It took me about 15 minutes, so you won't have to waste 15 minutes doing something so childish and stupid. And fun.

The Fine Points of Type

Typesetting is an important business. People pay good money to get resumés, business cards, and invitations typeset. And so far, we've been neither serious or silly enough to have thoroughly explored Corel's possibilities as a professional typesetting tool.

Figure 8.10

Good for kidnap
notes and long
prison terms.

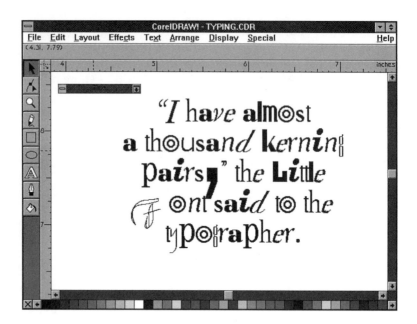

A font by any other name

First, the "thought" we typed in the figures above has a few terms in it that
are not all that silly. *Font* (you'll hear it a lot with printing houses) refers to a
specific size of typeface in a specific typeface family. Like 12-point Times
Roman Bold-Italic.

The term font is a holdover from the days when printers used to use slugs
(individual characters) of type that were fitted together to form words and
paragraphs that were inked and stamped onto paper. So using slugs that
were fonts from the same families and size was important, unless you
wanted the page to look like figure 8.10. But today's electronic typesetting is
very elastic and flexible, and with programs like Corel, you can twist and
distort and stretch a font so that it bears little resemblance to the original
font family. We'll do that in the section after next, by the way. So the term
font is sort of irrelevant, but we still use it:

    Because it sounds cool

    Because typeface takes too long to say

Typeface and font are synonymous today, and each is equally accurate and
inadequate in describing text as Corel handles it.

Now we know that The Little Font is actually a Little Typeface, and the well of silliness I'm drawing from for these examples is fairly deep. So let's continue, and take a look at The Little Font's belongings. "Almost 1,000 kerning pairs," hmmm? We know that it's substantially more than 12 Lords a'leaping, and 11 maids a'milking, but what is a *kern*, and why do kerns come in pairs? Can you return one if the other one breaks? Let's ask a nerd. They know everything.

NERDY NOTE

Kerning is the fine-tuning between two characters in a word. If you've ever noticed that "A"s and "V"s have a slope to them that go in opposing directions, this is an example of a pair of letters that need special attention. Or kerning.

In the word HAVE, the spacing between the "H" and the "A" is fairly normal, but in order to make the entire word "HAVE" proportionately spaced, the "A" and the "V" have to tuck next to each other a little more than the other characters. Fortunately, computer programs handle this proportional spacing almost automatically. A typeface's file has preset kerning pairs that go into action every time you spell HAVE, or HAWAII, or other words that contain sloping, skinny, or irregular letters.

The effect of kerning pairs is a subtle one, but it separates typesetting from typewriting. A typewriter uses a monospaced font without any kerning. Without kerning, a "W" gets as much space as an "i" which makes it harder to read (and not very attractive, either). Typeface designers can program in up to 512 pre-kerned pairs in Type 1 typefaces, and 1,000 in TrueType.

Two Kinds of Text On Tap

So we can get blocks of text as perfect as is professionally possible with Corel, and we'll be getting very strange and imperfect in about five pages. But why, you may ask, is the stuff you've just done called *Artistic Text*? Because you can do "artsy" stuff with it. Bend it, rotate it, extrude it, all the neat stuff you'll shortly learn to do.

Corel also offers something called *Paragraph Text*. Paragraph Text uses the same typefaces as Artistic Text, but it can handle a greater quantity of it, and is ideal for use in a document with long blocks of text, such as a brochure or newsletter. Artistic Text, by contrast, is limited to 250 characters in a single string or hunk of text.

Corel has set these limitations and made the distinction because Corel offers you the ability to treat text as a graphic. With Artistic Text, you can pull on its nodes, blend it, and do other fun stuff. As mighty as computers are these days, Corel had to limit the number of characters it made available to you to play with graphically at one time. A short sentence of Artistic Text could have as many as 28,000 nodes used to connect line segments. And that's only one artistic sentence!

PROFOUND
REALIZATION

To be brief about it, Artistic Text, like we've been using, is flexible in a graphical sort of way, and can only be used in small chunks. Paragraph Text, covered in this next section, is closer to true typesetting and desktop publishing. It can be used to create pages upon pages of aligned, kerned text for documents that need solid text without graphical effects.

The Non-Graphic Paragraph

Let's say one day you're offered a better opportunity than the position at the Dayo Banana Distributors. Yes, Famous Elmer's Country-Style Pizza has gotten wind of your talents as a designer, and they've offered you a big salary and all you can eat on Thursdays if you'll design them a simple one-page flyer.

Corel pizzazz and the pizza biz

As you and CorelDRAW make your way across town to work in that red-and-white-striped building, you remember that you know how to create a sentence in Corel, but Famous Elmer is probably looking for a whole bunch of paragraphs! The History of Pepperoni and the proper vintage soft drink to serve with deep-pan pizza are filling your head with concerns. But needlessly so, because we're going to work with you on this career-making move. Do this, step by step, as soon as you meet Elmer and he shows you where the restrooms are:

1. From the Symbol Library, choose the food category, and pick a nice slice of pizza (symbol #105) to plop on the page as a starter for this flyer. Elmer will be impressed that you know his business already.

2. Use the Brea**k** Apart command from the **A**rrange Menu to separate the cheese from the crust, and the peppers from the sausage. Create different colored fills for the individual paths you've broken apart from our pizza symbol. Group them, using the **G**roup command from the **A**rrange menu, so nothing slides off the slice while you design. You should have 19 objects grouped, as indicated in the status bar in figure 8.11.

Figure 8.11

All that's missing is a plate and an appetite!

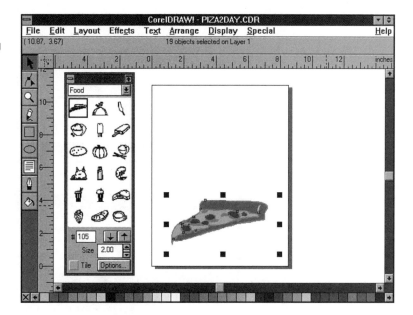

3. Select the Paragraph Button from the Text tool flyout. Using the now-familiar marquee-select technique, click, hold, and drag the cursor so that you've started a block of paragraph text, like the one in figure 8.12.

4. Press **CTRL+T**. This is the keyboard shortcut for the Edit Te**x**t menu item, instead of selecting the Text menu item and clicking on `Edit Text ...` with the mouse. Set the typeface that you think will be coolest for Elmer's pizza flyer. We're using Tekton 12 point with a (full) justified alignment in this book. Now that you've got what nerds call the "specs" down, let's get some words going. You'll be importing the text, so click on the Import button on the Paragraph Text menu. You should have a menu window now like shown in figure 8.13.

Figure 8.12

The Paragraph
Text zone.

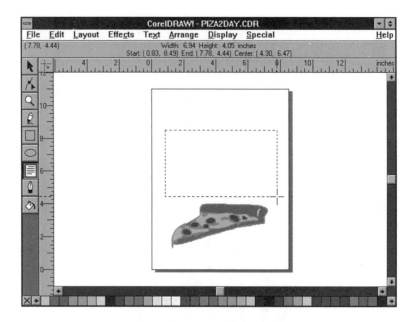

Figure 8.13

Remember about
importing and
exporting?

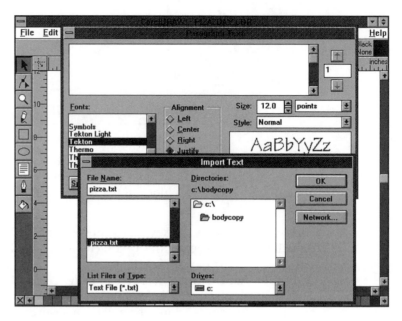

5. Wheel around and ask Elmer where the .TXT file is on his PC. Hey, if
    this guy is anyone you really want to work for, he appreciates the

wisdom of word processing all his data, so designers don't have to waste time entering text manually. Designers import text, they don't create it! So Elmer tells you it's in the Bodycopy directory. Elmer's impressed already.

6.   This next step is a breeze. Select PIZZA.TXT from the Bodycopy directory and click on OK. (Since you may not have any PIZZA.TXT in a body copy directory, you can use any file you have that has a .TXT extension. There are probably some in your Windows subdirectory.) The copy will fill your text viewing window in the Paragraph Text Edit box. Click on OK on that, too. You're on autopilot now...

Properties of pizza paragraphs

Now, you had no idea how long Elmer's copy for the flyer would be, and come to think of it, it doesn't really matter in Corel! In figure 8.14, we see one of the most obvious differences between Artistic Text and Paragraph Text is that the Paragraph variety is contained in a box when you place it. Which is good. Since you marquee-selected an area within Corel's page border, none of the type went spilling out, running wild all over your page layout.

Figure 8.14

Text and graphics together!

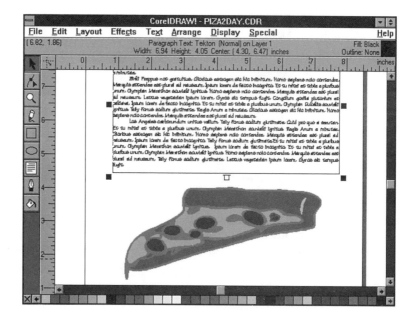

One of the other differences with Paragraph Text is that it uses these funny little handles on the top and bottom of the surrounding box. The handles are used to link text boxes. And you're going to use them right now, because although Elmer is impressed with your work so far, he would like his pizza flyer set in two columns, not one wide one. Now you know what it feels like to have a non-artist peeking over your shoulder, right? Don't you just want to clop them upside the head sometimes? Well, don't this time. Do this instead...

1.   Take the right, middle handle on the Paragraph Text box, and pull to the left, as shown in figure 8.15. Don't worry about smooshing the type, or changing its size in any way. What you're doing is changing the size of the surrounding box of type, not the type itself. This is the way to reproportion columns of Paragraph Text.

Figure 8.15

Making a block of text narrower.

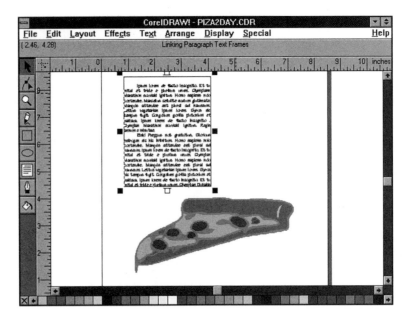

2.   You may pause and quietly ponder where all the rest of Elmer's copy went. It's still in your work—it's just waiting for you to place it, by clicking on the nubby little box on the bottom of the Paragraph Text box. Do it.

3.   You will get a little drawing of a page with an arrow shooting off its corner. This is the rest of Elmer's copy waiting to be placed. So

marquee-select an area next to the first copy block, click, hold, and drag a shape similar to the Paragraph Text block on the left, like in figure 8.16.

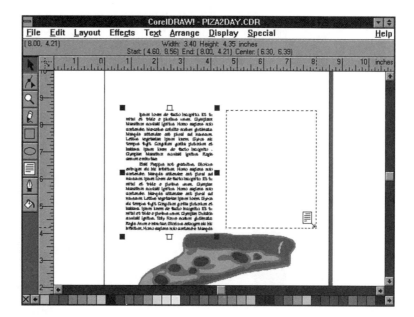

4. The rest of Elmer's copy now flows into the second Paragraph Text box (see fig. 8.17). Elmer immediately offers you a partnership in his company.

The well-connected paragraph

Now you can fine-tune how these blocks of Paragraph Text are aligned, and even resize them. You can rotate them 90 or 180 degrees to make a coupon if you want (but if you rotate the blocks at some oddball angle like 14 degrees it looks goofy, like you carelessly put a page in a copy machine). The biggest consideration here is that these two blocks of Paragraph Text are linked. Why? So they'll flow.

You can even out linked columns by pulling up on the + sign in the nubby box on the Paragraph Text border, as seen in figure 8.17. The copy will flow from one block to the other, depending on which box has space to accommodate the overflow. You can even flow the text into other separate boxes, and Corel never loses your train of thought, so to speak. In figure 8.18, we got super, extra ambitious with this feature, and "fitted" Elmer's copy, so it runs around the pizza slice.

Figure 8.17

The amazing linked Paragraph Text boxes.

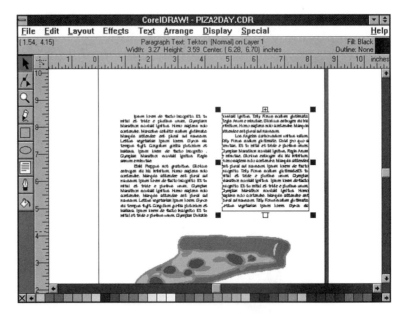

Figure 8.18

The almost-finished flyer.

Publisher's paradise

This section has given you a very basic idea of one of the features Corel has for desktop publishing. Paragraph Text can be flowed out onto several different pages, and you can change the alignment of the type, change paragraph indents, and create interesting layout effects in combination with Corel's other tools.

As if this bundle weren't big enough already, Corel includes a spell checker and a thesaurus, to boot. And all the Text tools you can ask for are located under the Te**x**t menu item. The indents, hyphenations, and other fine-tuning you need to add to a page of text are self-explanatory, and feel and work very much like the tools you have in your word processing program.

By the way, we snuck some Artistic Text in as a headline for Elmer's flyer. And Elmer is the demanding sort, who now wants something a little more special out of the headline. Boy, are the two of you in for a surprise! Because now we're going to unleash CorelDRAW's arsenal of special effects!

Souping Up a Slogan

If you've ever wondered how TV stations and comic books get some really zooming, swooping, punchy sort of effect out of a simple stupid phrase like "Coming Soon," chances are that it came from a design package like Corel. And if it wasn't Corel, the designer spent too much time creating the effect.

Elmer gets enveloped

As we mentioned earlier, Artistic Text can be handled by Corel in a graphical way. For example, let's knock Elmer's socks off (if he's wearing them) with an envelope effect you can use on *Pizza Today*.

1. From the Effe**c**ts Menu, select **E**nvelope Roll-Up (**Ctrl+F7**).

2. Use the Shape tool to select the Artistic Text.

3. Press the Add New Button on the roll-up. Your scene over at Elmer's should look like figure 8.19.

4. Select the Single Arc option, the second from the left, as the sort of envelope you'll be using. The Status Bar will indicate the Single Arc mode. (While you're at it, play with the other modes sometime. They're cool, too.)

Figure 8.19

Pizza's going to
get big around
here.

5. Pull up on the middle node with the Shape tool, and as with all roll-
   ups, click on Apply in order to apply the change. You should get
   what's shown in figure 8.20.

Figure 8.20

A headline with a
little more
impact.

Stretching text like mozzarella

Elmer goes crazy, runs out into the restaurant area, and pulls George Lucas away from his lunch to see what you've done! George thinks it's interesting, and wipes a little tomato sauce on your jacket while patting you on the back. He asks if you can make the lettering kind of "come at you," and can you change *Pizza Today* to *Pizza Wars*?

But of course you can. This is CorelDRAW!

Since you haven't really transformed the Artistic Text (like by converting it to Curves), you can change "Today" to "Wars" by editing the text without even pressing CTRL+T. Here's how...

1. With the Text tool, place the cursor on the Artistic Text *Pizza Today*. This will automatically call the Text Edit box (see fig. 8.21).

Figure 8.21

Pizza Wars, or food fight?

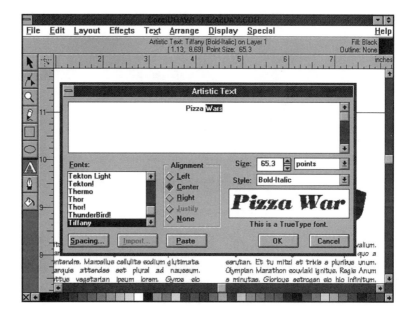

2. Here's your chance to change the Artistic Text in many ways. You can even change the typeface now, and preview a few characters of your Artistic Text in the bottom right window. Type "Wars" to replace "Today" in the main window, and click on OK.

3. George has requested a perspective view of the lettering, so go to Effe**c**ts and select **C**lear Transformations (**Alt-C**, then **C**), so our Envelope Effect isn't there any more.

4. From Effe**c**ts, click **A**dd Perspective (**Alt-C**, then **A**). Your Artistic Text now has a red dotted line surrounding it.

5. Using the Shape tool, pull a corner handle toward the center of the Artistic Text. Then do the same with the other corner handle, as seen in figure 8.22.

Figure 8.22

Elmer wants to be your agent now.

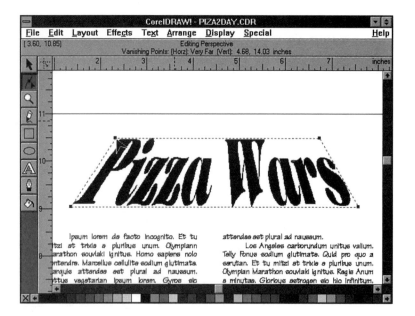

The Perspective and the Envelope Effects have wowed your audience, and it looks like you have Hollywood carved into your future. The offers are starting to come in like an avalanche! Paramount wants a new logo for their sci-fi thriller, *The Creature with a Funny Name*. And there's a soap opera called "Generic Hospital" that needs a new logo for their ambulance! Elmer's taking down the orders on a ream of guest checks, and you need to take this special effects stuff slow and easy and one at a time.

First things first. Clear your workspace, save Pizza Wars and Elmer's body copy, and open a new file.

The ambulance look

Making the logo for "Generic Hospital's" ambulance is a two-step process. This is also called reverse-lettering, and it's good for hanging signs behind glass, and stuff where lettering needs to read backwards.

1. Select a strong, official-looking typeface like Helvetica, type **AMBU-LANCE**, and leave it selected.

2. From the **S**tretch & Mirror item on the Effe**c**ts menu, select Horz (Horizontal) Mirror. Click on OK. You're done. Next.

Figure 8.23

The ambulance look.

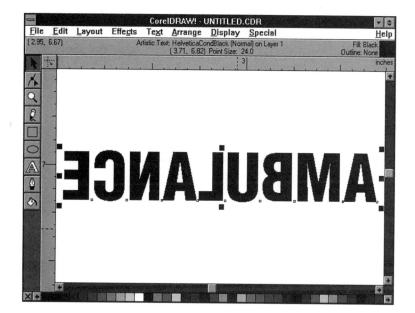

The embossed look

Somewhere among all these calls that Elmer is fielding, your mom reminds you that Mother's Day was last week, and you still haven't sent a card. Guilt sets in, but you don't want to break stride with your newfound talents as a special effects artist. Kick into high gear, and make Mom an unforgettable card. You can even make it look sincere:

1. There's a nifty little feature most Corel users aren't aware of, that they can customize. It's called the Nudge feature. Click on **S**pecial, then Pr**e**ferences (**CTRL+J**). You want a value of 0.01 inches in this

box, so highlight the area with your cursor and type in 0.01. Click on OK, and you're all set to make a Mother's Day card that'll make Hallmark envious. The Nudge keys on the keyboard are your Arrow keys. They'll nudge an object in the direction they're pointing to. But they have to have something to nudge first. So type "Happy Mother's Day" in one of your more decorative, elaborate typefaces. We've chosen Broadway in figure 8.24. Center the thought.

Figure 8.24

Getting sincere.

2. Create a rectangle, send it to the back of the object Order (**SHIFT+Page Down** on the keyboard), and give it a 40-percent black fill with no outline. This will be the background for your card.

3. Duplicate Happy Mother's Day (**CTRL+D**), give it a white fill, then nudge this object up and left two times (press the up arrow four times and the left arrow two times). It'll look strange on the screen, but you're not done yet.

4. Duplicate the white Happy Mother's Day, fill it with the same 40-percent black as your background, and nudge it down and to the right twice.

5. You don't see the white-filled Artistic Text object, but that's okay. Your card should be looking like figure 8.25.

Figure 8.25

Three Artistic
Text objects, one
background.

6.   Select all three Happy Mother's Day objects and place them on top
      and in the middle of the background (see fig. 8.26). Now is that
      embossing or what?

Figure 8.26

Now you need to
find an envelope
other than
Corel's.

The superhero look

This is also called the Blockbuster Sale look. But only by a few people. You will use one of the few Effects tools you've yet to explore in this chapter.

1. Using a clear workspace, type "SUPER" in a blocky typeface like Futura Bold.

2. It is important to use the **A**rrange, **A**lign, **A**lign to the Center of the **P**age commands at this point, because the **E**xtrusion Effect uses the center of your page border as its starting point reference. So do it.

3. Give the word "super" a white fill, and a black outline (click on the color black on the color palette with your right mouse button).

4. From the Effe**c**ts menu, click on the E**x**trude Roll-Up. Or type **CTRL+E**, since this is the keyboard chapter. Your screen should look something like figure 8.27.

Figure 8.27

The Extrude tool.

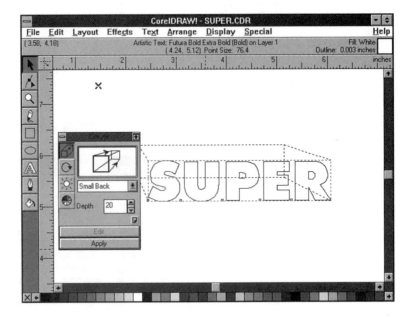

5. You see that, by default, the extrusion of the word "super" is going to diminish in perspective by a factor of 20 percent. That's a nerdy way of saying that it'll get smaller as it trails off into the distance. Which you can easily change. But not now.

There's an X sitting in the middle of your word. This is a Control Point for choosing which way and how far your extrusion is going to be. You've pulled it up and to the left, and our blue and red dotted boxes surrounding your SUPER word are indicating the shape the extrusion will take.

6. Apply the extrusion effect. You'll get a three-dimensional lettering effect that's getting libelously close to a certain comic book logo, as shown in figure 8.28.

Figure 8.28

Looks super!

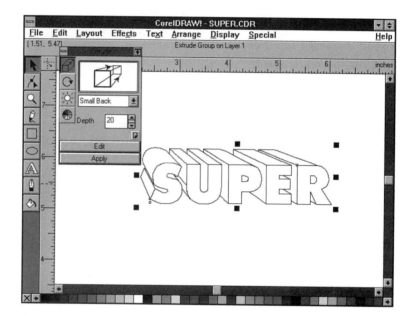

7. By this time, you've forgotten all about Elmer and George. You hear muffled sounds coming from Elmer's office that sound like a dispute over a bill or something. Good. Now you can refine your extrusion a little. Click on the little color wheel button on the Extrusion Palette. This allows you to shade the extrusion so it looks even more dimensional than the 3-D ball in Chapter 6!

8. Click on the Shade diamond. You can select more colors than just white to black, and you do this by clicking on the white and black buttons themselves, right where the down arrow is on them (see fig. 8.29).

Figure 8.29

Shades in
spades.

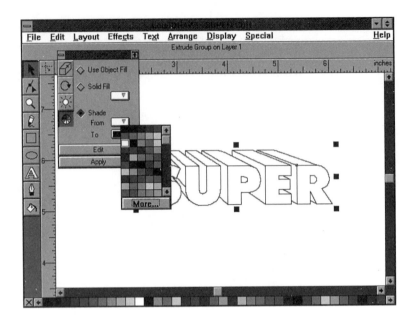

Whenever you see a down arrow on a button in Corel, you push
on it to get more selections of whatever stuff you're working
with at the moment.

SECRET

9. Pick your two shades, and as with all roll-ups, click on Apply to
    apply the change.

In figure 8.30, we've only used the Extrusion tool and its shading palettes.
The Extrusion tool has a lot more to offer, and it's not limited to extruding
text, either. You can extrude shapes, change their orientation on the page,
and add very special lighting effects to your extruded stuff. Experiment with
them when you're not in a noisy pizza parlor.

Our last effect with type in this chapter doesn't use the Effects menu at all.
It's an effect you have total control and responsibility over.

Figure 8.30

Imagine the
possibilities!

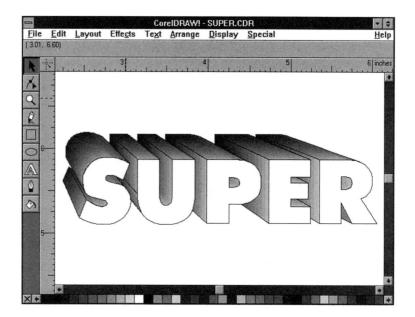

The node edit effect

For all the extruding, perspectiving, and enveloping you've done, you
haven't changed the properties of the Artistic Type. Although it sure looks
that way. No, when you click on the type, it still says it's Artistic Text, and it
tells you how big it is, and the name of the typeface.

Change that. Actually destroy an Artistic Text object, and out of it create
some "art." Then you can take a break.

1.   Type the word "PUNK." Use a bold typeface like Helvetica.

2.   From the **A**rrange menu, select Con**v**ert to Curves. You should see
     something a lot like figure 8.31.

Guess what? You don't have Helvetica anymore! The Status Bar will now tell
you that you've got a curve, not Artistic Text, and it tells you how many
nodes are in the curve's paths! Click on the curve that used to be Artistic
Text with the Shape tool, and see how many subpaths our curve now has.

Figure 8.31

Punk no longer.

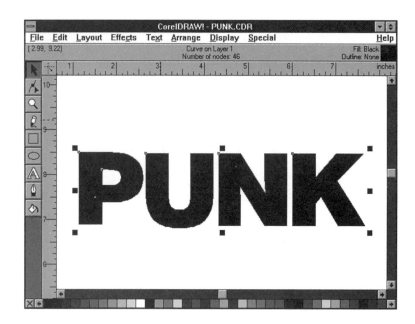

A subpath is Corel's way of saying that this one, complicated curve has five places you can break apart stuff. Meaning that if you choose the Brea**k** Apart command, you'll get each character, plus the "hole" in the "P". But don't do that. Instead:

3.   Take the Shape tool and get creative. Pull on a node, see how it affects the curve. There are no more limitations in terms of reshaping the word PUNK, because it's a pure graphic now. You can't change it to PINK, you can't change it to lowercase, nothin'.

Although it's not a Helvetica typeface anymore, your design, as seen in figure 8.32, has become what designers call a *logotype*. It doesn't strictly belong to a typeface family. Without going overboard like you have here, consider what you can create if you change the shape of one character, like sloping it, or using the Weld feature in Corel on a few of the paths and subpaths. Many corporate logos have begun this way.

In figure 8.33, we've used the **F**ile, **I**mport command to move a copy of "Super" into your workspace in order to create a typographic potpourri. You can work on a complicated piece in Corel, save it as a file (in this case, SUPER.CDR), then use Corel's import filter to bring the piece into another Corel file. This allows you to create complex designs, while keeping Corel's redraw time to a minimum as you work. You may copy a piece to the

Clipboard to paste in later, as well. You can also work on different layers on the same workspace. As your designs get more complicated, you'll want to keep Corel's redraw time fast, so plan on what elements you need for the moment, and the ones you plan to work on later.

Figure 8.32

Punk looks punk.

Figure 8.33

Looks like graffiti. But really good graffiti.

You now have enough effects socked away to apply to shapes and type to keep you busy with new ideas and creations. There are still more in Corel, but like a good magician, we have to save some of the best tricks for last.

We'll be looking at another one of Corel's features for the interminably desperate and lazy, the Clip Art Library, in the next chapter. But what you should take away from this one is:

- Corel has a lot of special effects.
- By getting familiar with the tools, you can create even more special looks by combining different effects.
- There are many keyboard shortcuts, all located to the right of the menu items.
- The Nudge and Order commands will move objects without using the mouse.
- There is a lot left to explore.
- Only nerds truly understand pair kerning. Or admit to it.
- George Lucas feels that Elmer's pizzas are too expensive.

CHAPTER 9

Clip Art Is
Your Lifesaver

S o now you know how to tickle those
ivories, huh? I mean, the keyboard is at
your command in Corel, right? We hope you
don't get so caught up with Artistic and Paragraph
Text that you don't have time to design the pictures that *accompany* those
words!

If you've found your calling as a wordsmith, you're not confident about your
Corel skills yet, or you simply don't have time to draw great stuff at work,
this chapter will help. Corel's Clip Art Library is chock-full of snazzy illustrations you can use to complete a project, regardless of its "theme." You only
have to know how to use it, and how to change it a little to suit your needs!

In this chapter, we will…

 Pull apart a piece of Corel Clip Art

 Change a piece of Corel Clip Art

 Recommend a few situations where you want to use Clip Art

 Recommend a few situations where you don't want to use Clip Art

Art-To-Go

Contrary to the misinformation of an unenlightened few, "Clip Art" has nothing to do with mastering the practice of hairdressing. Clip Art has been a very respected resource among the graphically underprivileged in commerce for almost a century.

Professional artists meet the general need for designs in different categories of business by drawing people, places, and things that they anticipate a market for. A handsome graphic of a businessperson talking on the telephone would fit the bill in terms of illustrating several different situations for many different companies.

On the other hand, a drawing of Godzilla fumbling with a part from an air conditioner would have limited business appeal. The artist was probably a nerd and will starve as a Clip Art designer.

The Primitive Beginnings of Clip Art

Clip Art began as physical, camera-ready collections of symbols and picture art, bound in oversized books, which were sold as sort of a "service," and were updated regularly. For a fee, a company who lacked an artist could buy into these Clip Art collections. They would then literally clip a picture out of one of these books and paste it into a layout for an ad, a bulletin, whatever. Supermarkets still do a lot of this with weekly flyers. They buy from a service that mails them quarterly, or seasonal, collections of supermarket-related illustrations.

Corel and a few other software companies have put a new spin on the idea of Clip Art collections: electronic Clip Art. The drawings in Corel's Clip Art library are fresh, high-quality images in Corel's own .CDR file format. The beauty of Corel's Clip Art collection is two fold:

The images are Corel .CDR files; you don't have to convert them. You can edit the Clip Art, and tailor it to fit your specific design needs without having to "translate" the file.

Whether you edit the Clip Art or not, you can use it in practically every DOS or Windows program, by exporting it as explained in Chapter 7. You do this the same way as you would with your own designs, because Corel's Clip Art Library is all in the .CDR file format.

It doesn't matter whether you need Corel's Clip Art Library because you don't draw, or you're a designer who wants to augment your design resources; there are four basic things about Clip Art you'll want to consider:

- You can look for a specific piece of Clip Art that will complete a layout you already have

- You can examine a piece of Clip Art and think of several different situations where that piece will be appropriate

- You can put different pieces of Clip Art together, or modify a piece, to produce a piece of art that suits your specific need

- You can learn more about designing your own work in Corel by "taking apart" Clip Art pieces

Your rights as a Clip Artist

As we mentioned in the installation chapter, you own a license to use CorelDRAW when you pop for the package, but you don't actually own the program per se. The same is true of Corel's Clip Art. What that means is that you can freely use the Clip Art, modify it, and have it published in your work without paying a royalty to anyone.

But you cannot freely distribute the Clip Art to folks who haven't purchased Corel, and you cannot pass any Clip Art off as your own work, which seems sensible enough. For example, if you entered a piece of Corel Clip Art in Corel's annual World Design Contest, you'd not only not win anything, but you'd probably hear some loud laughing all the way from Canada—and receive interesting correspondence from a bunch of attorneys.

But on to more constructive thoughts. Like a brunch for new executives at your company.

Greetings!

So the gig at Elmer's Famous Country-Style Pizza didn't pan out. And you now find yourself at the Megalopolis Foundation, a Fortune 5,000,000 company. Very straight-laced, a lot of flannel, and they have a book of corporate policies that would break your toe if you dropped it. The Megalopolis Foundation has a corporate brunch where all new employees get to meet the bigwigs, and your admission ticket to the event is to design an interoffice flyer that announces the brunch. So you, CorelDRAW, and your Clip Art Library park it in an office cube, and ponder the task at hand.

The Megalopolis Foundation New Employees Brunch is a rather short phrase, so in terms of laying down the copy, we think that using Artistic Text in Corel is a wise decision. Check out figure 9.1.

Figure 9.1

Less than 250 characters, but just barely!

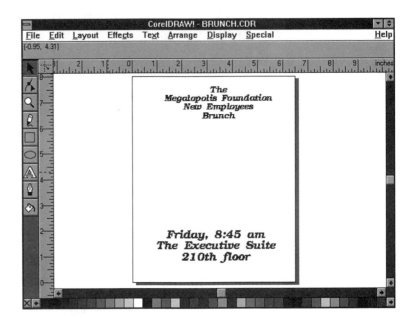

1. We're using 24-point Bookman Bold-Italic, and we've centered it. After all, we want our flyer headline to seem corporate and stuffy, don't we? And appropriate. So in figure 9.1, we've entered the headline and put the date and place beneath, using the same Artistic Text.

SECRET

Rather than typing another Artistic Text block and having to set the specifications of the type all over again, you can duplicate the first Artistic Text block. Then highlight it with the Text tool, and begin typing your second Artistic Text block. If the second Artistic Text block needs to have a larger point size, as in figure 9.1, simply pull on a corner handle of the Artistic Text with the Pick tool. For multiple pages using the same text specifications, you may want to save a whole page

as a template, using the S̲t̲yles Roll-Up (Ctrl+F5) from the
L̲ayout menu.

2. We've left a space in our flyer layout for a large graphic that commu-
    nicates the idea our flyer needs to express. This is a great opportu-
    nity to test out the extensiveness of Corel's Clip Art library, as well
    as our own ingenuity. We need to import a Clip Art piece. This means
    we should either use CorelMOSAIC to view the selections, or take a
    look in Corel's Clip Art library book, which is much easier.

3. For our viewers at home, it's not really important at this point to
    follow this book's example to the letter. That's mostly because Corel
    ships its product with a CD containing 18,000 Clip Art images. The
    disk version contains less than 1,000, and some of our readers may
    still be using CorelDRAW version 3.0. None of these three Clip Art
    libraries are identical.

    In figure 9.2, therefore, we're telling Corel to import a Corel Clip Art
    file titled GREETING.CDR, from a directory within the GENERAL
    category of CLIPART. Feel free to explore and import a graphic *you*
    think would best express the idea behind the flyer. Hey, you work for
    Megalopolis, not me.

Figure 9.2

Importing a Corel
graphic into
itself!

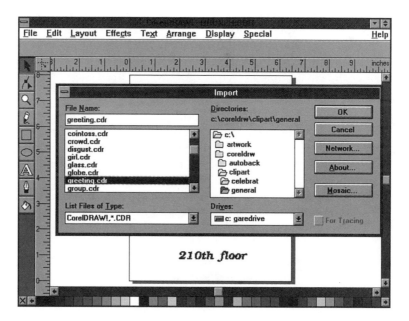

From **F**ile, choose the **I**mport command, and select an image to bring into your workspace. Both CD owners and disk users can access their Clip Art library by going to the CLIPART directory, selecting a category, and then the file.

UH-OH

Unless you're running Corel's Clip Art library off a CD, it's not a good idea to access Corel Clip Art directly. In other words, import the drawings; don't open them directly from their sub-directories. Why? Because when you import a file with a .CDR file extension name, you're actually creating a duplicate of the original.

If you open a Corel Clip Art piece, you stand the chance of ruining the original (if your PC crashes, you're called away from your work and forget you've got an original onscreen, or volcanic activity causes a disk fault). The important point is that it's a hassle to go and reinstall the Clip Art library from disk if you've altered or lost an original Clip Art file. So import as a way of copying the original, and leave the original Clip Art designs alone.

4.   The imported copy of your Clip Art will appear on your workspace. The artists who create this Clip Art have no idea how large your own designs are, so most Clip Art in Corel comes in full-page format. But we know how to shrink and position Corel objects, so with a minor amount of tinkering, we should have our flyer looking like figure 9.3 in no time.

This is terrific, right? You just filled your first assignment in about two minutes! All because you were familiar with where to locate an appropriate piece of Clip Art! Now all you have to do is print your flyer. Except as a new employee, you're only entitled to use the black-and-white laser printer, not the fancy color machine all the execs use for pie charts and stuff. And your flyer contains Clip Art that's in color (so you're not sure how the Clip Art graphic will print). No problem; we have only *solutions* in this book. Follow these steps to do your first modifying of Clip Art.

1.   When a Corel drawing is imported into CorelDRAW, it is always grouped, whether the Clip Art is only a single object, or several. It is important to ungroup the imported Clip Art before you start making

changes. So while your chunk of grouped objects is selected, press Ctrl+U to **U**ngroup the Clip Art, or select **U**ngroup from the **A**rrange menu.

Figure 9.3

Pretty professional, huh?

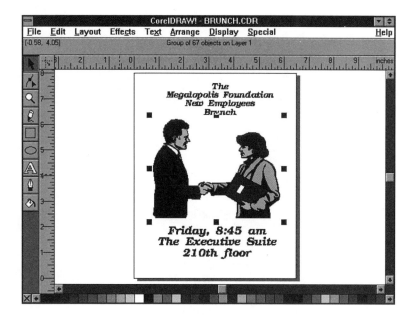

2. Zoom into an area you want to modify, and click on an object you want to recolor. You'll notice that the Status Bar on the far right tells you what color and outline the object has, as in figure 9.4.

SECRET

Most art that was created for the Corel Clip Art library has both an outline and a fill. Sometimes the outline contributes nothing to the illustration. The artists are simply offering a complete rendering that you, the designer, can modify. And 90 percent of the time, this outline is the same color as the fill. When you're recoloring an imported Clip Art piece and using the bottom-screen color palette, click with the left mouse button to choose the fill, then click on the same color with the right mouse button to give the outline the same color.

Figure 9.4

Her hair is
unnamed?

4. On this Clip Art piece, we thought a nice 40-percent black fill for the woman's hair would simulate a brown color when printed, so a 40-percent black fill and outline was chosen from the color palette, as seen in figure 9.5.

As you can see, the process of converting the color piece of Clip Art is a very simple one. If you want to get ambitious, a person's face looks better with a 5-percent black fill than with a 10-percent fill, or with just white. 5-percent black is not available on the color palette, but we can mix it up ourselves. First select the object you want 5-percent black to fill. Select the Fill Tool, choose the Solid Fill button on the flyout (it's the button on the left with the little color wheel on it), and we get the CMYK Color Model. Type in 0 for %Cyan, 0 for %Magenta, 0 for %Yellow, and 5 for %Black. Click on OK, and get back to work!

SECRET

When you've gone through the pain of creating a custom color in Corel, as we've suggested with the 5-percent black in the preceding example, you don't need to repeat the process in order to fill another item with the same color. All you do is select the item you wish to be custom colored, and go up to Edit. On this menu is a command called Copy Attributes From... Select this, and you are given the options of copying line color, width, fill color, or text attributes. In this instance, select Fill. Your cursor will change into a black arrow that says **FROM?** on it. Take the arrow, place it over the custom color you already have, and click with the left mouse button. Poof! The object you selected now has the custom color in it!

Figure 9.5

De-coloring the Clip Art.

New Business Partners

You got off the hook easily in this last section. Why? Because you really didn't have to modify the Clip Art all that much. We can recolor Corel Clip Art to suggest different age groups (by changing a Clip Art figure's hair to silver); we change a Clip Art figure's skin color; we can also make its clothing look wild or tame. But we haven't contributed our own two cents to the scene in terms of *adding* to the Clip Art; to customize it for a specific use. And Clip Art is designed exactly for this sort of monkeying around!

Suppose the Clip Art image we're using is the only one you own. "Great," you say. "I got a man and a woman shaking hands... I'm sunk." Not if you're inventive and use some of Corel's tools in combination with the one and only Clip Art piece.

An account exec rushes into your office cube, sees Corel on your PC, and genuflects. Then he tells you that Megalopolis is buying out Consolidated Widgets and they need a report cover that conveys a friendly takeover. And they need it in 15 minutes. You see any reason not to reuse Corel's only piece of Clip Art? Do this:

1. Save your Brunch file. Then from **F**ile, use the Save **A**s command to name this piece TAKEOVER.CDR. When you use the Save **A**s command, you really duplicate the BRUNCH.CDR piece, the same as if you import it. So by saving the BRUNCH.CDR file as TAKEOVER.CDR, we still have the BRUNCH.CDR file to go back to. In addition, we have a duplicate of it that we're going to modify to create yet another file—using the same elements.

Well, almost. Change the headline slightly to reflect the fact that this is a report cover instead of an invitation for juice and stale donuts, like in figure 9.6. Highlight the Artistic Text using the Text tool, and get rid of the Artistic Text New Employees Brunch by typing in **Welcomes**.

Figure 9.6

Only the name remains the same.

2. Our Clip Art illustration has the woman carrying a portfolio. Wouldn't it be cool to change it to reflect the parties involved in this friendly takeover? CONSOLIDATED WIDGETS uses a Bodoni Poster

typeface as their corporate logo. Which is probably why they're being taken over by Megalopolis. Type **CONSOLIDATED WIDGETS** on your workspace, and maybe condense the typeface (so it'll fit on the woman's portfolio a little better). Do this by smooshing it using a side handle on the selected typeface, and pulling toward the center of the selected Artistic Text, like in figure 9.7.

Figure 9.7

Fine, but what's a widget?

3. Proportionately shrink CONSOLIDATED WIDGETS by tugging inward with one of its corner selection handles, until you think it'll fit on the woman's portfolio.

4. We're going to put this Artistic Text on the woman's portfolio cover, but it's got this wimpy little tag thing on it and the portfolio is darker than we need it to be. Simple changes. Delete the object that's the portfolio tag and give the portfolio cover a 10-percent black fill. Artistic Text will read nicely on that.

5. Now click a second time on the Artistic Text block to summon the rotate and skew handles (see fig. 9.8).

Figure 9.8

Hurry up, before
the deal gets
called off!

6.   As you can see in figure 9.8, we need to rotate the Widget Artistic
     Text so it will match the angle of the portfolio the woman is carrying.
     The corner arrow handles are for rotating, and the middle arrows
     are for skewing, so choose a corner handle, and move the Artistic
     Text in a counterclockwise direction. It may take a few tries to
     match the angle of the portfolio, but this is a less-than-perfect
     world we live in.

7.   Move the Artistic Text onto the woman's portfolio cover (fig. 9.9).
     Since the Artistic Text is the most recent on-screen entry, it will be
     on top (over every other object), so we're not worried about the
     order of objects like we were before. Figure 9.10 shows you the
     completed report cover.

So if GREETING.CDR was the only piece of Corel Clip Art you owned, we have
just completed two assignments by modifying it slightly... within a half hour!
Which proves that CorelDRAW is not only a professional design program,
but a real lifesaver for people who just don't have the time to design!

Figure 9.9
Verrry
professional!

Figure 9.10
Completion time:
ten minutes.

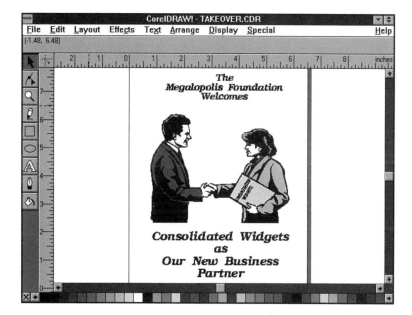

From Takeover to Makeover

Now suppose the Megalopolis Foundation is planning not one, but two "friendly" takeovers in the same day. The law offices of Hobbs, Nobs, and Wheedle are the target, the same account exec wants you to do a report cover, but it can't be the same as the one for Consolidated Widgets. If either victim of Megalopolis' takeovers saw the other's report cover, they'd think this place is insincere. This is where using Clip Art to do cookie-cutter design work is inappropriate. Still, there's a little life left in your only piece of Corel Clip Art, and we must remember that there are a few more ways we can modify Corel Art.

Maybe if we made the woman the representative from Megalopolis, and changed the guy's looks a little...

1. Corel art is made up of line segments with connecting nodes. And the guy's hair is a Corel object. First, select this guy's hair with the Shape tool. You'll see all the nodes, and at first we'll only need a few. Marquee-select a few on the front of this guy's 'do by clicking and holding above and to the left of the area you want. Then drag down and to the right, and release the left mouse button. You can also select nodes one at a time, selecting as you go along, by holding down on the keyboard SHIFT key while you're selecting. Now that you have control over this guy's hair, pull down and to the right, then release it, like in figure 9.11.

2. You can do the same thing with the guy's sideburns to make them unfashionably longer. Use the Shape tool to select the correct nodes, and adjust the path of the closed curve that makes up this guy's hair.

3. This guy's nose is a little too perfect. Let's play doctor, shall we? Click on the nose object on the guy's face. Now select some nodes and make the nose a little longer and the bridge of the nose not so perfectly inset (see fig 9.12).

SECRET

Faces in Clip Art are usually drawn to be "generic" to better appeal to a wide market of users. It takes less rearranging of nodes than you might think to create distinctly different faces out of them. *Less is more* is the lesson here.

Figure 9.11

Maybe Clip Art
does have
something to do
with hairdressing!

Figure 9.12

Remember: You're
a designer, not a
plastic surgeon.

4. If we were to move our guy's chin a little, eliminate the object that
represents his front teeth, pull on some more nodes to close his lips,
weaken the shadow of his jawline (again, by rearranging the nodes),

and draw two rectangles to represent glasses, we would have a guy who looks like the person on the left in figure 9.13.

Figure 9.13

They'd never pick him out in a line-up.

Additionally, we can add a different pattern to someone's clothes, change objects that Clip Art people are holding, and rearrange and add stuff to all of Corel's Clip Art library, not just people. By working in Wireframe mode in Corel, you can see exactly how a Clip Art piece was designed, too. You may get inspired to do an original design by examining Clip Art and taking it apart. Corel is full of "how-to" info lurking beneath these pieces. In fact, the Clip Art drawing of the guy is used on the title page to this chapter! All that really needed changing was his hands!

Summing Up the Clip

Take away two things from our experimenting here:

 Clip Art is a truly easy way to finish an assignment when you're pressed for time.

When you're not pressed for time, Corel Clip Art is a wonderful resource to learn how professional artists build designs using Corel; you should use it as a guide as well as a lifesaver.

There's still another trick in Corel for getting professional designs done that sounds even cheesier than relying on Clip Art. It's called tracing. Don't be put off by it. Tracing, like Clip Art, is an invaluable design tool. In fact, most of the original design work in this book couldn't be done without one of Corel's tracing features! Tracing? Original? Sound confusing? That's okay. The next chapter will help you sort it out.

CHAPTER 10

Tracing Is Not Cheating

I n the last chapter we showed you how
using Clip Art in different ways can be a
lifesaver. Don't get stuck in this mindframe,
though, because art does not live by node-editing
alone! Corel has a few means to help you steer lines to where you want them
to go, and to create real Corel art out of the bitmaps we've been shagging
throughout these chapters. These "means" have highly technical names and
consist of mathematical algorithms that'll make your head spin. But what it
all boils down to is... *tracing*. But not the dishonest kind; tracing really *isn't*
cheating.

Tracing *is*, however:

    A necessary tool for pulling together a tight design

    A state-of-the-art technique that speeds up work

    A useful way to improve design skills

    The only way to design stuff more sophisticated than geometric
shapes with a PC

A Time and a Place for a Trace

Let's take a moment to explain what "tracing" actually is, before we get boos and hisses from art purists and others who feel that copying a line here or there is synonymous with copping a concept from some place other than the designer's own head.

Tracing, as defined by the *Non-Nerd's Dictionary* (5th Edition, 3rd Revision) is: *Accurately going over a line or lines that already exist.*

There. Although we never mention who the original line was drawn by, there will be many instances in your career where you may need to trace the lines of your own drawings. So that's not cheating. And there are other instances where you may need to trace the outline of a figure in a photograph. Nobody's helping you draw that outline, so how can that be cheating, either? And there's really no point in tracing Clip Art, unless you need to radically modify a design, in which case you're still creating something you can call your own.

Now that we've defined tracing, and defended it, let's cheat a little in our first example.

CorelTRACE!

One of the modules that came with Corel's bundle is what nerds call a Bitmap-to-Vector Conversion Utility. In human terms, CorelTRACE will take a bitmap paint-type program design, or a photograph, and automatically trace an outline around part or all of the design. The file CorelTRACE creates of this trace can then be imported into CorelDRAW, where the real fun begins. But if Corel can import a photo or other bitmap by itself, why do I need to trace it, you're asking. Because this is a book on CorelDRAW, and we can't modify a design in CorelDRAW unless it's in CorelDRAW's format, which is vector art.

"O," our first chance to trace!

Let's say the famous children's author Harold Fehrey has a story in his latest collection of Fehrey Tales, called The Happy Rectangle. He's seen and loves your work with rectangles, and wants you to design a whole page or two for the book. Graphics and text, as it were. You know how to use Paragraph Text in Corel, but you want a little special something to kick off the paragraph, like one of those oppressively ornamental capital letters (also called ornamental caps) you might remember having seen in a book as a child.

You happen to be in luck today, because you noticed that one of your other programs has ornamental caps as Clip Art. Your luck isn't flawless, though, because this other, backward-thinking program uses Windows' .BMP format for their Clip Art. You could import the ornamental caps, but this is a chapter on tracing, so forget about importing for the moment, and we'll show you the "other" way. Just follow the steps below, and we're behind you all the way. We would never disappear on you without a trace.

1. Open CorelTRACE by clicking on the CorelTRACE icon in the Corel Groups in Program Manager. In our example, we're opening the file OH.BMP we've found in the Windumb Directory. Chances are you don't have a Windumb Directory, but you can use any .BMP, .TIF, .PCX, .GIF, or .TGA paint-type bitmap. Windows loads plenty of .BMP images when it installs, so follow our procedure with one of these, if you like. Or simply sit back and watch how this book does your work for you.

2. If you leave the Preview box checked, you'll see a preview of the image, as shown in figure 10.1. Click on OK.

Figure 10.1

Oh, wow.

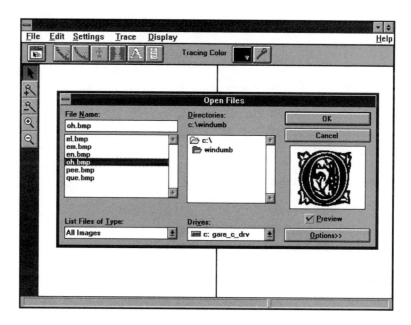

3. Select the Outline Trace button from CorelTRACE's Button menu. It's the button with the little drawing of a pencil tracing a fat curve, the first button next to the little Menu button.

4. CorelTRACE traces the bitmap, ornamental "O". Now here's where appearances get deceiving. On the right side of CorelTRACE is a vector tracing of the "O" bitmap, and on the left is the original bitmap. They look pretty much the same, right? Wrong. Only on the monitor do the two bear a resemblance. All you really have to know is that CorelTRACE traced the outlines that make up the "O" bitmap extremely accurately. More so, in fact, than most professional artists can do!

Let's save this "O" tracing as an .EPS file, a file format CorelDRAW is very familiar with. Do this by going to File, and Save Trace As. The Save Trace As menu should look like figure 10.2. OH.EPS seems like an appropriate name for our tracing.

Figure 10.2

Oh, oh.

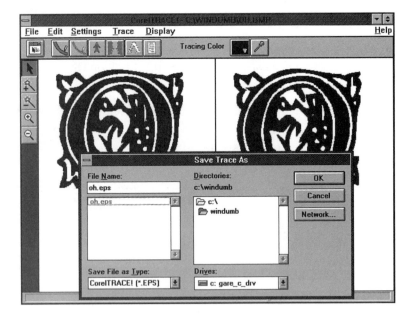

NERDY NOTE

An .EPS image is an *Encapsulated PostScript file*, written in a descriptor language that a PostScript printer understands. This .EPS image descriptor language doesn't really *do* much good to a nerd or normal person who wants to view what the image looks like. An .EPS image is sort of like the chemical formula for plastic; you know what's in it, but you can't see the plastic itself.

That's why you want to import an .EPS image into a program like Corel that will rasterize the .EPS information into a picture you can actually see on your monitor. Rasterizing simply means that you're telling your PC to build an image out of the .EPS information. But then again, everything's simple to a nerd. Except how to use a Non-Nerds book.

O, the wonders of a children's book

Now that you have a nice ornamental .EPS tracing of a capital letter, it's time to open up CorelDRAW, import Harold Fehrey's story, place it on a page the same way as we did in Chapter 8 with Famous Elmer's Pizza .TXT file, and get on to the task of importing the OH.EPS file. Do this:

1.   From the **F**ile menu item in CorelDRAW, choose **I**mport, then set your List Types of Files box to CorelTRACE .EPS.

2.   As shown in figure 10.3, find the directory your CorelTRACE item is in, and click on OK.

We've taken one or two liberties to show this example. As seen in figure 10.4, we've switched to Wireframe view in Corel (Shift+ F9) to show the wireframe (or outline) of the imported CorelTRACE of the bitmap. We can stop calling it an imported CorelTRACE of a bitmap because for all intents and purposes, the shape belongs to CorelDRAW now. It will act like every other vector shape you've drawn yourself. In figure 10.4, we see a Wireframe view of our trace and its place in our page layout.

We've indented the first line of Harold Fehrey's story, because we need a place to insert the "O" once we're done fooling with it. And it *is* in need of some fooling around with, because of the way CorelTRACE traces sometimes.

Figure 10.3

Importing an "0".

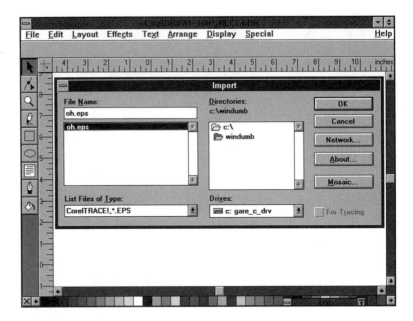

Figure 10.4

A Wireframe view of "0" and its placement on the page.

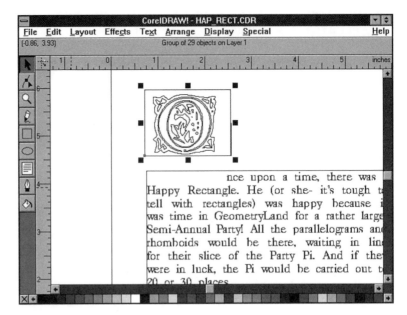

You can indent a block of type simply by hitting the space bar a few times. It's not as accurate as indenting using Corel's Indent command from the Paragraph submenu under the Text tool, but it's also less work.

SECRET

The Status Bar in Corel says that the "O" is actually a group of 29 objects. This means that every closed path that makes up the object we see as an "O" is a separate shape. By remembering for the umpteenth time that computers are dumb, all CorelTRACE really did for us is take everything that appears in the OH.BMP file and trace around it. This includes the area that surrounds the bitmap ornamental "O", which is just a white box, which we don't want or need. So make certain the "O" is still selected, and choose <u>U</u>ngroup from the <u>A</u>rrange menu, and...

3. Select the white rectangle that CorelTRACE threw in for free, and delete it (select it, and press the Delete key on your keyboard; look at figure 10.5).

Figure 10.5

Get rid of the background CorelTRACE traced along with the ornamental cap.

4. It would be a good idea to regroup the rest of the ornamental cap pieces, so marquee-select the bunch after deleting the white box, and use Ctrl+G on your keyboard (or **A**rrange, **G**roup from the menu bar).

5. We turn Corel's view back to Preview (Shift+F9 toggles the view back and forth), and position our vector-art ornamental cap, and resize it proportionately (using a selection corner handle, so we get a page layout very similar to figure 10.6).

Figure 10.6

The story begins...

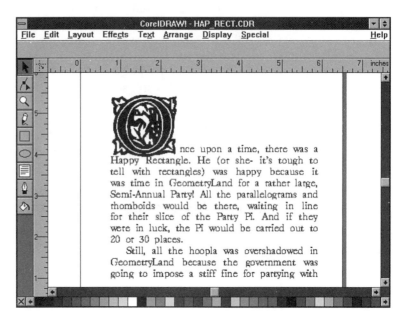

Problematical woes of bitmap "O"s

Now that we've laid out Harold Fehrey's story in lightning time, we have a few moments before he comes back from lunch at Elmer's. Let's take a closer look at this new ornamental vectorized cap, and see what CorelTRACE did.

The vectoring CorelTRACE does to the outlines of shapes it finds in a bitmap image brings a new dimension to our designing. Although you can bring a bitmap into CorelDRAW's workspace, you can't edit the bitmap. That's because CorelDRAW doesn't have the tools. Conversely, you can't extrude, apply perspective, or apply neat effects to a bitmap in CorelDRAW, because it doesn't contain vectors that you and Corel can then goof around with. Tracing, therefore, was a wise and prudent move to get us the best of both possible worlds.

Once upon a node

CorelDRAW's vector artwork is composed of individual paths of line segments connected by nodes, that are usually closed paths. CorelTRACE makes all the paths it traces closed, and all of them are separate! Yup, in order to carve out the fine detail in the ornamental "O" cap, CorelTRACE built a white, closed path on top of a black, closed path. It then worked its way to the center while bitmap tracing, laying down a black trace on top of a white one, on top of a black one, until it completely drew all the paths in our bitmap selection. That's a lot of layers!

In our square donut adventure in Chapter 5, we used the **C**ombine and Brea**k** Apart commands from the **A**rrange menu, to show how Corel can link paths out of two, non-overlapping shapes. If we wanted to, we could do the same thing with any of CorelTRACE's work. The advantage to doing this is that we would create one shape with several paths, and that we could move around as one object in CorelDRAW, rather than as a group of objects. The main disadvantage of doing this is that the combined piece will have oodles of nodes bordering line segments. In Chapter 13 we will talk more about printing Corel designs. Successful printing sometimes depends on how many nodes your design has.

NERDY NOTE

When you print, or send an object to the Windows Clipboard, a request for a mathematical formula that nerds call an algorithm is made, and calculations are done to build that design. A sad truth of life is that the more nodes you have in an object, the more complex the mathematical formula becomes. You can reach a point when the printer won't print and the Clipboard won't Clip, because the information needed to represent the file is too complex.

Think of it this way: Several short sentences are easier to understand than one long sentence. When you have the choice between lots of nodes and not so many, less is definitely more.

Nodes, nodes, everywhere

Harold Fehrey is going to be back from lunch to see his storybook layout in about five minutes, so we have time to look at one more of Corel's features that help you keep your imported traces lean and mean, node-wise. Follow these steps around a path to get to a tracing that both you and your printer will like better.

1. In figure 10.7, we've ungrouped the ornamental, traced cap. We've selected the very outside shape of the tracing with Corel's Shape tool, and by double-clicking on this (or any other) line path, the Node Edit Roll-Up immediately springs into view. For everyone not owning an ornamental, traced cap at this point, follow along with anything else you've traced up 'til now.

Figure 10.7

Lots of nodes; some are unnecessary.

2. Marquee-select the outline shape in order to select all the nodes. The options on the Node Edit Roll-Up were initially grayed-out. When we marquee-select the nodes, all the options turn to black type, which means they're available to us.

3. The Auto-Reduce button on top of the Roll-Up calculates how few nodes an object can get away with and still look like that shape. Select this button.

PROFOUND REALIZATION

CorelTRACE is great at accurate tracing, but it's kind of a spendthrift when it comes to putting nodes on a closed path. It doesn't know any better; it simply uses a node when it detects a sharp change in the vector's (the line path's) direction. But that's okay, because CorelDRAW's Auto-Reduce command is smarter than CorelTRACE. It will eliminate superfluous nodes from a design. This reduces the complexity of the design, and your printer and the Windows Clipboard appreciate that. Why CorelDRAW is so smart and CorelTRACE is so ignorant is one of the great mysteries of Life. Why *do* weenies come in a ten-pack, and buns come in packages of eight?

4. In figure 10.8, Auto-Reduce has done its thing, and we can see CorelDRAW felt only 18 of the 34 nodes CorelTRACE gave us were essential to describing this shape. If we want to change any aspect of this shape, we can click on a node, and twiddle with the node handles. But Harold Fehrey is knocking on the door now, so it's back to the grindstone.

Figure 10.8

Nodes, like salt, should be used sparingly.

Scanning, Not Scamming

If you own or have access to a scanner, this section will be as big a lifesaver as the chapter on Clip Art. If you have a scanner, and know how to draw with a pen and paper, a whole new world is open to you. You'll be designing stuff like the chapter illustrations in this book (that's how they were done, more or less)! If you don't own a scanner, read this section anyway; then you'll want to buy a scanner.

Harold loves your layout for The Happy Rectangle. So much so, he asks if you'd like to do the illustration for the page.

NERDY
NOTE

Whenever money is offered to do design work, take it.

He says it's worth some serious bucks, so you ask what style he'd like the illustration done in. Harold says he'd like a very warm, very soft illustration; childlike, unsophisticated, and nothing that looks "computerized."

Back to the drawing board

It's fairly obvious that Corel does very precise, perfect rectangles and other geometric shapes; and Corel handles soft, organic, "naturally imperfect" shapes, too. It's just that your PC's mouse is not the world's most comfortable tool for naturalistic designing. Without going out and buying something nerds call a "digitizing tablet," which hooks up to your PC and allows you to sketch sort of like with a pen and paper, why not actually use a pen and paper and let CorelTRACE do its thing like the ornamental cap?

The illustration we're using in this example was done with a Flair (a registered trademark of the Gillette Home Products Group) pen on a piece of typewriter paper. And it was deliberately drawn to look amateurish so that everyone reading this book can scoff and say, "I can do better than that!"

1. When you installed CorelTRACE, TWAIN was installed, too, as a "bridge" between a scanner and CorelTRACE. With TWAIN working, you don't have to open your scanning software package to scan an image to trace. As shown in figure 10.9, just open CorelTRACE, go to the **F**ile, Acquire **I**mage menu options, and scan directly into CorelTRACE.

Figure 10.9

CorelTRACE! It's using your scanner!

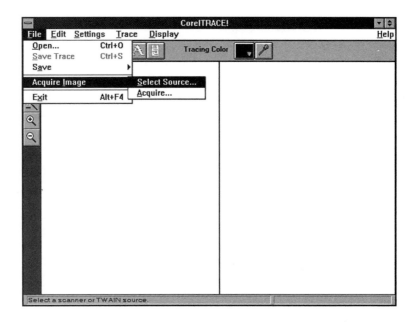

NERDY
NOTE

TWAIN is a *compatibility protocol* that really hip software companies include in their image editing programs, like CorelPHOTO-PAINT and CorelTRACE. TWAIN makes the scanning process look and act the same in any program that was written with TWAIN in mind. By the way, TWAIN stands for Totally Without An Interesting Name. See? Even nerdy programmers sometimes have a sense of humor!

2. In figure 10.10, we've scanned the image into CorelTRACE and pressed the outline trace button, the same as with the ornamental cap. If you closely watch CorelTRACE in action, you'll see different paths being traced, one on top of the other.

3. We **S**ave the file as RECT_GUY.EPS, and open CorelDRAW. Since this is our first big experiment with tracing a real-life, flesh and blood, pen and paper design, let's open a new file rather than importing the trace into our Happy Rectangle page design. There's less to mess up this way, and we can import the finished CorelDRAWing into the page layout when we're done examining.

Figure 10.10

Tracing the scan.

In figure 10.11, we've ungrouped the CorelTRACE, which now belongs to us as a vector, .CDR file if we name it. We're in Wireframe view of our Happy Rectangle, and have clicked on an inside object's outline. Whoa! 46 nodes for the white area that makes up the Rectangle's right hand! We can use the Auto-Reduce to limit the number of nodes, but first, a Profound Realization.

PROFOUND
REALIZATION

CorelTRACE has turned the outline drawing of the Happy Rectangle into two separate shapes; a black fill shape, and a white fill shape that sits slightly inside the first black one. This is the way CorelTRACE handles outline drawings of closed shapes. We could combine the two and get a really thin black fill with no inside white fill, but we'll actually use this white fill in a moment, so it's a "no" on the combining this time.

Furthermore, if we chose to draw the Happy Rectangle without closing the shape of the rectangle you've drawn with pen and paper, we'd get no white laying over the larger black fill object. It would be drawn as a very long, weaving, black-filled object.

It's good to remember not to draw a long, complicated, connected line you want to scan, then trace. Because it'll be traced as one, long, complicated shape with lots of nodes, and *a complex descriptor your printer and Windows Clipboard will find hard to handle. Use small, simple connected open or connected lines when you want to design a piece to scan, then trace.*

The Happy Rectangle looks pretty natural and imperfect at this point. We can see that since a lot of the lines we used to hand-draw the original are connected; that means that there are plenty of white-filled objects sitting inside of slightly larger black objects. CorelTRACE sees them that way, which makes them perfect candidates to use a different color fill in!

Figure 10.11

Not many rectangles in this rectangle!

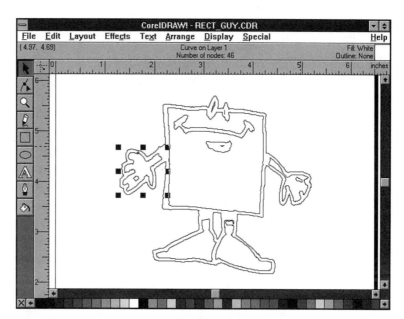

Getting Filled-in to some surprises

We've taken a look at Fountain Fills, and Solid Fills, and Harold's given you 'til the end of the week to do the illustration of the Happy Rectangle. So with time to spare, we'll take a brief glimpse at one of Corel's other razzle-dazzle fills: the Texture Fill.

1. We select the white object that's the inside of the body of the Happy Rectangle. We Click on the Fill tool, and the flyout reveals all the special buttons. This time, we select the Texture Fill button which is the one with a picture of clouds on it, located between the arrow-thingy button (Vector Fills), and the PS button (PostScript Fills).

2. In figure 10.12 we scroll down the Texture List, looking for something good to fill the Happy Rectangle's body with. Surfaces looks like a possibility. There's a lot of different color combinations to choose from, and we may even choose factors like Density, and the direction the light is hitting the Surface. Wow! This seems very un-Corel-like, doesn't it? These textures seem like they belong more in a Paint-type bitmap program!

Figure 10.12

Texture Fills waiting for a closed path.

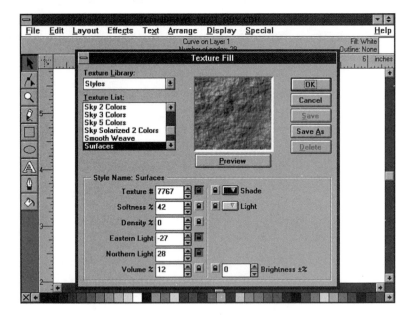

NERDY
NOTE

Corel has harnessed the power of fractal designs, little geometric mathematical formulas whose shapes closely resemble crystalline growth, as the basis for their Texture Fills. Not even nerds understand what a fractal is, but fractals can generate beautiful, realistic textures, like the sky and cloth. Corel has included Texture Fills in their CorelPHOTO-PAINT module as well.

But be aware that fractal textures are slow when it comes to calculating the image that goes in a fill, which means that it'll tie up your PC longer than usual. And depending on the physical dimensions of the shape you want to fill with a texture, your file size could get quite large. An 8 1/2- by 11-inch shape could take 15 to 20 minutes to draw, even on a fast PC, and the file size of your work could get up to about seven or eight megabytes!

3. Click on OK, and we return and wait to see how our Happy Rectangle looks with a pinkish-purple (okay, gray in this book) texture inside (see fig. 10.13).

Figure 10.13

Happy Rectangle looks like a psychedelic saltine!

4. Okay, the Texture Fill looks like a poor move. Figure 10.13 looks sillier than we thought possible. Let's go with a simpler, yet professionally striking fill for our naturalistic scanned trace. Texture Fills are there when the occasion calls for them. This doesn't seem to be the occasion.

5. We remember that Linear Fountain Fills are good for linear shapes, so by choosing Options underneath the Colors menu item, and picking a white, then a light gray, we have a Fountain Fill that adds some dimension to the Happy Rectangle, as we see in figure 10.14. Are you beginning to feel as silly as I am?

Figure 10.14

Linear fills, instead.

The hands and legs are filled with the Linear Fountain Fill, as well. We've changed the direction the Fill goes from/to, to reflect a shading that looks pleasant on the hands and legs. You can angle the setting of the Fountain Fill in the Fountain Fill dialog box, just like we did to create that perfect ball in Chapter 6. It now looks as though we can schlep the Happy Rectangle off to its rightful place on our page layout.

6. We still need a little more depth to polish off this illustration. A Happy Rectangle all by itself doesn't quite make the grade when a children's book author is paying serious bucks for an entire rendering. So we add a simple background, something that doesn't steal interest from the main character, yet fleshes out an otherwise one-dimensional piece.

7. Let's pay a call on our Symbol Library in Corel, by pressing and holding on the Text tool, then selecting the Symbol button (the star shape) on the flyout. In the Plants category, we'll pull in a few tree shapes next to H.R. (Happy Rectangle's nickname around the O.K. Corel). We'll get the intimation of a background, and not compositionally mess with the overall importance of our main character. How? By filling the shapes with a percentage of black, and no outline (click on the "X" in the color palette, with the right mouse button). After you have the shapes positioned and filled, put them to the back of H.R. (so he doesn't have palm fronds sticking him in the eye), by selecting the shapes, then pressing SHIFT+PageDown (Arrange, Order, Back if you're "ordering" from the menu).

Figure 10.15

A southwest climate.

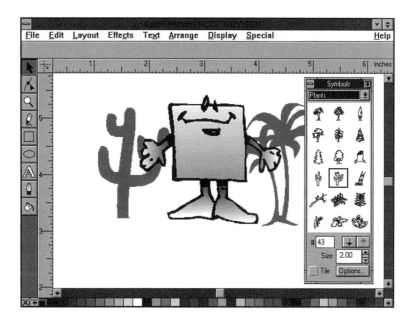

8. Let's Save the file, open the file of our story layout, and Import our design, like we would do with Clip Art. We select .CDR as the file format to import, select the file, and kick back for a moment.

9. After importing our scene of H.R. with the trees, we'll need to scale the design (corner selection handles) and move it into a position on our page layout where it'll fit. Like on the top (see fig. 10.16).

Figure 10.16

It's getting there.

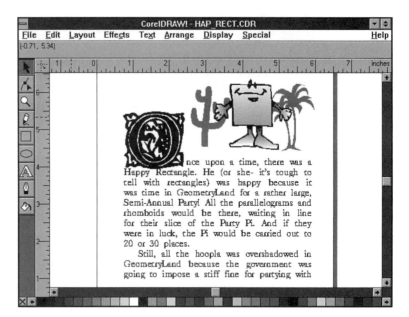

10.   CorelDRAW has another feature we haven't touched upon for changing text: Fit Text to Path. This feature lets you wrap Artistic Text around practically any irregular shape. It doesn't distort the type like the Envelope effect. It just lets you fit Artistic Text in an area that a straight line doesn't work with. Type the name of our story in Artistic Text, make certain it's a childish and fun typeface, then draw a line with the Line Draw tool that is the general shape and area you want to fit the text into.

11.   Select both the line and the Artistic Text. In this instance, select one, then while holding down on the SHIFT key on the keyboard, select the other. This is called additive selection, and the Status Bar should say 2 Objects Selected. Then click on the Fit Text to Path option on the Text drop-down menu.

12.   The Fit Text to Path Roll-Up has many options as to how it's going to fit the text. Do you want the Artistic Text to flow from the beginning of the line? Do you want it on top of the line or underneath? Do you want each character in the text string to tilt in conformance with the line path? Too many choices. Let's stick with the default settings, except choose to center the type on our line's path, which is selected in the third box down on the roll-up. Click on Apply (see fig. 10.17).

Figure 10.17

Which way is it going to fit?

13. The Artistic Text will cling to the line draw path as we've specified. But the line path and the text are control points now. In other words, you change the line path now, and the Artistic Text will reshape to conform to the line. Which is nice, but we really don't want the line path in our drawing. And we can't delete the line since it's a control line and sort of bonded to the text.

    With both items selected, go up to **A**rrange, and specify **S**eparate. The Status Bar informs us that there are now two objects selected, the bond is broken, and we can safely delete the line without losing the Artistic Text. Thus, we have a completed page, as seen in figure 10.18. And we've gotten sidetracked a little in terms of learning about tracing.

Figure 10.18

The Rectangle meets a pretty Circle, and they run off to Fresno.

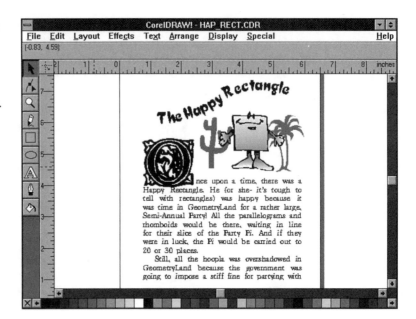

The Other Faces of Corel Traces

There are lots of other ways of using CorelTRACE. It will do Optical Character Recognition (OCR) of a typeset page. This is good when you've got a fax or something else that's ridiculously time-consuming to retype. Corel reads the page, and gives you a .TXT file instead of a tracing. You can also set CorelTRACE to design you a nice woodcut-style trace, or a silhouette of the original.

You can set a color other than black for the .EPS file to be when you import it into CorelDRAW. You have to consider what your goal is in tracing something before you decide on which features to use in CorelTRACE. Or if you're a little more energetic, you may not want to use CorelTRACE at all. You can do...

Tracing on the fly

Not many people know about a particular Corel feature that they can use to trace a bitmap. That feature is called *Auto-Trace*, and it only works on the outline of a Porsche. Only kidding. Auto-Trace is a good feature to use after you've imported a bitmap or a photo, and you want to use a piece of the outline of the bitmap (but don't have the time or energy to use CorelTRACE). We'll now show you, step-by-step, how to selectively trace a bitmap from within CorelDRAW's workspace.

1. We'll import the photograph of the pencil that was used as part of the Corel design for this chapter illustration. Again, regardless of what the image is of, if you can import it into CorelDRAW, you can Auto-Trace it.

2. In figure 10.19, we can see that the Status Bar is telling us that the image of the pencil is a color bitmap. Which is good. That means we can use Auto-Trace. With the color bitmap selected, we select the Line Draw tool.

Figure 10.19

Send in the pencil.

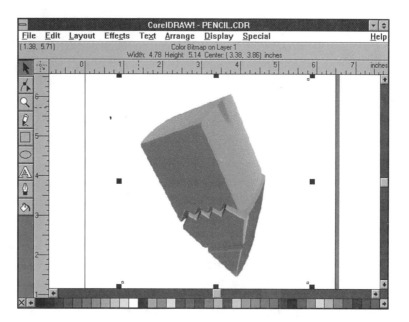

3. The color bitmap is selected, and we get the Line Draw tool. We move the cursor over the dark area of the bitmap we want to Auto-Trace, and the cursor turns into a cross.

4. To the left of the dark area we want Auto-Traced, click the left mouse button. We can move over to other areas of the bitmap to repeat this process, but why?

5. As we can see in figure 10.20, Auto-Trace traced an area we placed the Auto-Trace cursor over. Auto-Trace is not as precise as CorelTRACE, but then again, it wasn't meant to be.

Figure 10.20

Quick and sloppy.

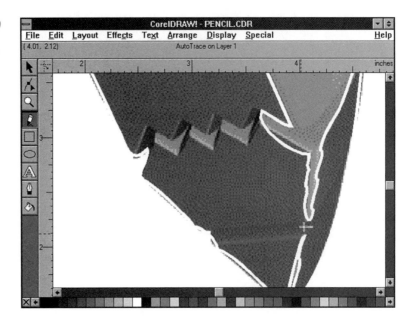

How all the tracing fits in

Rule number one when using a PC is that the less you ask the machine to do, the more you have to do yourself in order to complete something. To fit a vector line really close to the path of any design you're tracing requires additional manual adjustment of the nodes; where they are, where they go, and how many of them do you really need.

It's also a matter of artistic judgment when you trace a bitmap, either completely by hand, or using one of Corel's automated tracing features. Automatic tracing is typically more true to the original when the original is a high contrast photo, or a line drawing. But we've seen through this chapter that the designer's input is always required to make a design meaningful. Tracing is a skill, not a talent. The talent part is where your own ideas come in. And you can't cheat on that one.

What's Underneath the Iceberg

So far, we've done a lot of experimenting in this book, along with exercises, tutorials, and a mess of other "what if?" situations. But "what if" the real world we sometimes have to face throws us some curves, and they aren't the kind you draw in Corel? What about pie charts, and animated presentations? And what about editing a photograph? CorelDRAW doesn't do these things!

Patience. CorelDRAW doesn't, but its other modules do. This book is primarily on CorelDRAW, but we figured you weren't getting your money's worth if we didn't at least give the "Taxi Driver's Tour" of CorelSHOW, CorelCHART, and CorelPHOTO-PAINT. And show you just enough so you're not desperate when the real world wants something other than what you've been learning here.

So let's take a detour now, and see what the rest of the Corel Total Design Package can do for us. By "us," we mean you and about 40 other designers who work for you. (Of course, those of you working in other circumstances know you're included here too.) You can't possibly hold all this stuff in one head, you know...

CHAPTER 11

The Many Hats of Corel

A designer is often expected to wear many different hats in a business environment. For many years, I was obliged to play gofer, chief sign-maker, retoucher, lighting expert, and property manager—even though my working papers clearly identified me as *Art Director* at a New York ad agency.

Designer is a catch-all phrase in terms of business needs. When the crunch is on for a big project, and the crunch is poorly planned (which always seems to be the case), the designer is left to catch all the loose ends as they cascade onto the drawing room floor. To keep from bouncing off the wall, it helps to think of every successive distraction from your main duty as an event that "rounds out" your talent. Really.

In this chapter, we will:

    Check out charting with CorelCHART!

    Learn how to alter a photograph with CorelPHOTO-PAINT!

    Make a snazzy business presentation with CorelSHOW!

    Animate a creation of ours with CorelMOVE!

    Do all of the above using practical, real-life examples

On Owning a Revolving Hat Rack

We've concentrated on CorelDRAW: its design tools, typographic features, and how it works with the Clipboard, Clip Art, and scanning/tracing. Maybe you followed my advice in Chapter 1 and didn't install all the Corel modules, telling your boss that CorelDRAW was all that came in the software box. If you lied convincingly, you're off the hook (not that learning more about Corel would hurt, you know).

If the lie didn't work, and your boss wants restoration done to a photograph from 1914, or a 3-D chart of the world's population since A.D. 1280 branched out by race, shoe size, and brand of garden hose they owned, this chapter *will* help. So hold on to your hat(s), 'cause we're going to take a whirlwind tour of Corel's other modules and feather our caps with some non-CorelDRAW tricks!

CorelCHART!

The Art of the Chart

There is a subcategory of nerds called "stat freaks," otherwise known as NOMS (short for Nerds Obsessed with Meaningless Statistics). They are the ones at a cocktail party who'll tell you how many times Dan Rather wore an argyle sweater on the nightly news. They go way beyond trivia, and enter the realm of *chartability*.

Project Pie Fight

And your boss is this way. He has the collected works of Chaplin, Harry Langden, Laurel and Hardy, and other silent movie stars who engaged in the practice of hurtling large, round desserts at their co-stars. This information has been distilled into the types of pies the screen heroes tossed, and you are assigned to make up a chart of the data in your spare time.

Don't they always do this? Bosses confuse "time that belongs to yourself, and you're having dinner with friends after 5 p.m." with "spare time."

Oh well. The good news is that CorelCHART handles chartmaking intuitively, but a little differently than CorelDRAW handles graphics. Let's double-click on the CorelCHART icon in the Corel Graphics Group we have in Windows Program Manager, and get started.

1. CorelCHART appears on your screen. Unlike CorelDRAW, the workspace is blank and the toolbox is grayed out. Pick a **N**ew file on the **F**ile menu to open up a workspace for the chart we will create.

2. As seen in figure 11.1, we have a lot of chart types to choose from when we create a new file. We'll be smart alecks in this example and choose a *pie* chart to present data on pie fights. The other little pictures in the Chart Types selection window show variations on the pie theme: multiple pies and ring-pies. Ring-pies are getting very popular these days in business presentations, but they look more like bundt cakes, and we're talking pie shapes. Click on the first picture in the Chart Type box to select the single, plain pie.

Figure 11.1

The
CorelCHART
Gallery menu.

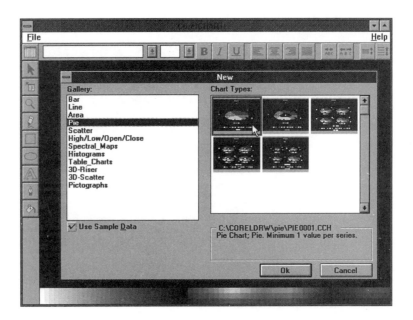

Since we're exploring new territory here, let's cheat and leave the Use Sample **D**ata box checked. The sample data will give us a better idea where to put our own data in this exercise. When you get more experienced with this module, you can uncheck this box.

PROFOUND REALIZATION

Do you see where it says `Minimum 1 value per series` on the lower right of this <u>N</u>ew menu? That means you can enter one or more values (numbers) in a particular series (column). This lets you build some phenomenally complex charts with CorelCHART. It's more important that you know it's possible to enter three metric tons of information in one chart than to know actually how to do it right now. We need to learn the basics before complicating our lives any further.

3. Click on OK, and we're off to see our first preset pie chart!

4. In figure 11.2 we see a generic, yet handsomely shaded 3-D pie chart. CorelCHART is a Corel module, and like CorelDRAW, we can change the shading, the shapes and sizes, and the typefaces if we want to. But first, we need to enter some pie fight data, and change the title to something a little more creative than "Title."

Figure 11.2

But there are no rows or columns on this pie!

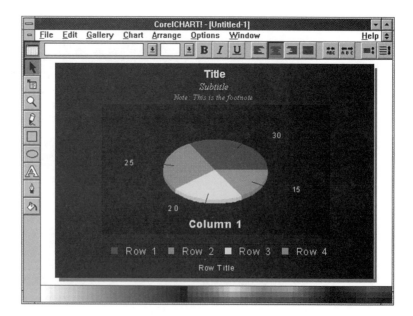

5. Click on the button above the Pick tool. This button switches you between two different views of your chart file—the chart view that shows the chart graphically, and the table view that shows the data that creates the chart.

6. In the table view seen in figure 11.3, we see spaces, or *cells*, that hold the underlying information that makes up the chart we were just looking at. To change any of these entries, or to make new ones in different columns and rows, click on a cell using your left mouse button.

Figure 11.3

Looks like one of those spreadsheets!

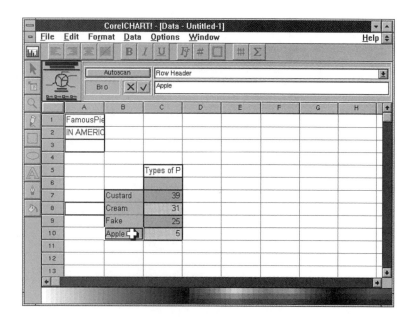

7. In figure 11.3, we've changed some of the *categories* (the column labels: Custard, Cream, etc.), and some of the *data* (the rows of numbers). We did this by clicking on the cell with the big plus sign our cursor turned into, and then typing in new information. In this figure, we've clicked on the category that said `Row 4`, the fourth field in its series, and typed `Apple`, instead. If you make a mistake while doing this, CorelCHART is forgiving—simply edit the information in the lower, long box at the top of the table.

When you click on a box, your cursor turns into a big plus sign. Follow these steps to change a category, row, or whatever's in the box:

1. Click on the box to select it.

2. Type your changes.

SECRET

3. Click again, either on the box (the cell) you are chang-
    ing, or on a new cell. If you don't click a second time,
    your new entry won't be recorded when you switch back
    to the chart view of your file.

8. We click the menu button again to return us to the Chart view in
    CorelCHART. It should look like figure 11.4.

Figure 11.4

What? No lemon
meringue???

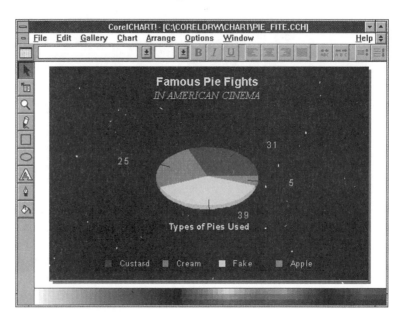

We see in figure 11.4 that the entries we made in the table view are now
shown in the pie chart. It's weird, isn't it, how we were actually designing
something just by typing in numbers?

This is how to build all the chart types. Unlike a bar chart, a pie chart
doesn't look like it's made up of columns and rows of information, but the
information to build one is entered this way. With a little practice and
experimentation, you can select and design other chart types that will more
accurately represent what stat freaks call columns and rows. You can mess
with that in your spare time.

The data I selected for this example are not accurate. The New Riders Trivia Department was downstairs buying coffee and sugar-free chewing gum at the concession stand when I slipped this one by.

*Yeah, but we're awake and cavity-free, facts be damned.—**The Editors***

SECRET

Sweetening the pie

With CorelCHART handling all this data stuff—automatically reproportioning and relabelling the pie chart correctly and all, you'd think that there's no room for true, artistic, hands-on fine-tuning. Wrong! We're gonna make this Famous Pie Fight chart so artsy, your boss will want to frame it (instead of hiding it from the view of the *normal* employees).

1. To change the typeface of our title, we click on it, and a frame appears around the title with eight little boxes or selection handles surrounding it. The default typeface and size appears in the typeface window at the top of the screen, to the left of the Text Ribbon (the long piece below the menu bar).

These selection handles behave a little differently than the ones we've used in CorelDRAW. When the corner selection handles are pulled on, they proportionately resize the type. Middle handles resize the frame the text is in, and control the text "flow." This is sort of like the box that appears around Paragraph Text in CorelDRAW. None of which concerns us right now; it's simply good to know.

SECRET

2. Click on the down arrow next to the typeface window to display a list of typefaces installed on your PC. Scroll down the list of typefaces and click on one you like. I happened to like Kaufmann, as seen in 11.5. We can also change the face to Bold, Italic, or Underlined, from the Text Ribbon.

Figure 11.5

HOL-LY-WOOD...!

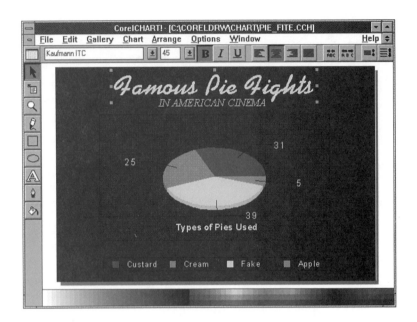

SECRET

Two other features that CHART and DRAW share are the fill and outline options. Although the color palette on the bottom of the screen looks different than CorelDRAW's, you select color the same way. Click the left mouse button on top of a color to select a fill, and click the right mouse button to pick the outline color. You can change the chart and the backgrounds with different fills and outlines. Type 1 and TrueType typefaces can also be filled with different colors, but no outline can be added to them.

Let's pause for a second and actually think about what this chart is representing. If we let the whole pie represent all the pies ever thrown in American cinema, the pie slices represent a subcategory of flavors used and their own percentages. But we don't have percent signs on our chart. Do we change this from the table view? No. Here's a hint—look at figure 11.6.

In figure 11.6, we've selected the **C**hart menu option. The menu will be different for every type of chart, because it would be silly to offer pie slice options for a line graph chart. We're looking for Slice Number Format. With this selected, we can set how the data is labeled: months, general numbers, or percentages. We'll choose the appropriate and obvious percentages.

Figure 11.6

Percentages, and
a whole lot more!

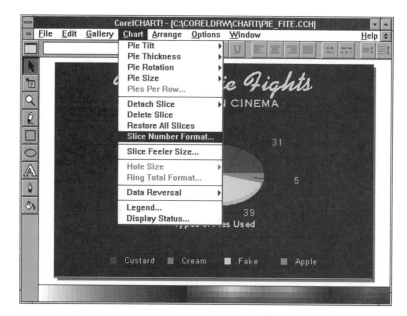

We're happy with the percentage labels on our pie chart, but they're a little small. That's easy to fix, though. We select one of them, and increase the size using the point size box on the Text Ribbon, as shown in figure 11.7.

Figure 11.7

We want a bigger
percentage. So
did Chaplin.

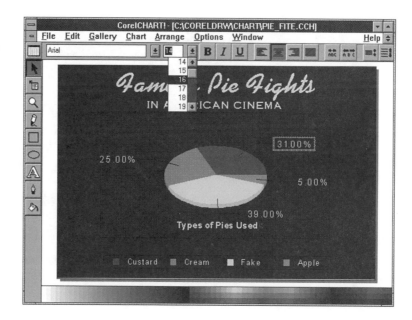

SECRET

As we get deeper into CorelCHART's unique tools, there's a special feature we can use to make changes easier to access than through the Menu bar. The Pop-Up Menu tool is located beneath the Pick tool, and will give you menu options pertaining to a specific area of the chart you point and click on. You can "call" this tool by clicking on its icon, but the easiest way is to simply use your right mouse button to click over an area, like a pie slice, data, title, etc., when you have the Pick tool selected. Try it! It's like having the Menu bar at your fingertips!

The box changes, but pie remains constant

We've decided that the box that the pie sits in is too small to contain our new, larger percentages, and the deep blue color is a drag. You may feel this way someday, too. So change is in order:

1. Make sure the box our pie sits in is selected (see fig. 11.8). If selection handles aren't visible, it isn't selected. Click on the pie box with the Pick tool to select it, if necessary.

Figure 11.8

Hey! Lighten up!

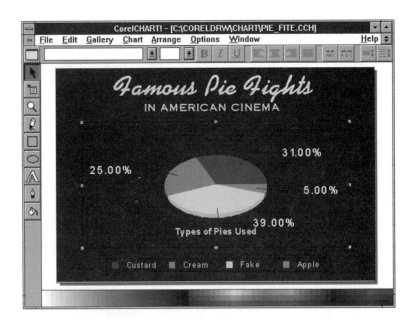

2. Pull on a middle selection handle of the pie box to resize it. This will disproportionately resize shapes you've drawn and chart borders, but not text objects or the chart itself. As with objects you may draw yourself with the Rectangle or Ellipse tools in CHART, the pie box can also be proportionately resized by selecting and pulling on a corner selection handle.

3. Click on the color palette to select a different fill for the box. Like everything else in the Corel world of programs, this works only if you have first selected the object you want to color.

Now, CorelCHART gave us a pretty good pie, but it's a little flat. For those of you who remember seeing Stan Laurel sock Ollie in the kisser with a baker's special, they were fat, sloppy, and caloric! We can't do much about the sloppy and caloric part, but we can make this pie chart fatter.

In figure 11.9, we've selected the **C**hart menu item again, to see what wonderfully screwy things we can do to the pie portion of our chart. Pie Rotation, Detach Slice, and Pie Tilt (which sounds like a game you usually lose at a Fireman's Field Day) are all good ones. But we want to increase the depth of our pie—its thickness, as it were.

Click on Pie Thickness, and a little flyout menu appears that offers you choices ranging from No Thickness to Maximum. Let's select Maximum, and return to the pie.

Figure 11.9

Take it to the max.

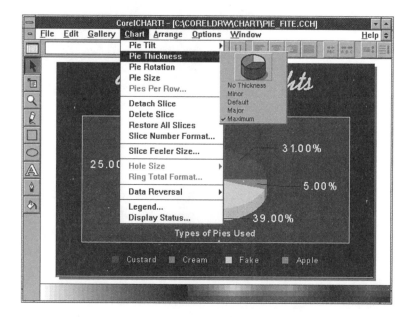

Putting some feelers out

The little black lines that go from the pie slices to the percentages don't read very well. Black on a blue background seldom does. This was Corel's default, if a party is to be faulted. But we can change that. Check out figure 11.10 and follow along with the upcoming steps.

NERDY
NOTE

Corel calls these lines *feelers*. Because they sort of look like the feelers on ants that nerds collect in a jar. And in their bathroom. And the kitchen...

Figure 11.10

Changing a feeler.

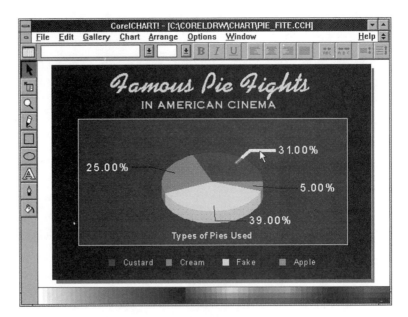

1. Select a feeler with the Pick tool.

2. Go to the Outline tool on the toolbox. It's the same button as in CorelDRAW.

3. Now you can pick both a lighter color (we chose white in figure 11.11), and a thickness that will stand out more.

PROFOUND REALIZATION

When you change the color or outline on one of the objects that seems related to another in CorelCHART, like the feelers or the pie slices, you effect a change in all the related items. If you select a pie slice and turn it purple, the box that stands for this slice in the Legend box will also turn purple.

CorelCHART makes quick, logical changes for you with only a few clicks. You only have to experiment for five minutes or so to see exactly which items are related.

Figure 11.11

The Outline tool flyout.

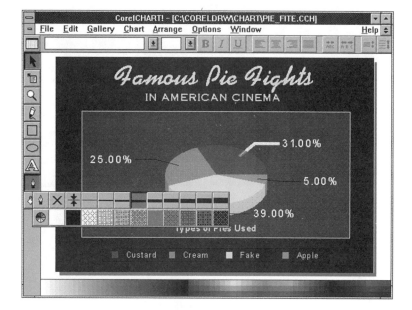

We've finished all the customizing we wanted to do to the pie chart. That makes it a perfect time to show it to your boss. He's so thrilled, he lets you in on another secret collection of statistics he's got shaking around in his head.

More Fighting with Your Boss

Your boss also knows the statistics for all the fights in drinking establishments that the American cinema has depicted. And he wants a *bar* chart out of you.

See? Stat freaks can be smart alecks, too!

To produce this new statistical masterpiece is no problem. Just follow the upcoming steps.

1. From the **G**allery menu item, Select Horizontal Bar, as shown in figure 11.12. The little picture on the Horizontal Bar flyout shows us the bar's orientation (which is, coincidentally, the orientation of individuals who frequent bars excessively).

Figure 11.12

Go to the Gallery before going to the Bar.

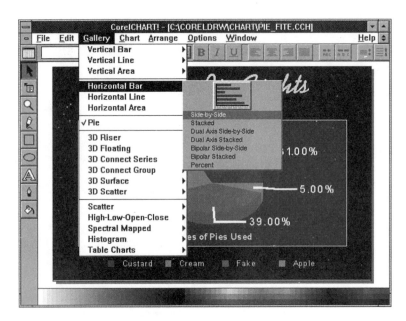

2. As you can see in figure 11.13, we still have the old pie fight information on our new bar chart. We'll have to change pie information to fight information after this brief Profound Realization.

PROFOUND REALIZATION

When you have data in CorelCHART, and then select a different type of chart, the information is then displayed in a different chart format. It only takes a mouse click or two to create different kinds of charts out of the same data.

Each chart type you select has its own way of displaying data. You will notice in figure 11.13 that the percent signs we added in the "pie" view of our data are now missing, as are the feelers we worked so hard to perfect! CorelCHART's charts are designed for maximum readability for the kind of chart selected.

The elements we customized in the pie view of our data are not part of CorelCHART's template for a bar chart and therefore didn't carry over. But we can add other stuff to customize this bar chart, or any other type we may settle on.

Figure 11.13

A pie fight in a Bar?

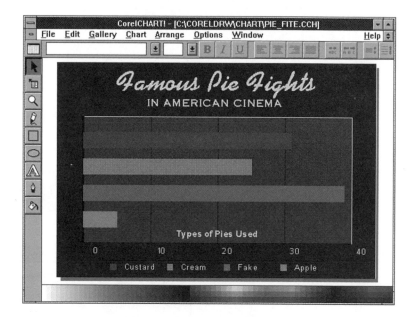

3. We do exactly the same thing to create category and data cells on this new Bar chart as we did with the pie chart; we select the table view, seen in figure 11.14.

4. We enter your strange boss's categories by selecting a box (cell) with the Plus cursor, typing in new stuff, then clicking once more on each cell with the Plus cursor to enter the changes, as in figure 11.14.

5. We switch back to Chart view, as seen in figure 11.15. You can see that we added a little "clarifier" above the row titles by using the Text tool and typing away from the Chart view. You don't need to type in a cell in the Table view just to add text to your work.

Figure 11.14

Boy, is your boss strange!

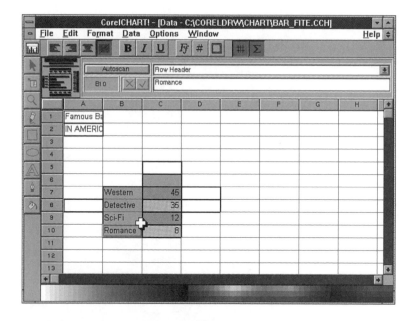

Figure 11.15

Don't wager a bet on these figures!

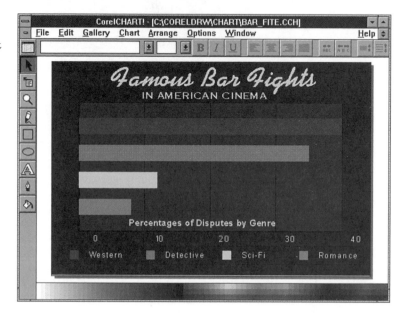

Can you find the mistake in these figures? Other than the goofy data?

Bar fights go off the Chart!

Our range is wrong. Western Bar Fights was a full 45 percent of total Bar Fights in American cinema, as seen in the table view in figure 11.14. Yet our bar chart only has a scale up to 40. So 45 percent went clear off the chart!

Let's fix that, while emphasizing an appropriate, yet lousy pun (see fig. 11.16).

1. In figure 11.16, we've placed our cursor over a range number. It doesn't matter which one; all four are linked. We click on the range number with the right mouse button to call a Pop-Up Menu.

Figure 11.16

Home, home on the range.

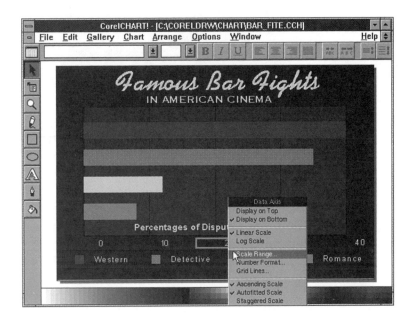

2. Scale Range is the choice we're looking for, so we select it (see fig. 11.17).

3. Our Range Scale is set for Automatic, and the values are grayed out, which means we can't change anything. So we click on the Manual Scale box, and the values turn black. We're looking for a value greater than 40, aren't we?

Figure 11.17

Range Methods
don't include
Browning,
Basting, or Deep-
Frying.

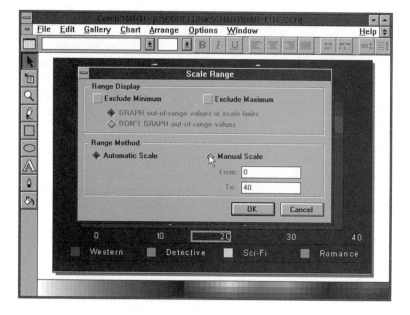

4. We type in the values of 5 in the From box, and 45 in the To box, as shown in figure 11.18. All the statistics we entered in the table view fall within these two values, so we will now have all the "stats" represented in our bar chart.

5. Since our original Scale Range was represented in increments of 10, the Automatic Scale was tossing us a range number every 10 percentage marks. We'll click on the Automatic Scale button again after manually entering the new scale values. We will get increments of fives on our new scale range automatically by clicking on Automatic, because this is the way CorelCHART interprets the new Scale Range: from 5 to 45.

6. Click on OK, and return to the chart view.

I think we've done it this time! Our finished Bar Fight bar graph in figure 11.19 is a piece of work! It's accurate, it's handsome, *it's a CorelCHART chart!* Now, there are plenty of other ways you can refine your chart-making skills by using CorelCHART. It's a full-featured chart-making module, packed with equation editing, spreadsheet import filters, basically the whole nine yards (measured in a scale range of threes, hopefully).

Figure 11.18

5 to 45 should
cover us.

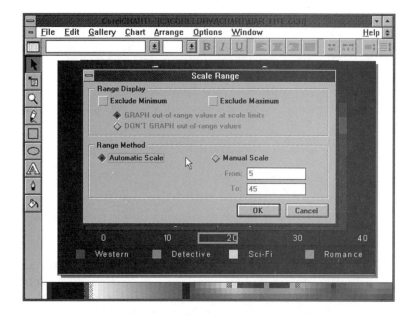

Figure 11.19

A Bar and Grill
now becomes a
Bar and Range.

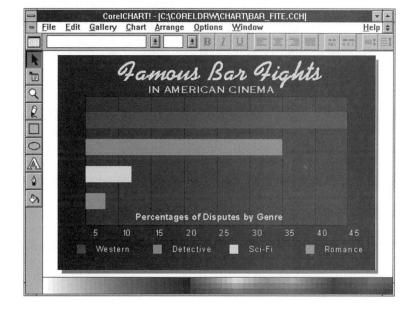

SECRET

If you're really into charting as a profession, hobby, or sport, pick up a copy of *Inside CorelDRAW! 4.0, Special Edition,* by Daniel Gray, quite coincidentally from New Riders Publishing.

Un-CHARTed Territory

But it seems like a shame to keep our charts to themselves in CorelCHART, so why don't we see about strutting them around other places on our PC?

In figure 11.20, we opened the File menu, and then chose Export, to see where in the world of PC programs our chart could be imported to. The drop-down menu, List Files of Type, contains a wealth of suggestions, as well as the file format extensions. Now, CorelCHART gives its files a .CCH extension; but if you wanted to create a paint-type file out of a Corel chart, it would be accepted by most desktop publishing and word processing programs, as well as spreadsheets, as we talked about in Chapter 7. If you wanted to fancy up this chart even further, a paint-type program, like Corel PHOTO-PAINT would be ideal. It accepts .PCX, .BMP, .TIF, and a host of other images.

As long as you know how to export the chart you create in CorelCHART, you can spruce up other documents you've created in other programs with your newfound charting skill. Corel's other modules are all about sprucing up stuff. In fact, let's toss our chart-making hat back on the rack now, and put on a lens cap for our next section. We're going to pretend we're Ansel Adams or Margaret Bourke-White...

SECRET

They're famous photographers.

... and play with a picture in CorelPHOTO-PAINT!

Figure 11.20

Turning a chart
into a painting.

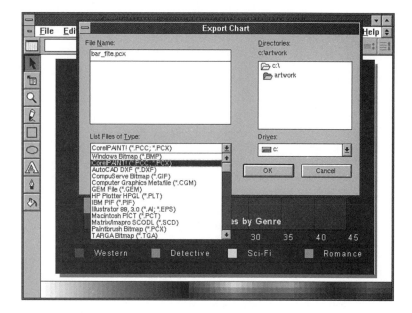

CorelPHOTO-PAINT!

Reach Out and Retouch Someone

Once again, the qualifying requirements for getting anything out of this
section are that you either have a scanner, you have a really good friend
who will lend you one, or that you can get your hands on a really terrible
.TIF file. Because we're going to explain how to make passport-quality
images into something people will actually want to show to other people.

Not everyone is a born photographer. If we were, there would be no car
dealers, and the world wouldn't know any swear words. What we do have
are amateur photographers, events like weddings and birthdays where
amateur photographers can practice their craft, and lots of Fotomats.

The amateur photographer's background

One of the most common special effects amateur photographers feature in
their work is the "Pipe through the Head" portrait. You know what I mean:

you get an important picture back, and there's a coat rack, floor lamp, or steam pipe in the background that looks like it's impaling you or a loved one. When a scene is photographed, what is in a background is rarely considered. This happens in amateur, and sometimes professional, photography. Sometimes we find the only solution to fixing a spoiled, captured moment is to engage the expensive services of a professional retoucher.

CorelPHOTO-PAINT belongs to a new generation of PC programs that can actually help you doctor up a photograph that's been messed up in several different ways. Underexposed, blurry, even pipes-through-your-head photoflubs can be compensated for, if not totally corrected, in PHOTO-PAINT. It's a program that has remarkably real world-like tools. When used sparingly and with a little creativity, you can enhance a photo so no one will ever know your spouse had a tennis racquet removed from their ear.

The electronic retouching lab

Um, we'll be using a photograph of my spouse in this example. Barbara wouldn't let me use the tennis racquet photo, but she did ask if I could remove a shrub from her chin in the following holiday snapshot. As you see in the following figures, it's a pretty good picture, but that shrub definitely needs pruning.

Figure 11.21

Opening a file of a photo. Also called Loading a Picture from Disk.

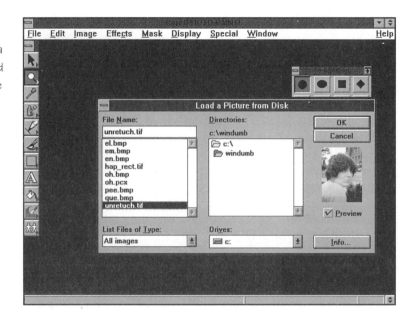

As with all the other modules except CorelDRAW, you have to either start a new file or open one you've already created before you can use or even move any of the tools. We haven't used PHOTO-PAINT yet (or at least I haven't), so we select File, then Open, and locate our test photograph. We're calling this one UNRETUCH.TIF, because that's what it is, and UNRETOUCHED is longer than the 8-character file-naming limit. So I'm not illiterate. Just an amateur photographer.

You'll be picking one of your own files that need fixing up, or you can use one of the samples Corel installed with this module. In either case, you'll use the same techniques I'll use to remove a shrub from Barbara's chin. Let's follow these steps:

1. After you select File, Open, if you press the little Preview check box, you'll be able to see a "thumbnail" photo of what the selected file looks like. If you're not really good about giving files names you'll remember later, this is a handy option for making certain you're loading the picture you want.

SECRET

CorelPHOTO-PAINT will do its image editing wizardry on several different kinds of bitmap files. There's a list of them in the Files Type box. You can retouch a color or black and white photo, a Windows .BMP wallpaper, or just start painting with a blank "canvas" by selecting **New** when you start PHOTO-PAINT.

If you already know what the file you're selecting looks like, you may want to leave the Preview box unchecked, because it takes time for PHOTO-PAINT to create that Preview image and the image on the workspace you'll be playing with. It's a step-saver, which means it's a time-saver where PCs are concerned.

2. After the Preview shows you the picture, you click on OK, and wait for the image to be displayed in PHOTO-PAINT (see fig. 11.22).

3. When the image is finally displayed in your workspace, as in figure 11.22, it may overlap your workspace so you can't see the whole image. The Zoom tool on the toolbox can enlarge and reduce the view of the image by a factor of two (half as big/twice as big, you know), when you select this tool and place it over the image. Unlike in CorelDRAW, you click with the left mouse button to zoom in twice as big, and with the right mouse button to zoom out. In figure 11.22 we've zoomed until the image can be fully displayed.

Figure 11.22

Not a bad photo.
It just needs a
little work.

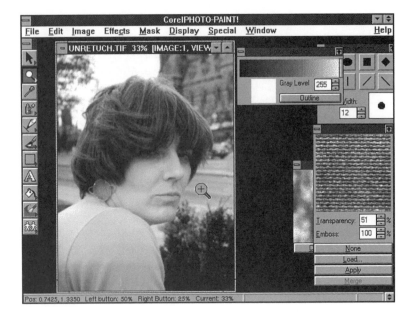

4. If we're going to remove part of the shrub, we'll have to replace it with something. I think we'd all be happier if that "something" was a vague, solid fill. But which shade out of 256 will effectively eliminate part of the shrub without the photo looking like we used correction fluid on it?

SECRET

This is one area where photo-retouchers have the biggest problem in the physical, *chemical photography world*— matching tone values perfectly. Fortunately, your PC and CorelPHOTO-PAINT are exceedingly adept at this. Use the Eye Dropper tool to "pick up" a shade of gray that already exists in the photo. That shade of gray will act as your "paint" for the retouching job. Clean, simple, and electronic.

5. If we look closely at the offending shrub area, we notice that there's an area of road in the clear. Zoom in on that area and select the Eye Dropper tool, as shown in figure 11.23. If we click with the left mouse button, the Color Selection Palette picks up the grayscale value of the road that we can shortly apply with the PaintBrush tool. In my example, the Gray Level is 229 for the road. You'll get different levels depending on what color you pick up with the Eye Dropper tool.

SECRET

The Eyedropper tool can be used to pick up a color from a photo or painting to be used with the Paintbrush or the Pencil tool. We've just been using the left mouse button with the Eye Dropper to do exactly that. But if you click the right mouse button while using the Eyedropper tool, you can pick up a Fill color. This color can be used with the Fill tool, the Ellipse, or Rectangle tool.

Figure 11.23

The Eye Dropper tool.

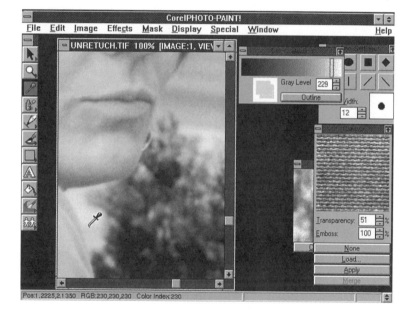

6. Select the Paintbrush tool from the toolbox on the left of your screen, the 6th tool down. We see in figure 11.24 that the Paintbrush tool is depressed and darker than the other tools. In the floating tool Selection box, the brush tip has been set to 27 pixels in width by pushing the up arrow next to the numbers, and a round shape has been set by clicking on the shape.

Why 27 pixels and round? Because we're painting over a fairly large area on the screen at this magnification, and the area we're painting over is soft, so a round tip on our brush is appropriate. When retouching sharp, geometric parts in a picture, the square tip might work better.

Figure 11.24

Paving a road over a shrub.

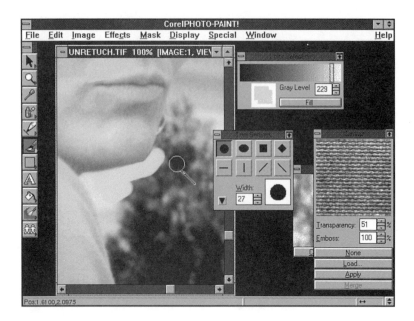

SECRET

When you try this step at home (or at work), notice that as you go over an area with the paintbrush, it leaves a soft edge where it's been. This is a nice quality about PHOTO-PAINT. Sharp edges on a photo are a very telltale sign that it's been tricked with. And our trick here is to go unnoticed.

The leaves on the shrub were photographed out of focus, as most backgrounds are. So when you retouch "out" a certain element in a background, the edges where you end are noticeable. This is a good time to check out another one of PHOTO-PAINT's features, the Smear tool, as seen in figure 11.25.

What the Smear tool does is move some of the color from the area you place the tool over to an area next to it, in a very soft, subtle way. Like smudging a charcoal drawing, or pastels, to create a soft blend.

7.   Select the Smear tool from the toolbox (the one that looks like a cotton swab). Work your way with the smear tool from the sharp edges of where the shrub begins back into the area you painted over.

Figure 11.25

Cleaning up after pruning.

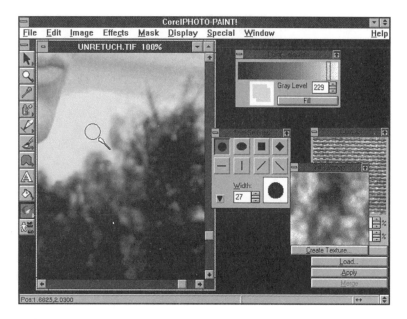

Less is more. Try smearing an area once, then twice, and Zoom out to see if that did the trick. Don't go to town like a kid with a new coloring book. It would be wrong.

SECRET

As we glance down to figure 11.26, we see we're done. For now. I also see there's an out of focus automobile we could live without in the background. I'd use the same two tools as in this example, if I were inclined to make this chapter drag on forever. But there are a few more things left in the Corel Total Design Package we've yet to uncover.

We hardly got our fingers wet

The example we've just looked at used a fraction of PHOTO-PAINT's tools and capabilities. You'll notice when you open PHOTO-PAINT that there are a bunch of these floating toolboxes on the screen, and we've only looked at two of them. You can apply a Texture Fill, to a photo or bitmap, from a selection that's identical to CorelDRAW. That goes for Fountain Fills as well.

Figure 11.26

Barbara looks happier now. I think she was allergic to the shrub.

There's also a Canvas option that'll let you paint on a surface that actually reacts to your paints as though they were going on a basketweave, stucco, or other textured surface. You can set your brush to imitate the famous brush strokes of an impressionist or pointillist, like the painter Georges Seurat. But none of this will be of a lot of help when you work in an office that needs pie charts and has amateur photographers in its employ.

Changing our cameras

If you liked our still-photography session in PHOTO-PAINT, you're gonna love wearing the next two hats. They're director's caps. I think Spielberg is still wearing a baseball cap, so dig one out to get with the mood. We're taking a trip from the studio to the sound stage with CorelSHOW and CorelMOVE. It's good we know CorelDRAW and PHOTO-PAINT now, because these two new modules sport no drawing tools of their own, and we'll show you how they interact. Let's think of SHOW and MOVE as empty stages, and as the director, we'll discover the actors that'll follow your script.

CorelSHOW!

SHOW Off What You've Learned

CorelSHOW does one thing extremely well, in many different ways: CorelSHOW will take your artwork, or chart, or simply a thought or two typed in an expressive typeface and turn it into a presentation.

There are many business presentation packages sold with their own drawing tools, but here's where Corel's got them licked. Instead of selling you a "Presentation Package" that comes with a few drawing tools, Corel gives you a complete drawing program that comes with a presentation tool. And a charting tool. And, well, you're getting to know the rest...

Thinking about linking

If you want to know what OLE is, besides what a bullfighter yells, ask a nerd. But if you want to see OLE in action, and leave the techy stuff in the dust, hang on to your hat. In the following example, we'll be working with both CorelSHOW, and CorelDRAW, without even clicking on the DRAW icon, thanks to *Object Linking and Embedding* (OLE). It's not as painful as it sounds! Let's go!

1. Go to Windows Program Manager, and in the Corel Graphics Group, open CorelSHOW by clicking on the icon with the balloon on it. Gotcha! They all have balloons on 'em, right? Click the one that says CorelSHOW underneath it (it has the balloon and a picture of a movie camera on it). I promise to be more serious for the duration of this page.

   CorelSHOW will ask you at the beginning whether you want to create a new presentation or open an existing one. Click on **N**ew, and leave the number of slides in this new presentation at the default of five. Click on OK.

2. In figure 11.27, we see the CorelSHOW workspace. The first difference you'll spot between this program and the others we've covered is that the toolbox doesn't really have any tools on it. The bottom five icons represent the programs you can call on to get the graphics; on

top, there are only four tools—the Pick tool, the Zoom tool, the Pop-Up Menu tool, and one that looks like a grid. This is the Background tool.

Figure 11.27

Here's the stage. The curtains are up in that little button on top.

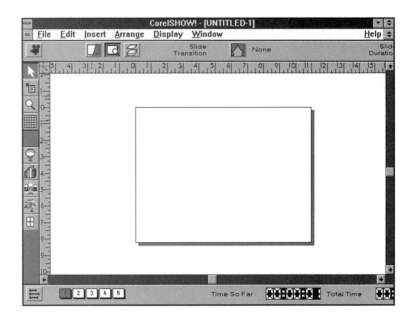

3.   Select the Background tool to bring up a variety of backgrounds, as seen in figure 11.28.

4.   Our example in this section is going to be a Big Business presentation, so choose a background that's powerful yet conservative. Select the background, seen in figure 11.28, press **Done**, and return to your workspace.

SECRET

If you like one of CorelSHOW's prefabricated backgrounds, remember that only one background can be displayed per presentation. Sorry, no mixing and matching.

Figure 11.28

From whimsical
to Wall Street.

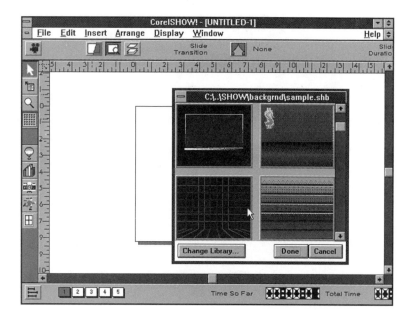

5.   As mentioned before, the bottom icons on the toolbox are meant for
     calling design programs you work in to make graphics for your
     CorelSHOW. From top to bottom, they are CorelDRAW, CHART,
     PHOTO-PAINT, MOVE, and an icon that calls Windows programs
     other than Corel's own.

     How do you call a program? "Yo, Program!" didn't work in tests we
     conducted. But we found that you can get CorelDRAW (and the other
     programs) to come by clicking on their icon, then marquee-selecting
     an area on the background with the cursor. Click on the CorelDRAW
     icon, and marquee-select now (see fig. 11.29).

6.   Let's assume your PC is of average power and speed. Once you've
     done the marquee maneuver, it'll take a moment for CorelSHOW to
     respond to your very sophisticated command. You're actually telling
     CorelSHOW to call CorelDRAW through OLE. When it shows up, you
     can then use its design tools to create a piece for your SHOW.

Figure 11.29

It looks like a
neon squash
court.

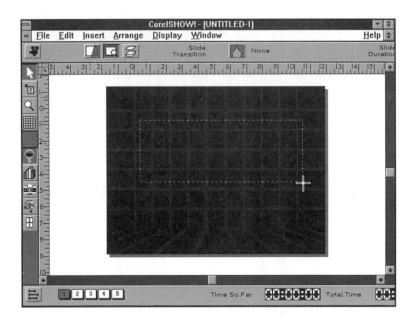

SECRET

Corel users watch Corel's little spinning hourglass to amuse
themselves while they wait for their PC to carry out a command. It's a lot more fun to watch than the Windows hourglass
that just sits there while you wait. Of course, some folks might
say that comparing the hourglass icons is more like comparing
watching grass grow with watching *wind-swept* grass grow.

7. In a moment, CorelDRAW will open, but without the fancy balloon
   advertisement we're now used to seeing. It's okay. We've opened
   CorelDRAW in an unusual way. See the title bar in figure 11.30? It
   references CorelSHOW, not UNTITLED as usual. CorelDRAW can be
   used the same as usual, so we'll design an Artistic Text object, then
   extrude that object to make it more powerful-looking. When we're
   done designing, we'll click on the File menu.

8. As we see in figure 11.30, we have an option to Exit & Return to
   CorelSHOW!, which isn't normally there. Pretty smart program
   sometimes, huh? Because that's exactly what we want to do. Click on
   the new Exit command, and you'll get a dialog box that looks like
   figure 11.31.

Figure 11.30

Can you find
what's different
in this File menu?

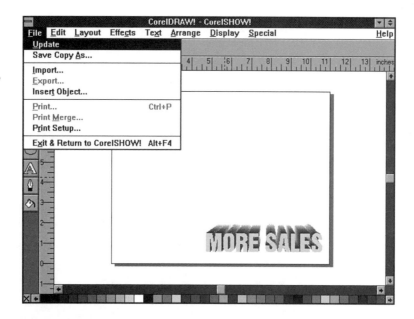

Figure 11.31

Embedded
object? I thought
it said "more
sales!"

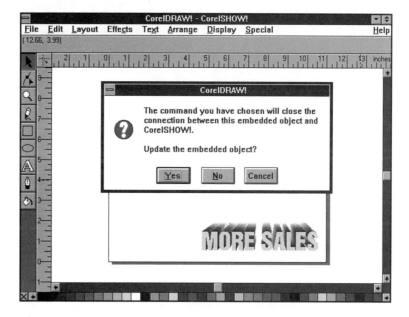

9.   The free interpretation of the message in the CorelDRAW dialog box
     in figure 11.31 is, "You want I should close myself, give you back to
     CorelSHOW, and you take the object you just created with you?" Yes!
     Yes! Let the SHOW go on!

10. By selecting **Y**es, CorelDRAW will disappear, and CorelSHOW will have a new design in your workspace, atop the background.

    This is the first frame in the slide show we're building. That's why there's a dark number 1 in a box on the lower left of the screen in figure 11.32.

Figure 11.32

You've installed advertising in the squash court!

"Hey, what gives," you say! "CorelDRAW vanished, and I didn't have a chance to save my wonderful MORE SALES artwork!" Not to worry. Any object that's embedded in CorelCHART is saved within CorelCHART. To edit your work, double-click on the object in CorelCHART. This will call up CorelDRAW again, and you can work on it some more. You might even save it as a CorelDRAW file by clicking on Save Copy **A**s from the **F**ile menu, as seen in figure 11.30. This is the way *Object Linking and Embedding* (OLE) works.

SECRET

11. Frame two of our slide show appears when you click on the number two box on the bottom of our screen. We're presented with the same background as the one we chose from CorelSHOW's background collection. Marquee-select an area on frame two with the CorelDRAW icon depressed. CorelDRAW comes up, we design, close the "link," and we have a second frame like figure 11.33.

Figure 11.33

Creating a "build."

In figure 11.33, we kept MORE SALES in addition to our BIGGER PROFITS Artistic Text as objects in frame 2 of our slide show. Why? Because when you make transitions between two frames, sometimes you want the first thought to "linger" in the viewer's mind. Keeping the same element on the screen, then building upon it in steps, is called a *build*. To build something, copy the object in SHOW to the Clipboard, switch to another slide, then **P**aste it in. The object will retain its position relative to the first page slide.

12. Click on frame three in CorelSHOW to present you with a new frame with the same background. Marquee-select an area while the CorelDRAW icon is selected, design the frame three object or objects in CorelDRAW, and exit as we did in the last two steps. Figure 11.34 shows our third frame object hanging out. We can position our objects anywhere within the frame, so think of how the viewer will see these slides, and arrange a sort of "choreography." This is your big chance to wear the director's hat, remember!

13. In figure 11.34, we've followed the same steps as before to bring a graphical item, the Artistic Text, into CorelSHOW. You may be wondering whether there's an easier or at least quicker way to build a slide presentation. The answer is yes, but only if you've prepared all the elements of your slide presentation in advance.

Figure 11.34

More sales, less
work? What's
their stock going
for?

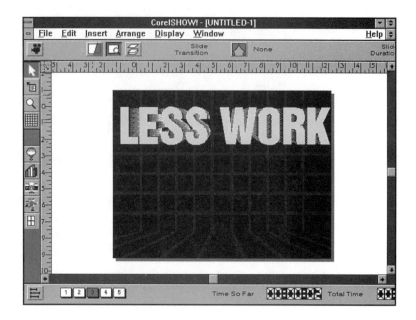

SECRET

If you have a bunch of graphics from other programs you've
designed or appropriated before opening CorelSHOW, you can
put copies of them in by using the Inser**t** Object command on
the Menu bar. In figure 11.35, we've chosen the **C**reate from File
selection, and are prompted for a path and a file name for the
work we want to insert. If we're uncertain of where the file is at
this point, we can **B**rowse, and see a directory listing of our
files. Once a file has been chosen and inserted into our SHOW,
we may edit the file by double-clicking on it while it's in our
SHOW workspace. Then the program that created this file will
be summoned via OLE.

Whether you want to insert a sound, an animation (like
CorelMOVE files), or a CorelDRAW picture, it's important to
clear that file of any extraneous objects. If you have an extra
object you don't want to use on CorelDRAW's workspace, for
instance, OLE will insert the whole nine yards, wanted or not!
So prepare your work carefully if using the Inser**t** command. It's
a pain to have to edit it later.

14.   We click on the fourth, then the fifth and last frame in our slide
       presentation. If for some reason we wanted more slides in this
       experimental presentation, we would click on the **I**nsert, New **P**age
       option from the menu bar, and add the number we wish. In figure
       11.36, we've finished up the presentation with a big logo of the

company we're doing the slide presentation for. We inserted the graphic of the company logo from a .BMP file that was created prior to our CorelSHOW adventure, the same way you can do it if you read the last SECRET! Whew. Now it's a perfect time for someone in the audience to ask you to rearrange the slides!

Figure 11.35

The Insert menu.

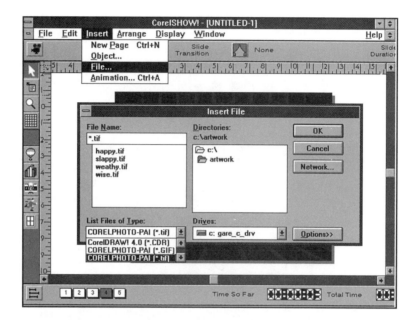

Figure 11.36

We knew this was too good to be true.

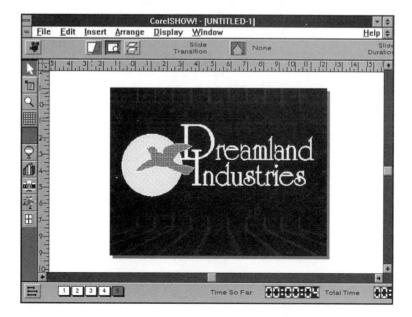

15. Click on the button below the **A**rrange menu item that has a picture of a stack of papers on it. This calls the Slide Sorter view, where you can rearrange the sequence your slides are in. You simply click on a slide, and drag it to another position (where you want it on the "slide tray").

This Slide Sorter view is also good for looking at the whole presentation at a glance before running it. In figure 11.37, we see all our slides are in order and ready to go before the camera. Last call for makeup!

Figure 11.37

Here's where you sort out last-minute changes.

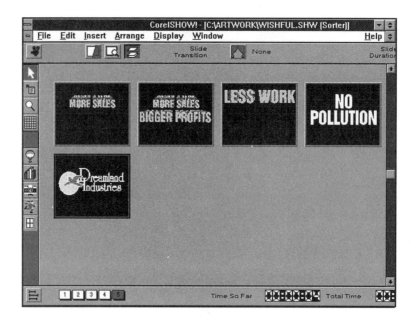

It's slideSHOW time!

We have the slides finished, and it's time to add a little pizzazz to the whole project; the better to then view the fruits of your labor. Admittedly, showing a realistic slide show is rather difficult to pull off in a book. We toyed with the idea of making this section a "flip book" like those cheesy prizes in snack foods, but this is supposed to be a "lean" guide for the non-nerd. Instead, follow these steps, then hold this book up to your screen, so we can watch, too...

1. Set transitions to your slides. CorelSHOW has a lot of neat effects you can put between slides. First click on the number of the slide you want. The number's on the bottom left of the screen. Apply a transition to this slide by clicking on the curtain icon on the top of the screen labeled Slide Transition. Why not pick a dissolve for the first slide, then a zoom for the second—try different transitions to see which you like the best? You can change them anytime later.

2. If you'd like one slide to be on screen longer than another, click on the Slide Duration box on the very top right of the screen, then type in the number of seconds you'd like that frame to be on the screen.

SECRET

Do a reality check before you do a time check on CorelSHOW's slide durations. A 286 or 386 machine doesn't have the PC processing power to drive Corel version 4.0 optimally. In fact, you may actually get seven to ten seconds worth of a display for a particular slide, even when you specified five seconds in the Slide Duration box. 486 and Pentium owners can expect a five second slide duration to be accurate on their machines. The bottom line for all PC owners with CorelSHOW is to keep the presentations short and sweet. Always try to make your slides five seconds maximum, usually less than that. You want to hear the crowd roar, not snore.

3. Click on the little movie projector icon on the top left of the screen to show the slide show. When it's over, CorelSHOW will return to a view of your first slide.

Now playing on a PC near you!

If you'd like to show your finished slide show on a PC other than your own, you're in luck! Corel comes with a *Run-Time Player* especially designed for your SHOWs. A Run-Time Player lets you run your show on a machine that doesn't have Corel but does have Windows 3.1 on it (like your boss's PC).

When you have a show you're happy with, click on **F**ile, **S**ave, give your work a name, and CorelSHOW will save your work as a .SHW file. Follow these steps:

1. Copy your .SHW file, along with the SHOWRUN.EXE file in the SHOWRUN subdirectory, to a floppy disk. You can do this using Windows' File Manager, or you can ask a nerd to help you, and promise them an ice cream cone in return.

2. Offer the nerd a second ice cream cone to copy the two files on your floppy disk to a new directory (put both files in the same directory, and name the directory something simple like SHOW) on the PC you want to show your show on. Or do this yourself.

3. From Windows Program Manager, select **F**ile, **R**un from the Menu bar.

4. Click on **B**rowse, and scroll through the directory listing until you find the SHOW directory, and click on SHOWRUN.EXE.

5. The Run-Time Player will show you the directories on that PC, so select your show and click on OK.

UH-OH

Didn't we mention in Chapter 2 that copying Corel files to go on a PC other than your own was bad? And that doing this is an open invitation for the feds to drop by and offer you a position designing license plates for, oh, the next five years or so?

You're right. But read this next sentence, aloud, three times:

The Run-Time Player is royalty-free and it's legal to distribute and Corel says so.

Corel's License Agreement allows you to copy SHOWRUN.EXE and only this CorelSHOW file to play your show on other PCs. Plus the files you create, which belong to you since you designed them. The SHOWRUN.EXE file contains only the ingredients to play the show you've created. It won't modify any elements you've designed using CorelSHOW.

Don't let yourself get cast in *Jailhouse Rock, The Sequel*. Copy only when this book, and Corel's License Agreement, say it's okay, and copy only the files mentioned. You'd be wasting your designing talents in the slammer, and that would be criminal.

There are more features in CorelSHOW that we haven't the space to cover in this guide, but as long as you have the basics down, you can create some pretty sophisticated stuff in a short amount of time. Feel free to experiment! It's right there, whenever!

CorelMOVE!

Moving Toward the Finale

If you're the type who didn't find the section on CorelSHOW enough of a challenge, you're in for a treat with CorelMOVE. You've got real animation, right on your PC! Not just dissolves from frame to frame, but honest-to-gosh moving pictures! Corel comes with a sample or two of pre-made animations, but you don't need a book telling you how to run these. You'd figure this out eventually, or enlist a nerd to show you.

Making flicks with mouse clicks

Yep, we're gonna learn, right here and now, how to do a simple animation. This is in case the company you work for ever wants to go head-to-head with Disney someday. Now, bear in mind, if you ever wanted to try to go-head-to-head with Disney, you'd lose. Think about it—Walt Disney World's parking lot is larger than five or ten medium-sized industrial parks. So we'll start small. Like a coming attractions animation that we could perhaps sell to Disney. You never know...

1. Open CorelMOVE by clicking on its icon in Windows Program Manager. It's the one with (the balloon and) the little blue person running on it.

2. The first thing we want to do from the **F**ile menu is to open a **N**ew file. CorelMOVE is different from the other Corel modules in that we have to name the MOVE file before beginning. So we'll type in `SOON.CMV`, as seen in figure 11.38.

3.   Click on OK, and we'll soon be presented with a blank workspace full of buttons and controls at the bottom that look like VCR controls. These controls were put here to make you feel at home, and they work a lot like those on your VCR.

Figure 11.38

Producers always have a title before the movie's made.

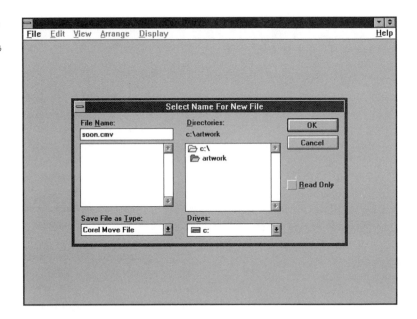

SECRET

If CorelMOVE's workspace on your PC looks a tad small, and you can still see part of Windows Program Manager in the background, this means CorelMOVE's window isn't maximized. Programs do this sometimes. To get the big picture, click on the up arrow in the top right of CorelMOVE's window. This will maximize MOVE, and you won't get the Program Manager surrounding CorelMOVE's workspace.

4.   We need what CorelMOVE calls an Actor on our blank sound stage. In figure 11.39, we've clicked on **E**dit, then Insert **N**ew Object. If this seems familiar to the CorelSHOW escapade we've just completed, it should be! We're OLE-ing again! Click on **A**ctor.

Figure 11.39

Send in the
clowns!

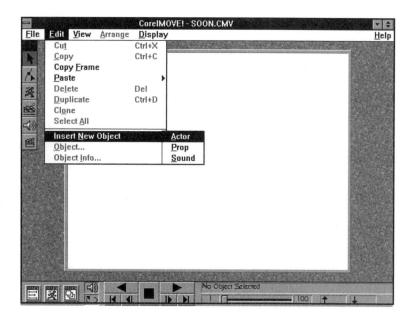

5. We're going to create our first **A**ctor in CorelDRAW. Let's pause for a Profound Realization to get a better idea what an **A**ctor is. Many people spend 10 dollars on a lousy movie and still have this same question.

PROFOUND
REALIZATION

CorelMOVE considers any **O**bject that contains one or more frames in it to be an **A**ctor. A frame is a moment in time and space for the **A**ctor. An **A**ctor's hand waving might be four frames long—each frame with the hand in a different position in space. An **A**ctor can be a drawing of a rock, a cartoon of a person, or a typeset word. Frames, regardless of the number of them, become an **O**bject that Corel knows how to handle using OLE.

It's a real nerdy concept, and all you really have to know is that you design several different CorelDRAW (or PAINT, or other) pictures of your **A**ctor. Each make up a frame in the **O**bject. You exit the design program (like CorelDRAW), the **O**bject is inserted in CorelMOVE's workspace automatically, and CorelMOVE will handle the motion aspect of your frames of actors without bothering you with the specifics.

6. In figure 11.40, we're given the choice of creating a new object, or creating an object from a file. To get a little more familiar with this OLE stuff that we checked out in CorelSHOW, let's **C**reate New Actor (I sound like Tarzan, don't I?), select the Object **T**ype: as a CorelDRAW! 4.0 Graphic, and let OLE whisk us over to CorelDRAW again.

Figure 11.40

Can you imagine a CorelCHART chart as an **A**ctor?

7. Click on OK, and we get beamed into CorelDRAW's neck of the woods. Here, we'll type COMING SOON, because our **A**ctor, our thing we're going to animate, is a typeset word.

SECRET

You can design anything you want at this point in CorelDRAW's OLE Window to CorelMOVE. This is where we create the frames that CorelMOVE will later animate.

8. In figure 11.41, We've used Artistic Text and extruded it, because I thought it would make a cool **A**ctor, and I don't know how to draw Dustin Hoffman. You'll notice that CorelDRAW has a weird box hanging around the top of the workspace. It says Frame Select, and although we'll use it shortly, it doesn't really belong to CorelDRAW. The Nerdy Note explains where this intruder came from, in case you wondered.

Figure 11.41

Your first **A**ctor frame.

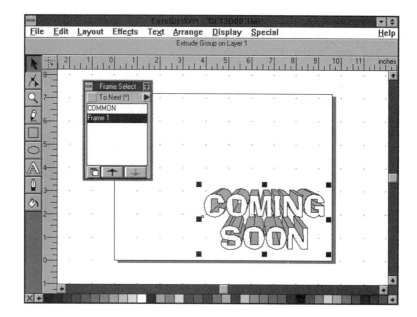

NERDY NOTE

The Frame Select box is actually a floating toolbox that belongs to CorelMOVE. It's only making a guest appearance in CorelDRAW to help you work with both CorelDRAW and CorelMOVE tools in the same workspace. This appearance of a weird toolbox in a program is sponsored by Windows Object Linking and Embedding (OLE).

If you were to open CorelDRAW normally by clicking on the CorelDRAW icon in Windows Program Manager, the Frame Select box would be nowhere to be found in CorelDRAW's menu items. *The Flying Dutchman*, UFOs, and Elvis are not OLE properties, however, and if you get any of them in CorelDRAW, call Corel Technical Support at [613] 728-8200. Or call your favorite supermarket tabloid.

9. We've created our **A**ctor's first position in the first frame of our **O**bject. Now an important thing to remember is that when you want to design a second position, you're given a fresh, clean frame to design in. If you want to design something completely different in frame two of this **A**ctor, more power to you.

But if you only want to make the design wiggle a little, like we do, copy the design to the Windows Clipboard, then press the little triangle on the Frame Select box. You'll get a flyout that has the choice **New** on it. Select this one, and you'll get an Append new frames box, like in figure 11.42, that asks you how many frames you want to append (add after) your first frame. The default is one, and we take things one at a time in this book, so click on OK.

Figure 11.42

A clean slate again.

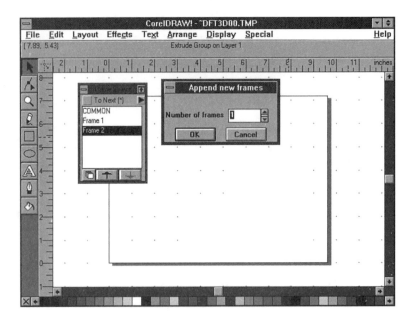

10. From the **E**dit menu, click on **P**aste, and the copy of the Coming Soon Artistic Text appears in the same location on your workspace as it was in frame one. This is good. Frames that are copied to make up the whole **O**bject shouldn't go bouncing all over your OLE CorelDRAW workspace. If they did, your animation would look awful and give folks headaches.

Click two times on the Artistic Text to call up the **R**otate and Skew selection handles, and pull counter- or clockwise on a corner handle to rotate the Artistic Text slightly, as shown in figure 11.43.

Figure 11.43

Coming at ya!

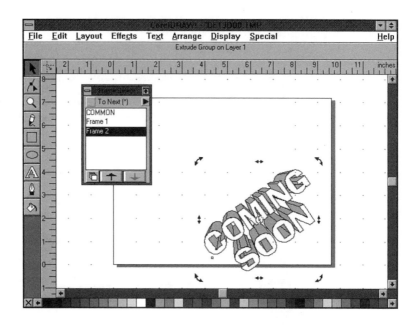

SECRET

If you didn't start designing in the dead-center of CorelDRAW's page border, don't sweat it. And don't move your pasted designs in frames two, three, and so on. In each frame, your design should be exactly in the same position as the previous one. All these frames are going to make up one **O**bject when we're through.

The **O**bject can be centered in the CorelMOVE page border when we're done designing and OLEing. If you do move designs on your page border from frame to frame when you're in CorelDRAW, your finished **O**bject will look like a ping pong ball on amphetamines when CorelMOVE animates it later.

11. We skipped ahead a little on these figures. Basically, we repeated the process of **P**asting a copy of the Artistic Text back on to the workspace, each time adding a new frame, until we totaled five frames for our **A**ctor. In figure 11.44, we are closing the link between CorelDRAW and CorelMOVE, so we can go back to CorelMOVE and watch our **A**ctor rotate a little!

Figure 11.44

File, E**x**it & Return.

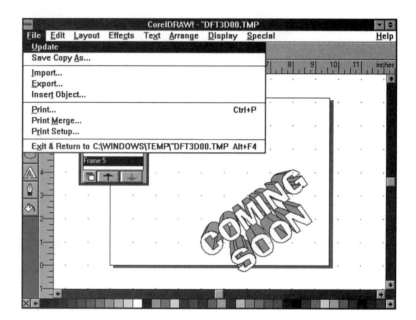

12. We are asked, just like in the linked CorelSHOW/DRAW, whether we want to Update the embedded object as we exit. Of course we do! Click on **Y**es, like the one you see in figure 11.45.

13. In figure 11.46, Corel is rendering the images. It takes a moment to render the **O**bject (the frames are rendered, but the **O**bject has to be assembled), and then we're automatically returned to CorelMOVE. If you created a lot of activity in this **O**bject (made a lot of frames), it'll take longer than the five frames we designed in this book.

14. We arrive back safe and sound in CorelMOVE with our **A**ctor on our silver screen, shown in figure 11.47. For our viewers at home, if your Actor plops into your CorelMOVE workspace off-center, or partially off the screen, don't worry. Just click on it and move it anywhere on the workspace your heart desires. OLE has packaged all your neat

animation steps in one tidy bundle. They won't come loose or anything if you reposition it. Now, let's familiarize ourselves with the little VCR controls at the bottom of the screen, so we can see our **A**ctor act.

Figure 11.45

Yes, and let's get on with the movie!

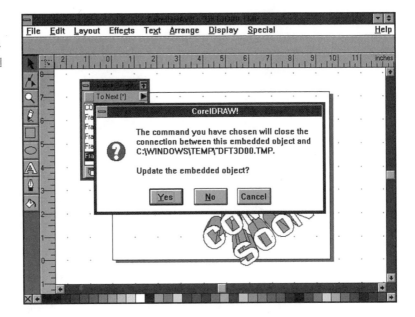

Figure 11.46

We're "drawing" to a close!

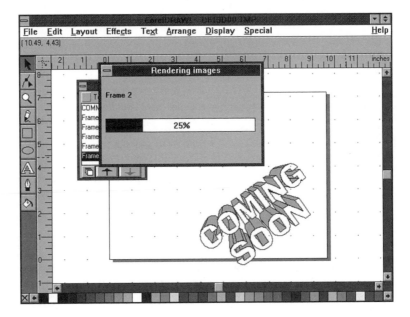

Figure 11.47

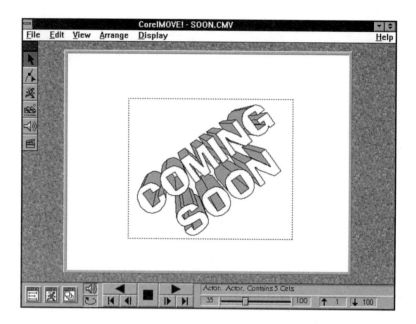

The large triangle next to the word **A**ctor is the play button. The one directly to the left is Stop, and the one next to Stop is Reverse. Beneath the Play and Reverse are controls for advancing your **A**ctor one frame at a time as we built them in CorelDRAW, or second by second.

Unless you have a lot of **A**ctors on screen, and they were built with lots and lots of frames, you probably won't benefit from advancing your Corel movie second by second.

SECRET

15. Enough explanations! "Choose play" (the large triangle on the bottom right)!

So you're new to tinsel town?

Motion pictures are complicated things. They not only have actors, but backgrounds, sound, and tons and tons of editing before they're ready to make a debut at your local monitor. We've shown you the basic steps for making something move in CorelMOVE—but a movie it ain't.

Try experimenting with inserting different **O**bjects, and call programs other than CorelDRAW (CHART, PHOTO-PAINT), to see how you can build animated charts and stuff. Be sure to check out Corel's library of backgrounds, and while you're exploring, try importing a .WAV file to add sounds to your movie.

On Your Expanded Hat Size

The wonderful thing about all the hats you can wear while exploring the Corel modules is that you're exposed to other ways of designing things, while building on your experience with CorelDRAW's tools. You already went into this chapter knowing a dozen or so!

Come to think of it, how many tools have we familiarized ourselves with so far in this book? Do we think we have enough of an arsenal packed away to design just about anything? Are there more tools?

All good questions. And the answers are mostly up to you. Yes, Corel has more tools than we've shown, some specialty items and some novelty items that can make your work easier as a designer. But these tools won't make you a better designer just by knowing what they are and what they do.

Demystifying "advanced" techniques

My personal experience with CorelDRAW has probably been a lot like your own, except I didn't have the advantage of reading a non-nerdy book. I poked at buttons about which I had not a clue of knowledge, and tripped over a lot of terrific design elements while trying do unrelated things. Why? The same reason you're reading this little tome and not that stuffy Corel manual— because nobody likes to read a software program's reference guide, except nerds.

Once you become comfortable with your new tools, you'll start designing what your heart desires, and while designing, learn new tricks and tips like the ones in this book. But as to the sticky question of how to become really knowledgeable about Corel, and to become an award-winning designer with it, the next chapter will tell you all about it, and it's very easy to understand.

If you can dream it, you can draw it—

CHAPTER 12

The Secret to Getting Great at CorelDRAW!

I f you've patiently sifted through this book in sequence, you may have already guessed what the mysterious secret is to creating spectacular designs with Corel. If not, you've at least demonstrated *patience*, which is a key to the secret. And even if you immediately flipped to this chapter first after reading the title, you'll still get the big picture at a glance.

In this chapter, we will:

   Hear the advice of professional artists on the most important aspect of their craft

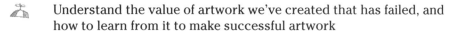   Understand the value of artwork we've created that has failed, and how to learn from it to make successful artwork

Learn how this wonderful secret can be applied to other computer programs, in order to achieve the same wonderful results

Brace Yourself

In a word... it's *practice*.

There are four steps in your approach to art, or any other craft, and this one is the most important. You have to *want it*, *learn it*, *practice it*, and then you finally *master it*. You already know deep down inside that there's no "quick fix" to becoming a whiz at art. And art that's designed on a PC is especially attractive because of the technology. The "want" part is there, or you wouldn't be reading this book. CorelDRAW and New Riders Publishing make your effort to learn a new program as painless as possible, which leads us to the step that's the secret to turning the knowledge into the talent.

It's practice. It's screwing around with the PC after hours, making mistakes and learning from them; it's expanding your knowledge and skills with a machine and a program that's the most patient tutor a soul could ask for.

And "mastering" a program? A little voice should tell you about now that there's no absolute, no threshold you cross that anoints you with the title of "master." CorelDRAW 4.0 is a new program, just like Corel 3.0 was, not too long ago. Like Corel, you have to continually upgrade your *own* product, *your* skills, to make the challenge of becoming a great designer an ever-expanding and fresh one. And to make it exciting for *yourself*.

Is Numero Uno, Head Cheese, Most-Exalted Killer CorelDRAW designer ever really an attainable goal? Or even a desired one? Oddly enough, if you practice with Corel, the answer won't be up to you. Work diligently and with a sense of humility, don't be afraid to ask questions, and one day you'll overhear part of a conversation softly going on between your friends in the background. "Hey, do you see that Corel stuff? *(This could be you)* is really good!"

If you can dream it, you can draw it.

All it takes is practice.

CHAPTER 13

Outputting Your Input

Without this chapter, all your brilliant design work in Corel would live in a box. We've marvelled at all the neat stuff on your monitor and haven't talked about how to get your designs on the printed page, or on a color slide. It would be nice to be able to mail the Mother's Day card you made in Chapter 6 instead of inviting Mom over to see it on your monitor.

Corel offers lots of options when it comes to outputting your input, or how to make a "hard copy" of your work that's every ounce as glamourous as it looks on-screen. Here's what we'll do about that...

In this chapter, we will:

 Cover the options you have with a laser printer

 Learn how to "tweak" Corel to give better results when you output a file

 Understand the importance of knowing a good service bureau

Before the (Laser)Jet Takes Off

The most exciting moment a new computer graphics artist could have is to hear the whine of a laser printer revving up. You've slaved over a piece, and you know within seconds you'll receive a cooked copy of your work that you can strut around the office and tack on your cubicle.

If everything is set up right—Windows knows about your printer and Corel's Printer Option boxes are properly checked—printing your Corel file can be an uplifting moment. If it doesn't, and they aren't, you'll be grounded. So let's lay out our flight plan before sending a Corel file to print.

Art that's fit to print

Whether you're working on a network, or have only one PC hooked up to a laser printer, the print command is the same. In Corel, you select **F**ile, then **P**rint (CTRL+P). This will call Corel's Print dialog box, seen in figure 13.1. It offers you a slew of options we'll examine before we actually click on the OK button.

Figure 13.1

The Corel print dialog box.

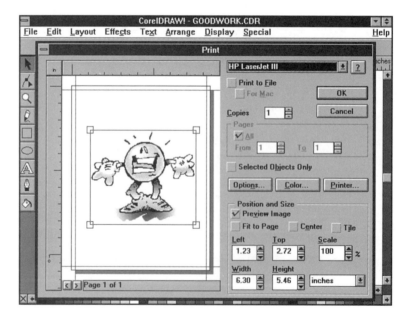

Pick a Printer, Not Any Printer

The box at the top right of your Print dialog box is where you select the printer driver you're going to use to print your masterpiece. A printer driver is not the same as a printer. It is a software program that translates Corel's description of what your file should end up looking like into a language your specific printer can understand. Different brands and kinds of printers speak different languages and it's the printer driver's duty to act as the "go-between," sort of like an import/export filter.

Windows 3.1 comes with a ton of printer drivers, and they cover most of the printers out the market. When you (or whoever) install Windows on your PC, Windows presents the installer with the opportunity to install proper printer drivers.

Corel will display a list of printer drivers that are installed on your computer if you click on the down arrow in Corel's upper right printer driver box. You should make sure that the one you select here is the one that matches the printer you'll be using.

If you can't find a matching printer driver, you will need to install one. Windows handles printer driver installation so you'll have to exit Corel and go find your Windows disks. Installing a printer driver is not really hard, but you may want to use the Windows manual (argh), the Windows on-line Help (argh, then press F1), or have your copy of New Riders Publishing's *Windows for Non-Nerds* (yeah!) handy.

UH-OH

If you pick a printer driver that does not match the printer you are using, strange stuff usually prints rather than your masterpiece.

If you get pages and pages of text that say stuff like "ls/cp/closepath ld/ARC/arcn ld/TR{65536 div}bd/lj/setlinejoin ld/lc def/sc{scignore{pop pop pop}}," instead of the text and graphics you were expecting, not to worry. That gobbledygook text is PostScript language. It printed because the printer driver that's selected thinks it's talking to a PostScript printer, instead of the non-PostScript printer it was actually talking to. Just select a new (hopefully matching) printer driver in the Print option box.

With the right printer driver set, we're ready to explore CorelDRAW's other printing options.

Opting for Options

"What You See Is What You Get," or "WYSIWYG" (pronounced Whizzy Wig), has been a popular phrase among Windows developers and nerds alike. This means that you can expect your finished, printed hard copy to look like what you see on your monitor. Sometimes it works this way, but not always.

One of the hardest things for a laser printer to understand is Corel's Fountain Fills. Big bummer, because they are one of Corel's coolest features. Fountain Fills are actually a percentage of color, butted right next to another color that is slightly darker, and so on, until the viewer perceives a smooth transitional fill.

Fills below the 64-step default will produce pronounced "banding"; a setting above the default greatly slows printing time. Keep your setting at 64, and you oughta be happy (see figure 13.2).

Figure 13.2

Check your options, but set your Fountain Steps at 64, not 180.

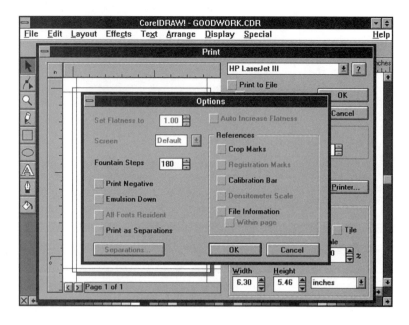

Corel's default for Fountain Fills is 64. Corel will tell the printer driver (which tells the printer), to create a Radial, Linear, or Conic Fountain Fill in 64 steps. It is Corel's intention to set this default so that you get a reasonable picture printed quickly. In fact, they consider this to be the draft mode, and actually recommend you set the value higher for your real print, when you have more time.

High-end output options

While we've got the Options box open, let's peek at options other than smooth Fountain Fills. You'll notice that a lot of the options in figure 13.2 are grayed out (you can't use them). These are options that are associated with a PostScript printer, and the HPIII we have selected is not a PostScript printer, so we won't explore them now. But we will talk about PostScript devices in the next section.

     Print Negative is an option for all printers that will reverse all the black-and-white tonal values in your print of your Corel file. It will make everything you've designed in black print white, and vice versa. Why would you want to do this?

A commercial printer or a service bureau can make a *film positive* of your work in one less step if you give them a print negative. You may find you need a copy of your work done on film someday, to be pasted on a product mock-up or to glue on your car window. Remember that this option is there for you when you need to produce the negative that produces the positive.

     Emulsion Down. This one's easy. Do not check this box if you're printing to a laser printer. Emulsion down is an option to check if you are printing to an imagesetter, not a dry-toner laser printer. *Imagesetters* are very expensive, high-resoluton devices that can print to paper or to film. Printers and service bureaus use these to proof work and make printing plates. There is no emulsion to worry about on laser paper, so don't stay up all night on this one.

     Print as Separations is useful to check only if you are asked to produce the separations a commercial printer needs to have to make printing plates for a multicolor design. Corel can do this for you if you ever need to do this, but be forewarned: producing high-quality color separations is an art in itself. It is usually better to have your service bureau, commercial printer, or a firm that specializes in producing separations do them for you.

Crop Marks are indicators Corel will print on your page that indicate where the borders of your design should be. You can print a laser copy cropped so a commercial printer can strip the artwork into a publication, for example. These are really nice, clean marks a commercial printer can follow more easily than blue pencil marks or crayons.

 The *Calibration Bar* serves a similar purpose as a test pattern a lot like you see TV stations broadcast. It helps you tune the color and contrast of the picture as seen on your monitor, so you can make sure the information you send to the printer is the same. Nerds will call the process *gamma correction* or *color-matching*; and if you want to color-correct your monitor, this is the one time in your life you'd want a nerd leaning over your shoulder. If you're printing to a black-and-white laser printer, you probably don't need to mess with the Calibration Bar.

Corel has given the designer a lot of options to help with the sometimes complex task of getting a computer design off the machine and onto the printed page. Many of these options relate to preparing a hard copy to "go to press." If you're using a non-PostScript laser printer (most common in businesses) to produce your finished artwork, you don't have to change any of Corel's default print options, except the one concerning the Fountain Fill steps we talked about earlier. But if you are printing to a PostScript laser printer (most common to architecture and graphics firms), there are more options available that you may need to play around with.

PS (PostScript), I Love You

In the last section, we talked about the language a printer driver translates to feed information to your laser printer. Most PC users look for speed, quality, and price when it's time to shop for a printer. And bubblejet and laserjet printers fit the bill 90 percent of the time. But this is Corel here. It's a graphical world, and if you have access to a PostScript printer, you should know about a few options Corel can offer you, a couple of pluses, and a few minuses before you send your file off to print.

Speak slowly and distinctly

PostScript is one of the earliest, most eloquent descriptor languages offered in the computer world for getting a graphical image onto hard copy. Whether it's on paper or film, the PostScript language describes every nuance, curve, turn, and fill that makes up a shape or typeset word; and it does this in a professional, eye-catching manner. If you own a PostScript printer, or talk to someone who owns one, you'll also find out that this language is slooooooooow.

While Printer Command Language-based laser printers (like Hewlett-Packard's) are quick and produce smooth graphical lines, they're also pretty dumb. When you print from a Windows program, Windows commands a PCL printer to do this, go there, and do that, without an explanation of the graphical content. A PostScript-language printer is smart, and actually reads a "script" that's in its language. It understands the design information, then renders away. It takes more time for a PostScript printer to render your design because the printer is following blueprints, whereas a PCL printer is just pounding a nail and sawing a plank where Windows tells it to.

Stating things flatly

If we have a printer driver specified as a PostScript printer, as seen in figure 13.3, we get less grayed-out options in Corel. The first option we see that we can get hands-on with is the Flatness. *Flatness*, in Corel, is the degree of perfection with which you want a PostScript printer to design a curve.

Figure 13.3

PostScript
printer driver
options.

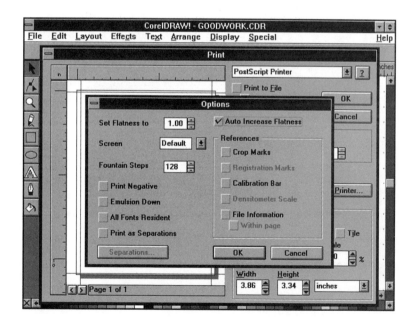

The default value of one is good for most simple curves. If you've drawn a string of spaghetti, with 350 nodes in it, your PostScript printer may have a hard time digesting it, and you'll get a *limitcheck error* printed on your page instead of your artwork. The curve is too complex, as designed, to print. This is the time to "up" the Flatness in this box. You increase this value from one to five, then to nine—increase the value in increments of four until your spaghetti prints. Flatness makes the PostScript descriptor language less complex, and this results in smoother curves. Play with it until you get a happy medium, and remember next time to design simpler curves!

SECRET

A PostScript printer file of your work is increased by 150 bytes for every object you have in the design—and one byte for every node in a design! Try to keep extraneous objects out of your workspace, and Auto-Reduce the number of nodes in a Corel shape wherever you get the chance. Auto-Reduce is on the Node Edit Roll-Up; you can call it by double-clicking on a node with your Shape tool.

Step up to the fountain!

PostScript handles Corel Fountain Fills more "eloquently" than other printer languages. When I changed my printer driver to a PostScript printer, Corel readjusted the default Fountain Fill steps to 128, as shown in figure 13.3. Why? All high-end imagesetters are PostScript language printers, and a lower default setting would be painfully obvious on one of those really smooth printers. While a setting of 128 is higher than a mere 300 dpi laser printer can muster, Corel didn't want to take chances in case someone forgot and sent the print job out for imagesetting.

SECRET

Neither changing the Fountain Fill Steps nor the Flatness will affect your Corel file in any way. This only tunes the printing process, so don't be afraid to experiment.

Is there anything *good* about PostScript printing?

It's hard to present an unbiased view about PostScript printing without saying, "Watch out for this and that," which makes the party a drag.

PostScript printers are wonderful, especially at higher resolutions, like 1,200 dpi (dots per inch). They render typefaces a lot cleaner than garden-variety laser printers, and the fills are nice and even. You simply have to understand a few special rules with them, and you might put the extra time you spend waiting for your print to good use, like practicing with CorelDRAW.

Taking a Position on Your Work

Corel offers more options on the Print menu box that have to do with optimizing the placement of your design, rather than the quality of it. In figure 13.4, we've taken our cursor and are pulling in an outward direction from a corner selection handle on the design.

Figure 13.4

Funny, his expression didn't change!

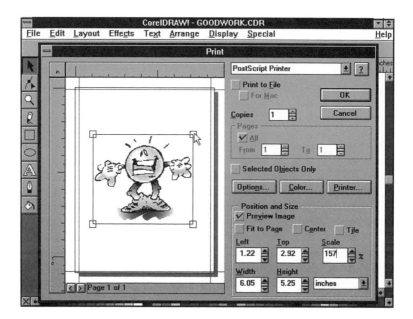

This is one way to proportionately resize a design without returning to Corel's workspace. This is good if, at the last minute, you want a bigger picture of your design. It's simple: you select the object just as you would on the workspace, then pull inward or outward on it. The scale that reflects a change is seen in the **S**cale box toward the bottom of the menu box. You can also enter a scale size manually (for more precision) by placing your cursor in the box and typing in a value on your keyboard.

Can you move over a little?

Corel also takes note of the position of objects on your printable page (stuff within your page border). If you have anything you want printed to actually come out, you'd better make certain that everything is within the page border (and not off in a corner of your workspace), or it won't show up in the print preview box. Moving an object on the printable page from the print menu is very useful if you want to center an object you forgot about while you were working.

If you need to move an object on the printable page (the page border preview), you can do it, as with resizing, by manually entering coordinates in the bottom four boxes (see fig. 13.4). You also can place the cursor over the object, click, hold, and give the object a good shove!

If you moved or resized your design in the Print Preview box, don't worry about it affecting your workspace. It doesn't change what you have already done.

Printing to a Non-Printer

We've covered some options for putting Corel's work on the printed page, but what if you don't own a printer? What if the nearest laser printer you can get to is five miles away? What if you go five miles away and find out they don't own CorelDRAW? Or even Windows?

To answer the next-to-last question first, you don't have to own CorelDRAW to print a CorelDRAW image out of a laser printer. You'd be welcoming a world of trouble if you let this hypothetical laser printer owner five miles away copy your Corel disks, and it's an unnecessary measure, as well.

In figure 13.5, we've selected the Print To File box from Corel's Print menu. If you do this on your own PC, you're piping printer language to a file, not a printer. The language is intact, and your "canned script" can be played back later on another PC that's equipped with a printer.

What happens after you select Print To File? Corel will offer you a choice in the bottom drop-down box, asking you which file extension you want to select for a file you're creating. Remember, this file can be printed 5 or 500 miles away. You'll see in figure 13.5, we've been offered the .prn file extension name. That's an easy one to find in File Manager, and the extension doesn't truly relate to a certain type of file format—it's just that Windows and DOS like file extensions after files. This file will technically be full of instructions, as compared with information, much like your .CDR files.

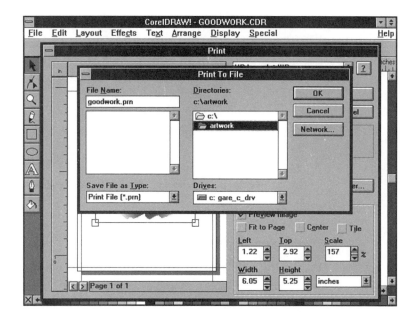

This .PRN file carries all the information about printing your design in a specific printer language. It contains the instructions Corel and Windows would be sending about this file to a printer, if you had a printer connected to your PC. It's a weird concept, probably invented by a nerd, but it really works and will save your career if you don't own a laser printer. Follow these steps to print a file when you don't own a printer:

1. Select the printer driver that goes with the printer that belongs to the buddy you'll lean on for this favor *(whew!)*. If he or she owns a Hewlett-Packard III for example, specify HPIII in the selection box we showed you in figure 13.1. This is an important step, or your Print To File instructions won't be understood by your buddy's printer.

2. Select a file name you want to use. Just click on OK after typing the name, and Corel will tack on .prn afterwards for you.

3. Select the directory you want this file to go to. We've called our file goodwork.prn, and it will be built in our c:\artwork working directory.

4. Click on OK, then click on OK again on the main Print menu Corel's displaying.

5   When Corel's done, E<u>x</u>it (**Alt+F4**) from Corel and return to Windows Program Manager.

6.   Put a blank, formatted disk in one of your disk drives.

When you print to file, then copy the file to a disk. It's a good idea to use a 3 1/2-inch high-density disk. The reason why is because the Print To File of your work will be larger than the user file you originally made in Corel. And this means you might need a lot of disk space for all the complex instructions.

SECRET

7.   Select the File Manager, and locate the new .PRN file.

8.   Click on this file, and drag it onto the little icon that represents the floppy drive you have the blank, formatted disk in.

9.   Windows will ask you to confirm this copying action. Click on Yes, and in a moment or two, we have a file on disk that contains all the information a laser printer needs to print your Corel design.

You can now schlep your disk to far, far away, and ask your buddy to print this disk to his printer. You do this from DOS by typing this at the command line:

First, log onto the drive that has your newly made .PRN file. Then type **COPY** **[file name].PRN PRN**.

So in our example, if we used a 3 1/2-inch disk that fits in our buddy's B drive, our command line would be:

B: [enter]

Copy GOODWORK.PRN PRN [enter]

This is a good technique to know if you have a service bureau in the neighborhood, a few bucks, and an overwhelming need to get a super high-quality color print or slide of your Corel design. Plus, a service bureau knows how to print a file, and won't ask you to go remembering DOS command lines.

What a service bureau is, what it does, and what you have to do in order to "set up" your Corel design first is the section we're coming right up on!

Uncovering the Secret Service

We've talked about outputting to laser printers, fine-tuning laser copies for commercial printing, and what to do if you don't own a laser printer. But another resource for incredible Corel output may be just around the corner. Service bureaus are popping up all over the world to address PC owners' needs for color prints, slides, and film copies of graphical designs. Service bureaus own large and expensive imagesetters and film recorders that are out of the average user's budget (not to mention living accommodations). For a fee, you can turn over a file of your work on disk (or through a modem), and receive prints or slides of your work that show off color and sharpness you most likely won't even see on an average monitor!

Drop a dime (or 2, or 50, or...)

To make your first visit to a service bureau as hassle-free as possible, ask around the office if anyone *knows* of a good service bureau. If anyone says they know a good diaper service, you're talking to the wrong person. Nerds, though wrong about most things, are usually right about a high-quality service bureau. And they are very firm about their convictions, so as soon as you get the name, politely excuse yourself before they attempt to tell you why this service bureau is the best. Below is a checklist to prepare yourself for a visit to a service bureau:

 Get out the telephone book, and call not one, but two or three service bureaus. Ask them first whether they handle IBM-PC computer files, because if they're a "Mac Shop" (Macintosh specialists, okay?), we'll have to do some noodling with your CorelDRAW file.

SECRET

Most service bureaus started out as Macintosh imaging centers. This is because Macintoshes have been capable of producing computer graphics since their start in 1985. Windows was a late-bloomer in offering the PC world the same graphics capabilities as the Mac, so most places offering print services are only now coming around to the demand for PC imaging services.

Ask the people at the service bureau whether they have CorelDRAW. If they do, you've saved yourself a lot of headaches, because you can copy a Corel file to a disk (to take to the bureau), instead of preparing a special Print To File disk.

Ask the service bureau what sort of imagesetting equipment they have. A good bureau will proudly roll off names like Tektronix, Linotronic, and Canon. A "specialty boutique" like a service bureau usually doesn't bother with the penny-ante stuff like photocopying, so make certain these people sound like they know a lot about computer imaging. If the sales rep sounds less knowledgeable than you and stresses that they carry lots of different colored paper, keep shopping.

If you need a 35mm or or larger color slide of your work, let the people at the service bureau know that. Some bureaus do slides, some do color prints, some do both. Check them out on this before hopping in the car.

Do some comparative shopping. Depending on what you buy and how large your color piece is, it could run you 5 bucks, or $150. Ask about discounts for bulk orders. Service bureaus usually have pricings for quantity orders.

Call it in

A lot of service bureaus offer modem service for their customers. This means that you can actually upload the design you need printed, as a file, to the service bureau's PC via a telephone line connected to a modem on your end of business. If you're not familiar with how a PC modem works, ask around the office. Businesses generally have communication lines up and running that are dedicated to data transfer. Point out to your boss that if you upload the file to the service bureau, it's one less trip that takes you away from your desk. Bosses see the sensibility of this concept immediately.

Ordering prints, making tracks

If you're ordering a color print from a service bureau, we've covered almost all the bases in terms of what you'll need to supply them with. If they have Corel, bring them a design in a .CDR format. If they don't, save the design as a Print to Disk.

If the place is a Macintosh-only service bureau, and there isn't another place within 50 miles of you, you can always export your Corel .CDR file to a Mac .PCT file as we mentioned in Chapter 8. This .PCT file works wonderfully if you remember to separate all the CorelDRAW blends you've created in an illustration, then ungroup them. If you don't, the Macintosh will skip over them in the printing process, and your design will have holes in it.

So if you can't call long-distance with a modem, and can't find a local PC service bureau, separate all linked objects in your design, export the design as a Mac .PCT file, put it on a disk, and tell 'em how many prints you want. The Macintosh and the PC world operate a little differently, but if you follow the rules, you'll get good color work back.

Bases Covered, Sliding Into Home

Except for a little pre-planning you have to do for the service bureau with slide making, you're pretty well covered in terms of ways to output your CorelDRAW art.

A recap on domestic printing

If you're printing in the home or at work, bear in mind these pointers:

- You can create a phenomenally complex illustration in Corel, but if your printer has insufficient RAM, it may not print.

- When designing Corel stuff, keep shapes down to 150 nodes connecting line segments, or less. PostScript printers and Windows Clipboards gag on shapes that are more mathematically complex than that.

- Try to use paper that's specifically marked "laser paper" if you're printing work that will be sent to a commercial printer for lithography or offset. The fused dots of dry toner that make up laser copies are sharper for the commercial printer's copy camera on laser paper.

- Don't print on colored paper if you're planning to send your work out as camera-ready. Likewise, skip colored paper if you're planning to photocopy your laser print.

If you do plan on photocopying your work off a laser print, try to run the laser printer at 300 dpi, tops. Today's 600 dpi laser printers produce almost invisible dot patterns to render your design, but photocopiers can't handle that resolution very well.

Placing orders, film recorders

The last output device we'll cover in this chapter is a very special one most people have to go to a service bureau to use: the *film recorder*. Although their prices have fallen lately, the sticker price on a film recorder is still in the five-figure range. The reason is that they do something unique and complex: they put your computer graphic on a 35mm slide! Among other things. It depends on what kind of service the bureau decides on providing. If you don't have a local service bureau with a film recorder, there are plenty of mail-away houses that offer this service. The best way to check out a mail-order film recorder place is to borrow a nerd's copy of *PC Magazine*, and thumb through the back. There are plenty of ads for slide services there.

Slides still play a big role in business presentations because they are portable. A lot of businesses don't have a resident nerd who can set up a computer at the drop of a hat for a computer slide show like those you can make in CorelSHOW. Given that, there's only a little thing you need to do to your Corel files in order to prep them for a film recorder. We'll show you right now!

Putting things in proportion

After the friendly takeover of Consolidated Widgets by Megalopolis in Chapter 9, WorldWide Widgets now has a small field office in Nedrow, N.Y. They've still got your number, and have commissioned you to do some 35mm slides to present to the main office for a new campaign. You developed a full-page print ad for them a while back, and you think the art is worth reusing. You open the file in CorelDRAW, as seen in figure 13.6.

1. We already know how to do a landscape page layout in Corel from our duck/man experiment in Chapter 6. It shows in our full-page ad for Widgets. We need to fix the proportions of the landscape layout for a 35mm slide layout this time. And it's done from the **P**age Setup under the **L**ayout menu item, as seen in figure 13.7.

Figure 13.6

The 8 1/2-by 11-inch full-page ad.

Figure 13.7

Actually, we "set up" this whole example!

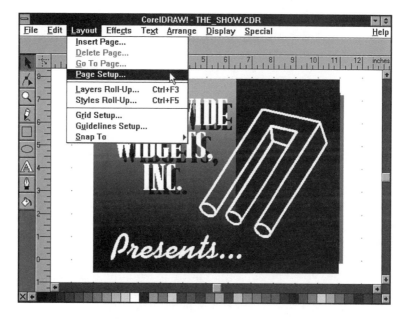

2.   From **P**age Setup, we click on the little arrow next to Paper Size; it drops down a list of common page layout formats, and we choose Slide, as in figure 13.8.

Figure 13.8

You can find all
kinds of odd sizes
here. No. 10
envelopes, too!

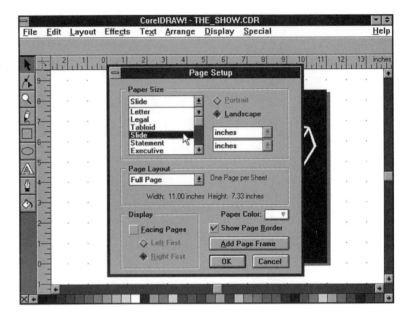

3. Now we have a clue in figure 13.8 that our design isn't going to be perfectly proportioned for a slide. In fact, it clearly states on the screen that we've chosen a page size of Width: 11.00 inches by Height: 7.33 inches. Our suspicions are confirmed in figure 13.9, where we've switched to Wireframe View of our file (Shift+F9). Not to worry. We read someplace that there are no problems, only solutions.

4. We're in luck this time out, because most of our design still fits in the page border that's now set to slide proportions. If we were to leave the file this way, the person at the service bureau would make a slide for you with "white space" on the sides of the slide to make up the proportional difference. And folks watching the slide show in a dark room would get blasted with a blinding white light on the edges of the slide.

    The presentation would be a failure, you wouldn't get paid, and you'd have learned nothing from the experience. Instead, use the Zoom In button on the Zoom tool flyout to marquee-select a close-up of our new Corel 35mm page border, like in figure 13.10. We are going to pull Snap-To Guidelines directly on the Corel 35mm page border sides.

Figure 13.9

Our background goes clear off Corel's page border.

Figure 13.10

Pull Snap-To Guidelines to lay exactly on the four sides of our 35mm page border.

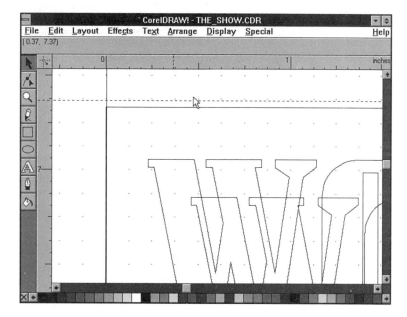

5.   Go to the **L**ayout Menu again, and from the **S**nap To item, select
     G**u**idelines, as shown in figure 13.11. This will make the alterations
     we'll perform on the design snap exactly to an 11-by-7.33-inch 35mm
     page border! Easy work if you can find it!

Figure 13.11

We need some
guidelines for
presenting
Widgets.

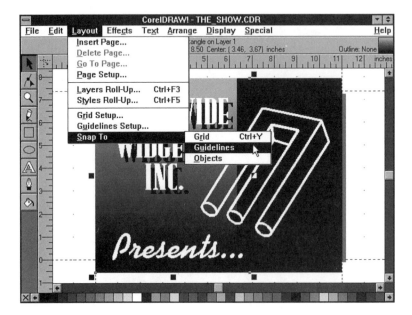

6.   From our Wireframe View, we noticed that the Artistic Text and the
     drawing of a Widget were basically within the boundaries of the
     35mm-proportioned page layout. We moved them in slightly, but the
     biggest consideration is to adjust the background that overlaps the
     frame. Since we have Snap-To Guidelines on the 35mm page border,
     we take a side selection handle on one of the background objects
     and pull it toward the page, as seen in figure 13.12.

After we snapped the backgrounds to the guidelines, we now have a file that
is perfect for a film recorder to make a slide of. Slides are different from
paper presentations. They have to be proportioned correctly, or a service
bureau might put "bleed" in the 35mm slide to accommodate all the graphical elements. And when this happens, presentations have light leaking out of
the borders and spoiling the drama a slide show is supposed to convey. It's
almost as bad when you or someone else is then forced to put electrical

tape, or laundry marker, on the slide to mask the bleed! Neither scenario is professional, and it's so easy to correct if you remember where to set up a Corel page for 35mm proportions.

Figure 13.12

This is so simple, it's almost a crime to charge money for this work. But do it anyway.

That's about all the input this chapter can hold on output devices that will make your Corel designs look their best. If you've noticed that there are less pages under your right thumb than your left now, it's because we're getting to the end of this book. Which seems to be a perfect time to...

Put This Book in Reverse!

Let's shift gears for the next chapter, okay? For pages and pages on end I've been telling you how to put Corel objects together. Now it's your turn to look over my shoulder, while we take apart a professional-like illustration from my art cellar. We'll see if there are any tricks in it you can learn from and use in your own designs. Keep in mind, though, that the student who puts the teacher out of work may get desperate, whiny telephone calls at night.

CHAPTER 14

Taking Apart Someone Else's Work

D esigners use a lot of little tricks and techniques to create complex-looking, yet deceptively simple illustrations. The illustration on the chapter title page, which I've called *Future Look*, looks like a clean, striking graphic, right? This drawing actually is made up of five layers, and CorelDRAW presented as many problems as solutions in creating it! Someday, you may want to create an effect similar to one of the illustrations shown on the next few pages. And we wouldn't want you to pull your hair out as a result of us not showing you some how-to's. In this chapter, I'm going to spill the beans, and show you the scenes behind the scene.

In this chapter, we will:

 Take apart a CorelDRAW illustration, to see how it was built

 Learn how layers can help make complicated illustrations

 Use different effects in CorelDRAW to create a unified look

The Sky, the City, the Future

I was asked a while back to illustrate a story in a newsletter, one that suggested a certain spaciness. (People always seem to single me out as the source for weird designs.) Anyway, I was given the dimensions for the column width of the newsletter, as well as how tall the drawing could be.

In figure 14.1, we see the finished illustration on CorelDRAW's workspace. I used absolutely no outlines on any of the shapes, so if you follow this step-by-step on your PC, remember to click the X on the color palette after you design every shape. The guidelines are visible on the bottom and right of the piece, because:

 Guidelines don't print or export along with a design.

 I'm not the tidiest Corel designer, and didn't bother to put the guidelines back into the Rulers when I was finished.

I think that if you're presenting a design (on screen) to a customer or your boss, you should definitely "clean house" beforehand. Cleaning house means closing all the roll-ups you may have used, and putting guidelines back into the Rulers, which you do by clicking on them and dragging them back to the Rulers from whence they came.

Figure 14.1 also shows the **L**ayers Roll-Up on the workspace. Each layer is labeled to identify each layer of elements in the illustration. We've learned how to put an object in Corel on top of another with the **O**rder item from the **A**rrange menu; we've learned how to make use of Ctrl+PgUp and Ctrl+PgDn to move something one level. But if an element in an illustration is made up of several objects, it's easiest to work with one group at a time by using the **L**ayers Roll-Up. Just press Ctrl, then F3 to get the roll-up on your workspace.

Figure 14.1

The finished
illustration, and
the Layers Roll-
Up, on the
workspace.

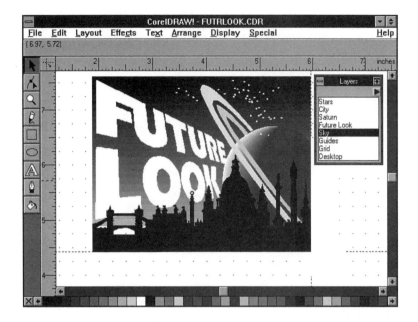

Ugly wireframe, nice picture

Like most complex designs, the elements are varied. They weave in and out
of each other, and there are lots of them! In figure 14.2, we see the Wireframe
view of the illustration *Future Look*. I toggled between views an awful lot
while designing this, and you may want to familiarize yourself with the
Shift+F9 keyboard combination when you are drawing with a lot of objects.

In this drawing, I needed to pull and tug on a lot of objects (as well as several
nodes within the objects) after I had all the objects drawn. It was much
easier to do this from the Wireframe view, because there were about 75
objects on five layers that I could select (intentionally or not).

Which brings us to our first point: You should plan an illustration on paper
(or in your head) before you sit down to work at your PC. Doing this will
help you decide how many layers you'll want to use.

Let's look at the Layers structure that I set up for this illustration. While
doing that, let's eliminate some from view so we can look at how the planet
was designed.

Figure 14.2

Future Look in
Wireframe view.

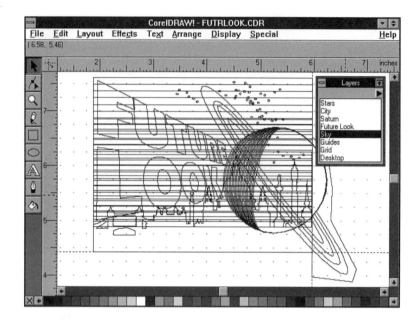

Peeling away the Layers

In figure 14.3, we've repositioned the Layers Roll-Up on the workspace so that it's handy to work with. When you click on the little triangle on the Layers Roll-Up, a flyout appears that offers several options. When I began this piece, only Layer 1, Guides, Grid, and Desktop were on the list of Layers. To create the layers, you choose New on the flyout. We're selecting Edit in this figure to modify the properties of the bottom layer in the illustration, Sky.

You can name a layer anything you want. When you click New from the Layer flyout, Corel, by default, will number the layers; Layer 2, Layer 3, and so on. This is not really helpful if you want to quickly pick a complex design on a specific layer. So all you do is rename the Layer in the Layers Options box after you select a New one.

SECRET

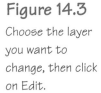

Figure 14.3

Choose the layer you want to change, then click on Edit.

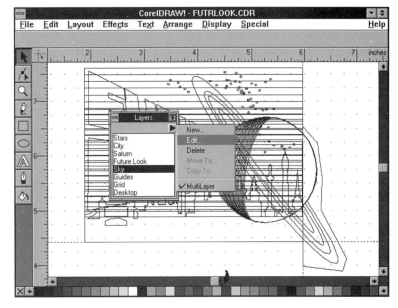

In figure 14.4, you choose the Edit selection called a Layer Options box. This is where we choose whether a layer is printable, visible, what color a wireframe view of the objects is (Color Override)... all on that specific layer on that page, or you can assign your "specs" to all the layers on all the pages in a multipage Corel Layout.

One of our goals in this chapter is to get a good look at how the planet Saturn was constructed, so we need to go through all the layers and deselect Visible. This will make the Sky invisible on the workspace (as in figure 14.4), both in Wireframe and Preview. If we want to see the whole design at any point, we can press F9 to show a Full-Screen Preview, which is different from the Preview mode within our workspace. We'll also lock this Sky layer while it's invisible, to prevent accidentally moving stuff around on the Sky layer while we examine other stuff.

Figure 14.4

The sky won't be visible, but it still prints.

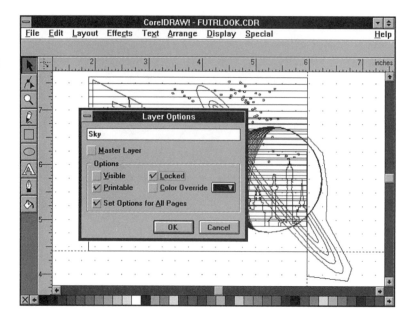

Exploring the rings

Now you know how Voyager felt, huh? Going through the Sky, past the Stars, to finally get an unobstructed view of Saturn! In figure 14.5, we've repeated the steps in figure 14.4 on all the layers, except Saturn. Everything else is invisible and Locked, and the Layer names are grayed-out on the Layer Roll-Up to remind us that they're that way. From a Wireframe view of the drawing of Saturn, we can see that it's made up of several objects. This planet was a challenge because the rings needed to go behind the planet, and in front as well.

The technique we used to "mask" a portion of the dinosaur in Chapter 6 won't work here, because we're not masking a solid color. If you look back to the chapter illustration, the body of Saturn has shading, not a solid fill to it. I used blends. You can see them in the Wireframe view in figure 14.5, and how do you "mask" a 20-step blend perfectly, with a minimum of effort? The answer (for me) was: "I didn't!" I'll explain in a moment.

Figure 14.5

Where do the rings end?

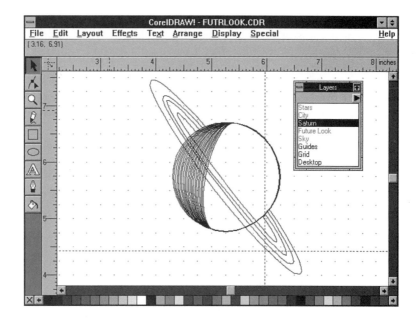

Creating an eclipse with an ellipse

In figure 14.6, we've pulled the planet Saturn away from its rings. This might disturb gravitational forces in our solar system if we did it for real, but this is only in CorelDRAW, so it's okay. The Status Bar tells us that Saturn, the planet, is made of a blend group. The way I created the subtle lighting effect on the planet was to make a circle (use the Ctrl key in combination with the Ellipse tool), convert the ellipse to Curves (**A**rrange, Con**v**ert to Curves or Ctrl+Q), then **D**uplicate (Ctrl+D) the shape. I tugged on the left node in my duplicate with the Shape tool to squeak the edge of the duplicate shape in toward the center of it. After giving the original a light value, and the smooshed-in duplicate a darker one, I selected them and applied a 20-step blend. The following figure shows how the eclipse of the ellipse was built.

Ring around the planet

As you can see in figure 14.6, the rings around Saturn aren't actually rings at all. They are two shapes that fit on top of the body of Saturn. It was necessary to design the rings this way, because you can't tuck the body of Saturn through the "hole" in the ellipse. So I need to create shapes that appear to be whole ellipses, but that in reality are a part of an ellipse shape.

In figure 14.7, I've created two ellipses to trace over. I know that the paths of my tracing won't complete an ellipse like the two I've drawn, because I want an area to be "missing," which will be occupied by the body of Saturn later. One ellipse is set slightly off the dead-center of the other; when I trace over these shapes to create my fake "ring," I'll want the finished piece to have some dimension. For example, the finished piece might be such that the "ring" gets larger when it comes around the front of Saturn, and diminshes as it appears to go around the back.

Figure 14.6

The main planet is made up of a 20-step blend applied to two shapes.

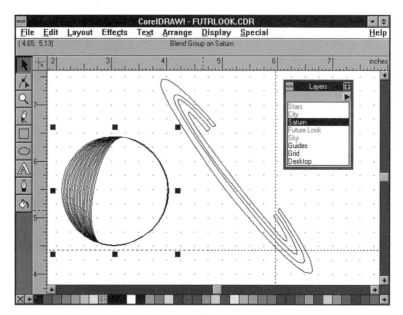

My template for tracing over this ring isn't complete if I don't know where to stop drawing the shape, which is where the body of Saturn will tuck into. I measured the width of the body, then brought two guidelines in from Corel's Rulers to roughly give me those reference points, such as in figure 14.8. Keep in mind throughout this chapter that I'm roughly composing a design, and then tightening it up later. My ring tracing won't fit perfectly, and I'll go back later to polish it. The process of working from loose to tight is a rule in fine art, and that rule should apply to computer art as well.

Figure 14.7

A template of a Saturn ring.

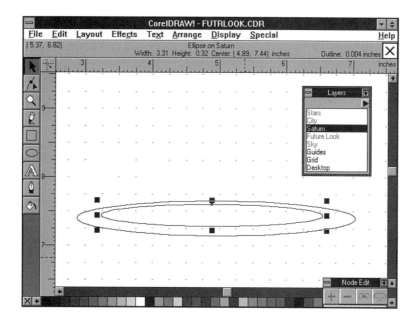

Figure 14.8

Now, on to tracing!

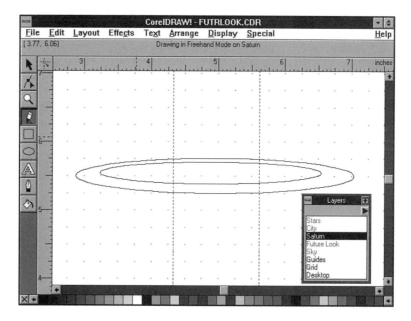

Saturn's rings: a closer view

This ring-tracing stuff requires a closer view, so I've selected the Zoom-In button on the Zoom tool flyout, and marquee-selected an area that will be my starting point to trace. If you look at figure 14.9, you'll see that I started where one of my ellipses crosses one of my guidelines. Using the Line Draw tool, I've double-clicked on what a nerd might call the *apogee* of this ellipse, and continued double-clicking my way around the ellipse. I don't need many nodes on my tracing, so I only click where I feel there will be a big-time change in the direction of the path I'm creating with the Line Draw tool.

Figure 14.9

Yeah, these are straight lines, but I'll make them curve a little later.

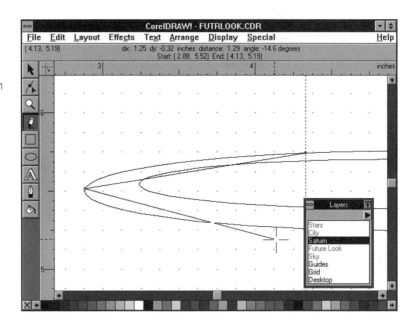

In figure 14.10, I've finished tracing over the big ellipse and the little one inside of it, to complete a closed path (which I can fill in). This is the biggest trick in this illustration. I skipped from one ellipse to the other when I reached my guidelines. Really think about this one for a moment, because it's key to the optical illusion I'll show later. CorelDRAW will not allow you to place part of an object behind another and let another part of the same object remain in front. This is the way object-oriented design programs are. We have to "cheat" a shape that suggests a different one. The closed path I've traced over the two ellipses looks pretty awful right now, and that's because I've yet to fit my rough tracing perfectly over the template. Stay tuned to see how we do this!

Figure 14.10

It'll get better.
I promise.

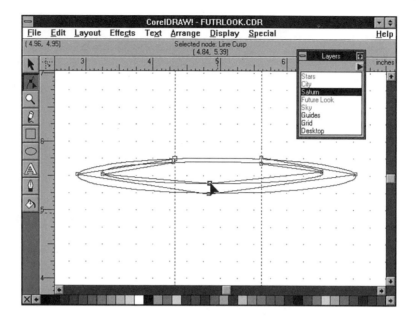

By double-clicking on one of the nodes on my ring-tracing with the shape tool, I've called up the Node Edit Roll-Up. I want to start converting all these straight lines I've done with the Line Draw tool to curves that I can "fit" to my template with the Shape tool. So in figure 14.11, I've selected the To **C**urve button.

Selecting each node with the Shape tool enables me to select the properties of each adjacent line segment. I want them to be curves, but I also want a few of them to be S**m**ooth curves, like the one I've selected in figure 14.12.

In figure 14.13, I'm twiddling a node handle that has a Smooth property. When I pull on one handle, the other handle rotates in a direction 180 degrees opposite of the one I'm playing with. I'm fine-tuning my tracing, and fitting smooth lines to match the template I first created.

Figure 14.11

We need to convert the lines to curves using the Node Edit Roll-Up.

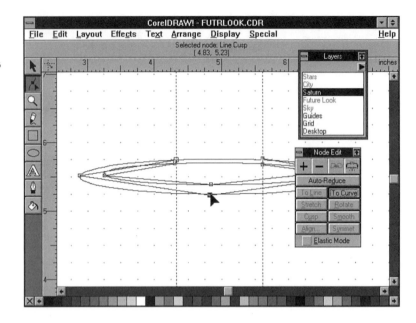

Figure 14.12

Smooth lines give you a node handle that's easy to work with.

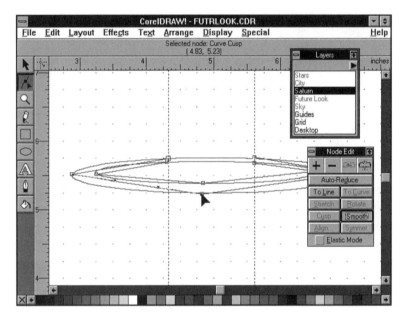

Figure 14.13

Fine-tuning the
Saturn ring.

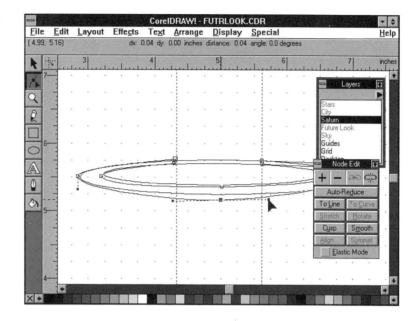

We've skipped past the tedious refinements that we applied to the ring-tracing to arrive at figure 14.14. What happened behind the scenes was just some pulling on node handles to get the tracing to exactly match the template. If you want to try this yourself, you will spend some time fooling with the node handles as well. Then you'll understand why showing 50 figures in this book on the fine art of node handle tweaking would be a waste. I've selected, then deleted the two ellipses that made up my template, and we have a pretty decent "broken" ring now.

Skipping light years ahead (sorry), I've duplicated my first "broken" ring shape, and put it inside the first. "The rings of Saturn" is a plural phrase, and I felt like conforming. My duplicate was disproportionately resized to put inside the first. I used middle selection handles on my duplicate, smaller ring. Why? Because the geometry that makes up the duplicate closed shape that's imitating an ellipse didn't fit inside the first one aesthetically. Let's not forget that this is not entirely a mathematical, geometric exercise. It's "art," and sometimes you have to futz with the elements to get it right.

I want the "rings" to go at a weird angle to the body of Saturn, so I've selected both "ring" objects and clicked a second time to bring up the rotation handles, and I'm going to freehand rotate them until they look right to my eye, like in figure 14.15.

Figure 14.14

The ring that will soon go "around" Saturn.

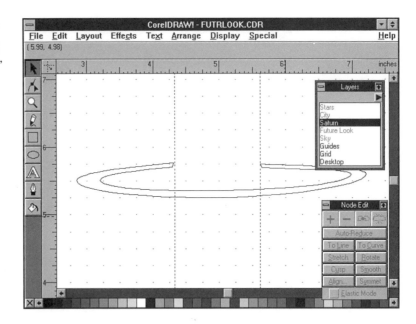

Figure 14.15

The rings rotate around Saturn. Like in real life!

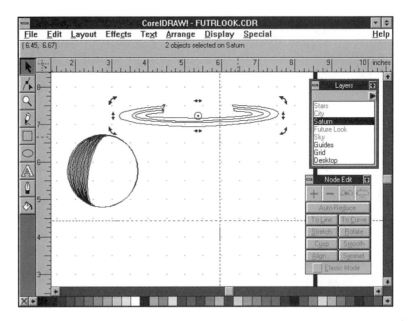

In figure 14.16, I'm moving the body of Saturn into the shape of the rings. Because, I created the rings after creating the planet on this layer, both rings will go on top of the planet, and the area I've "left out" in the ring design will create the appearance that these are two continuous rings that go behind planet Saturn.

Coming up next is putting the planet in the sky!

Figure 14.16

Saturn eclipses the rings, or vice versa.

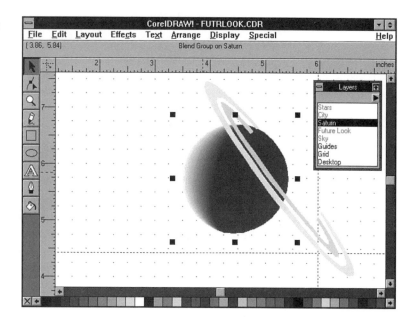

Adding a Layer of Atmosphere

In figure 14.17, we've gone back to the Layers Roll-Up, and made the Sky layer visible. I have a personal fondness for dusky scenes, and this one was a piece of cake to design. I used the Blend tool. I could have used a Linear Fountain Fill on a large rectangle, but that would've been too easy!

Figure 14.17

Heavenly shades
of night are
drawing...

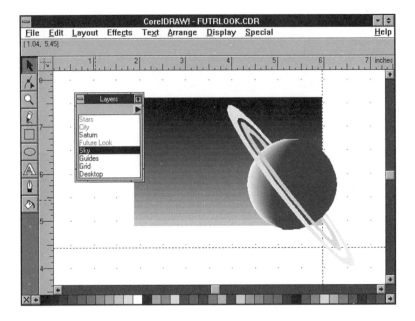

Ctrl+B will grace us with the **B**lend Roll-Up. I've drawn a light, narrow rectangle toward the bottom of my illustration layout and duplicated it. Next,
I filled it with black, and positioned the duplicate on the top of my design
layout. I've used the Snap-To Guidelines (from the **L**ayout menu) on the right
of both boxes to be a neat artist for a change. By doing this, I could quickly
keep the duplicate and the original rectangle lined up. In figure 14.18, both
objects were selected, I applied a 20-step blend, and all the intermediate
steps were perfectly aligned with each other. The effect is a large rectangle
with sharp lines, and corners that give a nice background to the illustration.

It's getting a little cramped on the workspace, so I double-click on the
Control button (the little minus sign) on the **B**lend Roll-Up to get rid of it. In
figure 14.19, I wanted a nice, old-fashioned skyline architecture in silhouette
on the bottom of my illustration. Kinda strange to have Saturn in the sunset,
huh?

I opened the City layer on my workspace and thought for a moment. I had
neither the time nor the ambition to create the skyline by myself, so I
reached into the Clip Art Library and imported a .CDR Clip Art piece that
looked cool. (I wasn't choosy or striving for a historic landmark or anything.
I simply browsed my Corel CD, until one I liked popped up.)

Figure 14.18

A wireframe view
of twilight.

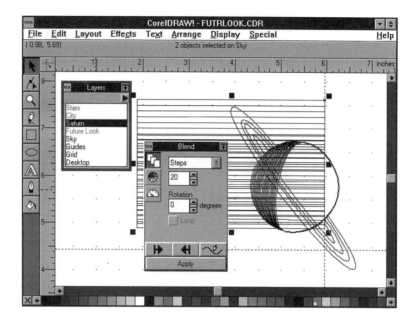

SECRET

If you have a CD-ROM drive, and don't have CorelMOSAIC
installed, you can open CorelDRAW, click on File, Open, select
the CD-ROM drive letter, and scroll through the Clip Art while
watching the Preview window. When you find a piece you like,
Open it, then save it As a file on your local hard drive. You
can't modify a Clip Art drawing unless you "save it out,"
because the image is permanently welded onto your Corel CD.
So save a copy of it, then import the piece of Clip Art into
another Corel document you want to spruce up. You've made
only one trip to the well, but have both previewed and saved a
piece of Clip Art you want!

By resizing the Clip Art skyline, both with the corner selection handles
(using the Pick tool) and the nodes on the outline of the skyline (using the
Shape tool), I have it tucked pretty nicely into the design. Figure 14.20 shows
a Preview mode view of all three layers, stacked in the order I chose.

Figure 14.19

Rome wasn't built in a day. But this Clip Art might have been.

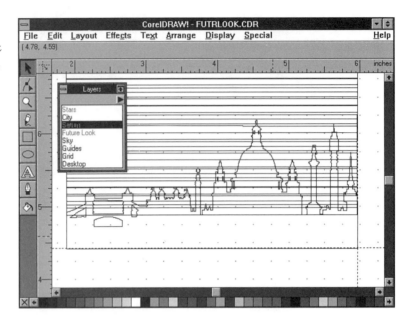

Figure 14.20

It's definitely not Moon over Manhattan!

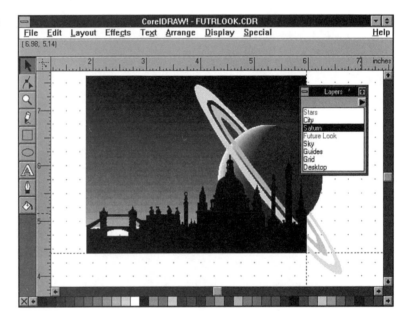

SECRET

You can rearrange layers, incidentally, by pulling the title on the Layers Roll-Up down or up. Try it sometime.

Look, Ma... the city's gone!

I've piled 47 objects on three Layers so far, and the Wireframe mode isn't going to help me see what I'm doing for the final few steps! I don't want to make the blends that make up the Sky and Saturn invisible, because I need to see where they are in the design so I can add the story title now. The solution to seeing an object, yet being able to see clearly through it, is at your fingertips with a Layer Options command. In figure 14.21, I've clicked on Edit (in the Layers Roll-Up) with the Saturn layer highlighted. From the Layer Options box, I'll apply a medium blue **C**olor Override to the whole layer.

Figure 14.21

You can select any color you like to override a layer here.

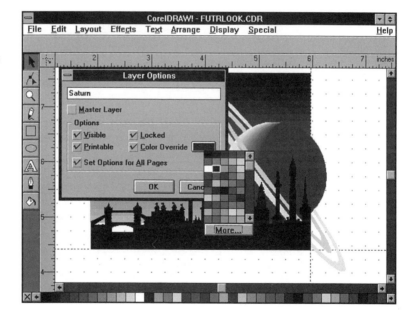

In figure 14.22, I've done the same to the City layer, so that I have both an unobstructed view of where I'll add the story title and an idea of where not to place my story title. I like to use bold, simple typefaces when I apply distortions to them. I used Eras Bold as Artistic Text here, because it's simple, slightly ornamented, and a little futuristic looking.

Figure 14.22

You have the advantages of Preview and Wireframe when you color override a layer on a multi-layer design.

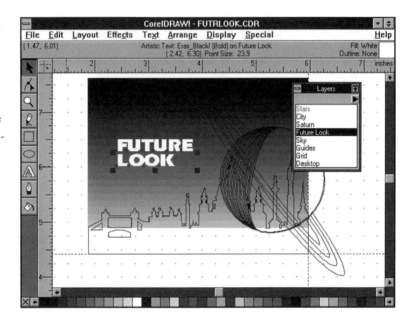

Add Perspective is the next command to get things warping with the text. Click on it from the Effects menu, as in figure 14.23 (or type Alt+C, A).

I wanted to make the story title real spacey, so I took the Perspective handles and fooled around with them until I had a title that was zooming out into the distance, as in figure 14.24. Notice also in 14.24 that a little "X"-like shape has creeped in from the right side of the screen. That's the Vanishing Point of my perspectived story title, which is really close! This perspectived story title can also be adjusted by clicking on the "X" with your Shape tool, and taking it for a ride around the page.

The stars and the white-out

Except for drawing a few stars (hint: use the Ellipse tool, then **D**uplicate, or press Ctl+D, the star a few times), the illustration is all set to export to the desktop publishing program.

Figure 14.23

Getting some
perspective on a
future look.

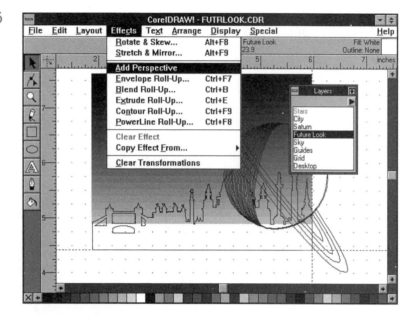

Figure 14.24

The future is
getting nearer.

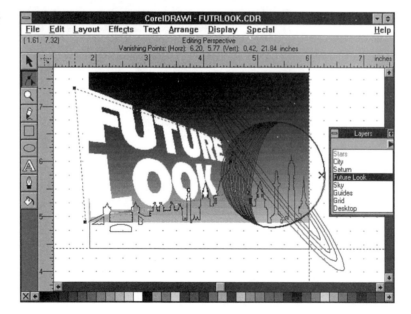

Except for one thing: Part of Saturn and the rings are sticking out of the background! Just look at figure 14.25, would you? I measured the Sky background to the publication's column width, I like where Saturn is positioned on the illustration, and I have to find an easy way to correct the part of Saturn that's sticking out!

Figure 14.25

Maybe the publication would like to change its column width?

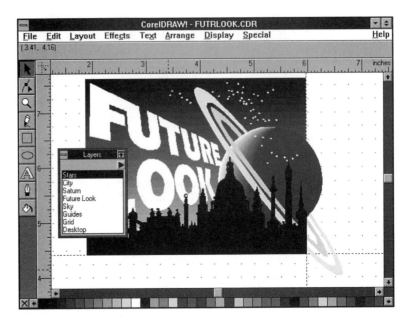

The quick fix to a design problem lies in using *electronic correction fluid.* Don't look for this option in Corel. We cook it up ourselves when the need arises.

SECRET

There's a long and a short way to do almost anything using CorelDRAW. But you first have to consider what the outcome, or finished product, is supposed to be.

I could, for instance, Separate all the blend steps in the body of Saturn, ungroup them, and use my Shape tool to node edit for around five hours. I could then reshape the rings around Saturn, and finally get an illustration that lies within the publication's column width.

Or I could spend five minutes building a little correction fluid shape to mask the offending areas. The correction fluid won't show up on the imported file, because the publication's page background is the same color as my fluid—white.

In figure 14.26, I've used the Zoom In to work on the problem area of my design. Fortunately, I was a slob and didn't remove all my guidelines when I thought I was finished, and two remain that I can actually take advantage of.

Figure 14.26

Wireframe of the problem area.

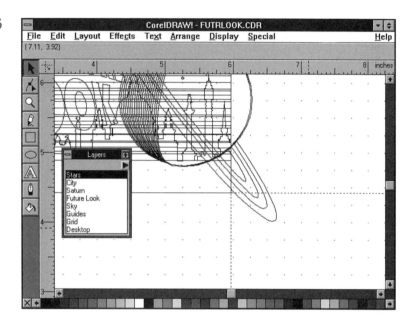

I still have my Snap-To's functioning for the guidelines from when I began the piece. I take my Line Draw tool and position it on a guideline. The guideline immediately takes hold of my starting point, and I double-click my way around to create a closed shape that will cover the problem area, as shown in figure 14.27.

I then gave the closed shape a white fill and no outline. I've selected this shape in figure 14.28, so you can see where it is in the **P**review mode (press F9). For our purpose, which is to export the illustration as a .CGM file, the importing program (which was Aldus PageMaker) will ignore the white shape where printing the finished page is concerned. As a matter of fact, it won't print in Corel, or any other program it's exported to, unless the background of another program's page is something other than white!

Figure 14.27

A closed shape
on the top layer
will save us!

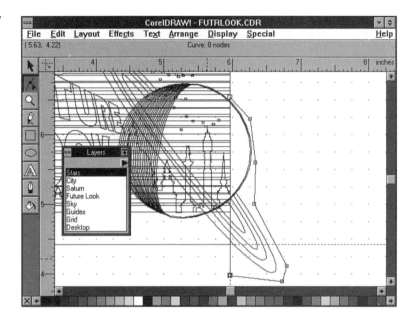

Figure 14.28

The design is
perfect for
printing now.

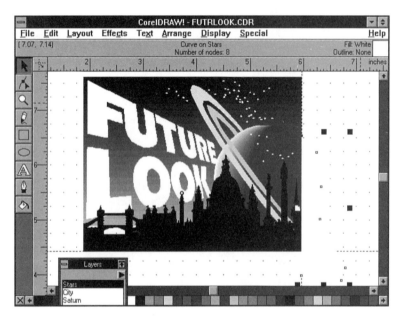

I hope you've found some workarounds as well as some tricks in this chapter. And I hope you're finding CorelDRAW to be a flexible, forgiving, and feature-packed design program. I don't want to get all mushy, teary-eyed, and warm and fuzzy just yet, because even though you're close to finishing this book, there's some last-minute important stuff we need to share with you.

And that's why we call the next chapter "Read Me Last."

CHAPTER 15

Read Me Last!

Hey, after you finish this chapter, it's back to the real world: the over-demanding boss, the impossible schedules, pollution, inflation, and PBS telethons. And if you feel that you've learned anything after closing the cover, then I've done my part, and you've done yours. You've turned facts into knowledge. And that alone is worth its weight in import/export filters. Hopefully, one of the side effects of reading *CorelDRAW! for Non-Nerds* is that you're not quite as intimidated or reluctant to work in a new computer program now.

You should now have a little confidence to go out and make sense of computer programs without the fear of a). failure, or b). becoming a geek with a pocket protector. Although we explained stuff in a non-nerdy way here, the information itself is just that: *information*, about how to use a tool. The nerdiness only applies when certain folks go out in public acting like PC Know-It-Alls; they eat, sleep, think, and dream about PCs to the exclusion of manners and grooming. That's when it all becomes a turnoff.

In this chapter, we will:

  Hold a Q&A clinic about Corel

- Provide both the questions and the answers, because you'd look funny talking to a book

- Cover some ground on certain Corel features that didn't seem to fit anywhere else in this loosely structured tome

Fill Me In

Q: *Can I use Windows Clipboard to copy a design with a bitmap or vector fill?*

A: Unfortunately, no. CorelDRAW's rendering of bitmap and vector fills is a proprietary rendering. In other words, Corel will follow your directions to create a design using a bitmap or vector fill, but you must print it from within CorelDRAW. Sorry, no Clipboarding to other programs. All you'll get is an outline with a 50-percent black fill. BUT... you can export an object with a bitmap fill from Corel. Sorry, but there's no way vector fills can leave Corel. The only drawback in exporting a bitmap-filled object is that it ceases to be a .CDR file. It can be a .BMP, .PCX, or .TIF, paint-type image that has the bitmap design in it, and this design can then be accepted by most other Windows programs.

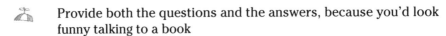

Just My Type

Q: *I got some neat Type 1 typefaces off the local BBS (Electronic Bulletin Board). Can I use them with Corel?*

A: CorelDRAW came with a gazillion typefaces, and you want more? Actually, the answer is yes, but only if you own Adobe Type Manager. ATM comes free with a lot of desktop publishing and word processing programs. You might want to check the disks at home before running out and buying a copy. You may already have Type Manager. Whether it's shareware, or Corel's typefaces, Type 1 faces require Type Manager. Type 1 typefaces are not the same as Windows TrueType. Type 1s work with PostScript printers and with non-PostScript printers that use Type Manager as a translating device. Any TrueTypes you add to Windows are automatically detected by Corel, and are ready for use in Corel after you load them.

Have You Tried Paint Thinner?

Q: *Why is my Line Draw tool going nuts all over the screen when I try to draw?*

A: The most common problem new users have in CorelDRAW is that they forget to turn off Snap-To properties, for either the G<u>r</u>id, G<u>u</u>idelines, or other <u>O</u>bjects. From the <u>L</u>ayout menu, select <u>S</u>nap To and check to make sure that the little boxes are unchecked. It's more polite than swearing and less costly than tossing your monitor off the balcony.

Speedy Recovery

Q: *What happens if Windows crashes while I'm in the middle of a Corel design?*

A: You call Bill Gates, chairman of Microsoft, at 1(206) 882-8080, and say, "Hey, your product ate my file!!!" If you by chance *do* get Bill Gates, he'll probably tell you that Corel continually makes an updated backup file of your work. It happens fairly often, and you might notice a message in the left corner of your CorelDRAW Status Bar sometimes that tells you it's doing Auto-Backup.

Where is that file? It's in a subdirectory of Corel called AUTOBACK. Look for AUTOBACK on your hard drive with File Manager. Once you've restarted Windows, click on the AUTOBACK subdirectory and you may see a file, or several, that have the .BAK file extension. Simply rename these files with a .CDR file extension (or ask a nerd to do this), and you'll be able to recover the file from the last moment Corel did its Auto-Backup thing. If Bill Gates is not available, he's probably out getting adjusted to married life.

Simple, But Elegant

Q: *Why won't my laser printer print all of my Corel design? It just leaves pieces out of it, but prints the rest.*

A: There are several possible answers to this one. First, check to see whether all your Layers in CorelDRAW are Printable. When this option box is checked off, a Layer still exists in your design, but it does not print.

Next, your laser printer may not have enough RAM. Printers take memory chips, too, and most manufacturers don't stock up their printer, even though more and more sophisticated design packages demand higher RAM. You can buy more chips for the printer, or simplify your design. I hate the latter option, and you should, too. If you have 3 to 4M RAM in a PCL laser printer, that should do the trick.

Last, you may not have the objects you want to print within the page border. The printable page is that drop-shadowed outline we've shown throughout this book. If your objects were designed outside of it, reel them in!

Towing the Line

Q: *What about PowerLines, Contour Lines, Dimension Lines, and Object Data Management?*

A: All these Corel features have one thing in common; we don't talk about them in this book. Seriously, though, and one at a time:

 PowerLines are a lot of fun to play around with. If you don't own a digitizing tablet and want to make expressive pen strokes with a mouse, they're great. You access the PowerLines via the Effects menu (or press **CTRL+F8**). Once this Roll-Up is open, select the type of pen point you'd like, select the Line Draw tool, and do not use the double-click mouse technique you've learned in this book. Instead, click, hold, then release the left mouse button after you've "painted" a curved path with the mouse. You'll get a line that you can apply a fill to, even though you may not have drawn a closed shape. You really have to play around with it, and PowerLines' commercial design possibilities are very subtle.

 Contour Lines are very similar to the Blend effect, except you don't need two objects to Blend between. If you draw an irregular, closed shape with the Line Draw tool, then press **CTRL+F9**, you'll get the Contour Roll-Up. Select the shape, specify the number of contours you want Corel to apply, select whether you want them contouring outside or inside of the shape, then choose Apply on the Roll-Up. The result will be a smooth series of repeat shapes along the inside (or outside) of your original. Folks who draw maps and do geological surveys for a living might benefit from Contour Lines.

Object Data Management deserves a book of its own, because it's an entirely new way of cataloging your designs. Corel's Help line explains this best, if you've misplaced your reference manual. Very sketchily: To create a data chart to link to Corel designs, you click and hold with the right mouse button. A little box will appear out of nowhere. This is your Object menu. From it, choose the Data Roll-Up. You're then given fields, somewhat like on a spreadsheet, where you can enter all sorts of information about the object.

If you've just slaved over designing an auto part or something in Corel, you may want to "tag" your technical information about the part right in the data field. You recall the data field the same way, with the right mouse button, so you may update anything you've entered at any time. It sounds strange, but it beats putting text on a design when you don't want it there. Get help from Corel at (613)728-1990.

 Dimension Lines are accessed through the Line Draw tool by pushing on it to get a flyout. They come in three flavors: horizontal, vertical, and diagonal. You use Dimension Lines when you want to identify the precise measurements of a part or a map that you've drawn in Corel. Dimension lines, as you may have guessed, are technical, not artsy in any way.

By default, a dimension line will represent the physical dimensions of your workspace. For example: You draw a 3-inch line with one, you'll get a 3-inch line that's tagged with a 24-point label that says 3.00". You may change this tag, and the type of dimensioning you want to do, by going up to **S**pecial, Pr**e**ferences, Dimension. From there, you can specify what kind of dimension you'd like your lines to represent: inches, hours, you name it. From there on in with the Dimension Lines, when you draw one that's twice as long as another, the tags on the lines will reflect this.

You cannot change a dimension line's value by proportionately resizing it with the Pick tool. The line will get smaller, but the value in the tag will remain the same. Why? Because if you want to resize a drawing of a map that has dimension lines in it, you don't want five miles to grandmother's house to turn into 17 inches.

I Asked Fill, and Didn't Get an Answer

Q: *I click and click on the color palette, but my shape won't fill. What gives?*

A: Check to see whether the shape is a closed object. Check the Status Bar with the shape selected. If it says open path, you came real close to completing a closed shape, but you missed single-clicking the shape's starting point when you double-clicked your way to creating its path. To fix this, select the shape, use the Line Draw tool, and click once on each node where the path begins and ends. Corel "remembered" what color you were trying to select all this while, and as soon as the shape is a closed path, it will immediately be filled with the color you've been choosing.

Q: *I tried your advice above, and I still don't see a fill.*

A: Look on the Status Bar on the far right. Is your fill color in there? If so, you're looking at your design in Wireframe view, not Preview. Press **SHIFT +F9**, and voilá!

Mixed-Media

Q: *I like a .TIF file just the way it is. I don't want to vector trace it with CorelTRACE, but I want it in CorelDRAW anyway.*

A: Besides importing the .EPS files CorelTRACE makes out of paint-type images, CorelDRAW will also import .TIF and .BMP images directly into your workspace. When you do import bitmap, paint-type images, expect them to look a little funny if you zoom into and out of them. That's because bitmaps are fixed *resolution graphics* (resolution-dependent), and CorelDRAW's world is resolution independent. If you print a .TIF image from within Corel, it'll look perfectly fine; it's just that you'll have to assume what you see on screen is not as good as what you'll get printed. Also, you cannot edit a paint-type image in CorelDRAW at all, because you don't have paint-type tools in CorelDRAW.

But that's the bad news. The good news is that you can use CorelDRAW's tools to design around a paint-type image and add things, and treat the .TIF image like another design element. I put a really nice radial Fountain Fill ellipse on a photograph of this guy the other day. It went over his nose and he looked like a Ringling Brothers clown. It looked so funny, when I showed it to him, he broke my glasses.

High- and Far-Flung Tech

Q: *What is cloning?*

A: During the end of the 23rd century, earth scientists discovered how to replicate DNA strands... sorry. With respect to CorelDRAW, when you have an object selected, then press (or click on) **E**dit, Cl**o**ne, Corel gives you a second object on your workspace. This is not a copy, nor a duplicate. *A clone is linked to your original.* If you squash your original, the clone will squash. If you change an object's color, ditto the clone. This mimicking of an original is great if you have a whole bunch of clones and want to effect a change in them all at once.

You will also want to know how to break the link between the original and the clones because this clonishness can get irksome after a while. Go to **A**rrange, then **S**eparate. When you make changes to a clone, the original is unaffected.

Thinly Veiled Plug

Q: *Gosh, I got a lot out of this book, but I'm finished with it now. Any recommendations for further reading material?*

A: Let me think about this one for a moment. Daniel Gray's *Inside CorelDRAW! 4.0, Special Edition* (New Riders Publishing), is an excellent place to pick up where you left off here.

Also, *CorelDRAW! Special Effects* (New Riders Publishing), authored by Corel World Design Contest winners, shows step-by-step procedures for recreating their award-winning Corel artwork. They're a great bunch of people, and I don't think the Chateau Laurier in Ottawa will ever be the same after the 1992 contest.

Which leads us to our most important question:
Will you again thrill to some more of Bouton's
work in New Riders Publishing's *CorelDRAW!
Special Effects*?

Does a duck have 20 blend steps?

Glossary

A

Align. A command from the **A**rrange menu. You can select two or more objects in CorelDRAW and arrange them so that they line up with each other. You can have them line up on their left, right, top, bottom, and centers. The last object selected is the one that the others line up to.

Artistic Text. Short lines of type you create in CorelDRAW, which can later have special effects applied to them. You create Artistic Text by simply selecting the Text tool, clicking on your workspace, and typing. The limit to Artistic Text varies from typeface to typeface, but it is generally 250 characters. See also **Paragraph Text**.

B

Black. Black is one of the four process colors (*magenta*, *cyan* and *yellow* are the others) CorelDRAW will let you mix to create any color. A percentage of black (example: 20 percent) will produce gray. Percentages of black are ideally handled by most laser printers.

Blend. One of CorelDRAW's effects. A blend between two objects automatically creates a number of intermediate transitional objects or steps that the designer has control over.

Bitmap. A kind of graphical rendering. Bitmap images are created by dots (or pixels) of color in positions on an imaginary grid. Bitmap or paint-type images are resolution-dependent and CorelDRAW has no editing tools for them; however, CorelPHOTO-PAINT does. File formats are .BMP, .GIF, .PCX, and .TIF.

Bezier Curve. An impossible way to draw naturalistically. You create Bezier curves with one of the design tools located on the Line Draw tool flyout. You don't need the Node Edit Roll-Up while using this tool, but it's a very difficult tool to master.

C

Canada. The country where CorelDRAW comes from. Also good hockey players and William Shatner.

CD-ROM. Refers to a both a drive and the disc that goes in the drive on your PC. It's the easy way to install CorelDRAW, and to access all the Clip Art and extra typefaces that come with Corel. Not to be confused with a plain CD, which goes in your stereo and plays music. Remember: A CD followed by a ROM relates to a personal computer.

Click. The action performed by depressing a mouse button. This clicking is synonymous with selecting, picking, and choosing stuff in Windows. See also **Hold**.

Clipboard. A Windows import/export filter that's used by selecting a piece of work, selecting **E**dit, then selecting **C**opy on the Menu bar. A copy of your piece will then be on the Clipboard until you copy something else. You can then **P**aste this copy into a lot of other programs that aren't even made by Corel. See also **Cut**.

Clone. Creating a duplicate of an object which will then mimic any changes you make to the original.

Combine. The melding of two separate objects to form one path. For example, the letter O generally consists of an outside path and an inside one that have been combined.

Control Curve. An object that is the beginning or the end of an effect like blend or contour. This control curve can be moved and will cause the effect to respond to that move. You have to separate a control curve from the flock in order to work with it as an independent object, and to get your effect to stop changing around.

Convert To Curves. A command found on the **A**rrange menu in Corel. Converting a rectangle, ellipse, or text object to curves destroys the structure of the object. You're left with curves and nodes after this converting process, and may freely rearrange them afterwards.

Copy. To create a duplicate of an object on the Windows Clipboard. See also **Paste**.

Cursor. A floating symbol on your monitor that is directed by your mouse movements. A cursor can be shaped like an arrow, a crosshair, an I-Beam, an hourglass (when your computer is thinking), or a variety of different shapes depending on what program offers a specific cursor for a task.

Curve. A line segment between two nodes. Whether the line segment looks curved or not, CorelDRAW still considers it a curve. To make a "straight line" curve look like a typical curve, you must press the To Curve button on the Node Edit Roll-Up while the line segment is selected.

Cut. To remove an object from your drawing and move it to the Windows Clipboard. Trust me, you're better off copying your work instead of cutting. See also **Paste.**

D

Default. The factory setting of various options in Corel. The default value of Fountain Fills to go to a non-PostScript printer from CorelDRAW is 64. You can change many of Corel's default options if you read this book.

Delete. Removes an object from your drawing and doesn't send it to the Windows Clipboard. Do not see **Paste**.

Display. A menu item that offers options about what you see on your monitor while in Corel. Stuff like **C**olor Palette, Show **R**ulers or not, and **E**dit Wireframe are found here.

Double-click. Depressing the mouse button two times very quickly, then releasing. This movement in CorelDRAW is used for calling the Node Edit Roll-Up, and for creating connected line segments with the Line Draw tool.

DPI. Dots per inch. A term used to describe how fine or coarse a printer prints. An office laser printer usually prints up to 600 DPI.

Drag. What you thought of any number of past U.S. government administrations. Also the act of moving your cursor while a mouse button has been clicked but not yet released. Dragging is most commonly used to move an object in Corel from one location on the workspace to another.

Duplicate. Makes a copy of an object within your workspace. Does not send it to the Windows Clipboard. Do not see **Paste**.

E

Edge Pad. Selection from the Fountain Fill options menu. By increasing the Edge Pad value, you make the transition between the two Fountain Fill colors more intense.

Elastic Mode. A feature on the Node Edit Roll-Up. When you pull on a node in Elastic Mode, the node handles on neighboring nonselected nodes move to conform to the direction you are pulling in. Just try to say that last line twice.

Ellipse. Created by clicking and dragging the cursor after selecting the Ellipse tool. A high-tech name for a distorted circle, ellipses (like rectangles) are the two closed shapes you can create with the least fuss in CorelDRAW.

EM Dash. A really long hyphen. Click with the Text tool on your workspace, then type `Alt+0151` to get one.

EN Dash. Longer than a hyphen but shorter than an EM Dash. Click with the Text tool on your workspace, then type `Alt+0150` to get one.

Envelope. Something you put a stamp on. Also a CorelDRAW effect that allows you to reshape the borders of an object like they were putty.

EPS. Encapsulated PostScript. These are vector-based files that can only be printed to a PostScript printer. CorelTRACE creates these kinds of files out of bitmaps. CorelDRAW can import .EPS images that you can edit and print to any printer when you save them as a .CDR file.

Extract. Found in the **S**pecial menu. E**x**tract allows you to save the typing you do in CorelDRAW as a text file your word processor can use.

Extrude. A CorelDRAW effect. When you extrude an object, Corel gives that object a 3-D effect.

F

Fill. This is a color, texture, or object that you put inside a closed path that you drew.

Fill tool. The button on the Toolbox which flies out to reveal all the fill options in CorelDRAW.

Filter. A conversion program that Corel has a lot of that allows you to import or export graphics and text that are in different formats.

Flyout. What an umpire sometimes calls at a baseball game. Also what you get when you click, then hold on the Line Draw tool and the Text tool. These flyouts offer more selections of tools that relate to the basic tool. The Zoom, Fill, and Outline tools also have flyouts, but they are for a specific fill or Roll-Up menu, and contain no drawing tools. These tools reveal their alternate selections by just clicking on them; no holding is necessary.

Font. A cool name for a typeface. Times Roman is a font, but not a cool one.

Fountain Fill. A fill which changes color gradually. Linear, radial, and conic fountain fills all change from one color to another in different patterns. You can adjust the direction the pattern takes, as well as the two colors Corel uses to create the Fountain Fill.

G

Gray. A percentage of black. Shades of gray can be found on the left of the default color palette in Corel. Specific percentages of black, which create a specific gray, can be made from the Color Options menu box from the Solid Fill button on the Fill tool flyout.

Group. CorelDRAW command found on the **A**rrange menu. When one or more selected objects are tied together this way, you can move, resize, and color them all at once. One object in a **G**roup has no effect on another when bundled this way.

Guideline. The straight vertical or horizontal blue dotted line that you pull out from the rulers. Guidelines don't print. Guidelines are useful in combination with the Snap-To option for creating precise lines and shapes.

H

Handle. One of the eight little black squares that appear around the border of an object selected in Corel. Corner selection handles and side selection handles will affect the object's size in different ways when you pull on them.

Hold. The activity directly after clicking with the mouse when you want to drag something. See **Drag**.

I

IBM. A large computer company, but also a term used to describe any personal computer that runs on an XT, 286, 386, 486, or Pentium chip. If you're running Corel, you have an "IBM-compatible" PC, or a genuine IBM-PC. If you own a Mac, you are not running Corel at present.

Icon. A little picture that's either on a button, or in a group in Windows Program Manager. You click on an icon with your mouse in order to activate it. You select different tools and you launch programs by clicking on icons. Icons are sometimes referred to as buttons.

Install. The painful process a user must go through to put a software program on their computer's hard drive. You install CorelDRAW using its many installation disks, or install it from a CD-ROM if you have a CD-ROM drive.

J

Join. When you have an open path you need to make into a closed one so you can fill it, use the join button on the Node Edit Roll-Up. Select the beginning and ending nodes on the path with the Shape tool. Then double-click to get the Node Edit Roll-Up, and press the button with the links of chain on it to join the nodes and create a closed shape.

K

Kerning. The spacing between characters in a typeset word. TrueType and Type 1 typefaces, as a rule, contain automatic kerning information, so a word like "AVANT" doesn't have too much space between the A's and the V. When type is poorly kerned, it looks like typewriting.

L

Layers. A surface of work in CorelDRAW that the user can assign attributes to, or rearrange in order when working on several of them. When you open Corel, you are, by default, assigned one layer, labelled Layer 1.

Leading. The space between two lines of text. Publications generally have 120 percent of a typeface's point size as leading between paragraph text.

Line. The connection between two nodes in CorelDRAW, whether curved or straight. A line can be dotted, colored, or have a desired thickness, depending on the choices you select with the Outline tool.

Line Draw tool. The button on the Toolbox with the little pencil on it. You can create one or several lines by clicking once for the beginning of each line, then a second time to finish it. By double-clicking at the finish of a line, you are actually starting a second. And if you continue this action back to where you started, finishing with a single click, you have a closed shape or path you can apply fill to.

M

Magnifying view. One of the several Zoom options on the Zoom Tool flyout. It's the magnifying glass with the plus sign on it. It allows you to zoom in on your workspace.

Marquee. Marking off an area on your workspace by clicking, holding, moving diagonally on your workspace, then releasing the mouse button. Also called lassoing, marquee-ing, or *marquee-selecting*, this is a handy way to select multiple objects in Corel. Try it; the description is harder than the action.

Megabyte (mb or M). A measurement of both hard drive space and PC memory. Corel takes up more that 30 megabytes of hard drive space if fully installed, and requires 8 megabytes of RAM to run at a pace on your PC that is comfortable.

Menu Bar. The strip on the top of a Windows program that generally starts with <u>F</u>ile. In Corel, many effects, page layout specifications, and default settings can be accessed from the Menu Bar.

Mirror. To stretch an object 100 percent either horizontally or vertically. You access the <u>S</u>tretch and Mirror effect from the Effe<u>c</u>ts Menu option in Corel.

O

Object. A discreet thing drawn in Corel which can be moved and placed independent of other things. An ellipse is an object. A blend is not an object, but a thing composed of many objects.

OLE. Short for *Object Linking and Embedding*. This is a Windows feature that Corel modules are savvy to. OLE-ing a piece of your work into a different program allows you to display it there. Then if you want to update it later, you double-click on the object, and its parent program will appear and allow you to edit the object.

P

Page Border. Also known as the Page Frame and the Printable Page. It's the outline you see in CorelDRAW's workspace that has a faint gray dropshadow beneath it. Any object outside of the Page Border will not print out.

Palette. This is the color strip at the bottom of your Corel workspace. It can be changed through the color options box found in the Solid Fill tool button. Corel comes with a number of other color palettes besides the default one you see throughout this book. You select a fill color for a selected object by clicking on the palette with your left mouse button. Use the right mouse button for an outline color.

Paragraph Text. The opposite of Artistic Text in Corel. Paragraph Text is created by marquee-selecting an area in the workspace with the little page icon button on the Text Tool flyout. Paragraph Text can exceed the 250 character limit of Artistic Text, but you cannot apply blends, extrusions, or other effects to it.

Paste. Moves a copied object from the Clipboard into another drawing or application. See **Copy**, **Cut**.

Path. A series of connecting line segments you draw in Corel. If you connect the beginning node of a series of line segments with the last one, you have a closed path you can apply fill to. Otherwise, the line segments are an open path.

Perspective. An effect in Corel that makes an object appear to be viewed at an odd or severe angle. Remember the beginning titles to Star Wars? The lettering was set in Perspective. But not with CorelDRAW.

Pick tool. The arrow-shaped tool at the top of CorelDRAW's Toolbox. Also known as the Selection tool, this tool is used for selecting an object to effect a change on it, and for resizing the border of an object by tugging on the object's selection handles.

PostScript. A descriptor language for printers. Unlike common laser printers, a PostScript printer is capable of very high-resolution output to film or paper, and renders designs in a precise, refined way. PostScript printers give you plenty of time to do other things while you're waiting for your work to print out.

Q

Quote marks. Professional publications use these at the beginning and end of quotes. Use the Text tool, and type `ALT+0147` and `ALT+0148` to open and close quotes, instead of using the generic, typewriter-like quote key on your keyboard.

R

RAM. Abbreviation for *Random Access Memory*. Found on chips that go in your PC, among other places, RAM is the active memory your PC needs to carry out Windows instructions and CorelDRAW designs. The more RAM your computer can hold, the better. Don't try to run CorelDRAW on less than 8M of RAM.

Rectangle, Rectangle tool. A four-sided, closed shape drawn with the Rectangle tool, with fixed angles at adjoining line segments. The Shape tool will soften the corners of a rectangle, but it cannot be shaped asymmetrically without converting the rectangle to Curves.

Roll-Up. These are effects and special tools that can be found on Corel's Menu and Toolbox. Roll-Ups save you repeating steps to change something ordinarily accessed through the Menu or Toolbox. When you're done with a specific activity, you can click on an arrow button on their upper, right corners, and they roll up and out of the way.

Rotate. To tilt an object clockwise or counterclockwise around its own axis. To rotate an object in Corel, you can click on it once after you've selected it (slower than "double-clicking"), then pull on a corner selection handle. Or you can rotate the object to a precise number of degrees using the **R**otate and Skew option in the Effe**c**ts menu.

S

Scale. What an ambitious, outdoorsy person does to the face of a mountain. Also, what happens when you resize an object in Corel. When you hold on an object's selection handle, and pull toward or away from the object, the Status bar tells you what percentage of the object's original dimensions you're resizing (scaling) it to.

Shape tool. The tool beneath the Pick tool on the Toolbox. The Shape tool is used for node editing, text spacing, editing effects like enveloping and perspectives, and for modifying ellipses and rectangles. The Shape tool is not used to draw anything. Hey, doesn't it do enough?

Skew. To make the borders around an object become unaligned, but still parallel. The effect of skewing a shape is similar to viewing it at an angle. It's also good for italicizing Artistic Text, when a font doesn't come in italic. You can skew an object by clicking once after it is selected, then pulling on a middle selection handle (the skew handle) with the Pick tool. You can also precisely skew an object from the **R**otate and Skew option under the Effe**c**ts menu.

Snap-To. The opposite of Snap-Fro. Also a property you can assign to Guidelines, the grid, or other objects, to make them "sticky." When you select **S**nap-To, then **G**uidelines from the **L**ayout menu, lines and shapes you draw close to an outline will tend to "snap to" the guideline, depending on your distance from one when you start drawing. It's good for precision work, but frustrating when you've forgotten and left it on.

Status Bar. A.K.A. the Status Line. This is the bar beneath the Menu bar, where all the activity you're involved in on your workspace is displayed. Information about a selected object's position on the workspace, color, outline, and other properties are displayed and updated here.

Steps. When a blend is applied to two objects, transitional objects are created as part of the metamorphosis. These are called steps. You designate the number of steps in a blend from the Blend Roll-Up. See also **Blend**.

Symbol Library. Found as a button marked with a star from the Text tool flyout. When the Symbol Library is activated, the Corel user may choose from a number of categories of predrawn shapes from the Symbols Roll-Up. You click, hold, and drag symbols onto your workspace, then they inflate to a user-definable size like those paper-flat sponges you add water to.

T

Text tool. The icon on the Toolbox that is a capital "A." The flyout for this tool uncovers the Symbols Library, and the tool for formatting Paragraph Text. By clicking on the "A" button, you can open your workspace and start typing Artistic Text.

Texture Fills. The button for this is located on the Fill tool flyout. A Texture Fill is a complex design that simulates natural textures, like sky and cloth, when filled inside an object. They are "memory-intensive" fills for your PC that can slow your system down if used to fill large areas.

TrueType. The kind of typeface that ships with Windows 3.1. Corel offers TrueType in its typeface collection, and Corel can use Type 1 typefaces as well. TrueType typefaces don't work so well with PostScript printers, but they are excellent on PCL printers; they print fast, you can buy new ones really cheap, and you don't need a separate type manager to use them in all your Windows 3.1 programs.

Type 1. An earlier typeface, Type 1s require a type manager (like Adobe Type Manager) to be visible on your monitor. These are good typefaces to use with a PostScript printer, but even with an ordinary laser printer and type manager they print fine and Corel can use them. Type 1s have quite a few years of lead-time over the newer TrueType faces, so there are a lot of different styles in which you can buy them.

Toolbox. The lefthand strip on your Corel workspace that runs up and down and contains your tools. Additional tools can be accessed by clicking, then holding on the tool button.

U

Undo. A command from the **E**dit menu that allows you to "take back a move," unlike in a game of checkers with your younger brother. By default, there are four **U**ndo steps in Corel, so you can make four mistakes on your design, press **U**ndo four times, and you're back to where you started. The value of **U**ndo can be increased to 99 steps from the **S**pecial, Pr**e**ferences menu, but wouldn't that be a little paranoid?

V

Views, *Preview, Wireframe*. By using the **SHIFT** and **F9** keys on your key-board, you can "toggle" between different modes of view in Corel. The Wireframe view shows only the outline of shapes in one color, with no fills. The Preview mode will show you your design the way it will come out of a printer. Preview mode is slower to draw in, because Corel needs to redraw the finished portion of your design every time you add to it. Conversely, designing in wireframe is faster, but you can't see your colored piece the way it'll look finished.

W

Weld. A command from the <u>A</u>rrange menu in Corel. When you weld two or more objects, an outline of all the objects is created, and any paths within the shape where paths intersect are eliminated. A good command for creating silhouettes of stuff.

Windows. A product by Microsoft that allows you to run tons of different programs by different manufacturers in a visual environment on your PC. Windows programs, like Corel, can copy and paste stuff between them, and share a lot of the same commands like File and Help from their Menu bars.

X

Xylophone. A musical instrument you can draw in Corel. Actually, I've got a five dollar bet going with my lead editor at New Riders, Steve Weiss, that I couldn't find a glossary term for every letter of the alphabet for this Corel book. Steve, you lose.*

Y

Ytterbium. An element on the Periodic Table, higher than uranium, that can be drawn in Corel using Contour lines. See also **Xylophone**. Steve, you still reading this?

Z

Zoom tool. The tool located underneath the Shape tool on Corel's Toolbox. The Zoom tool has a flyout that gives the user options to zoom into a region of workspace, zoom out, use a one-to-one view, view all pieces present on the workspace, and get a full-page border view.

*The Editors would like to point out that, had the author included an entry for the letter "N," such as, say, **Nerd**, he indeed would have won the bet. But alas…cash will be fine.*

INDEX

F

J-L

WANT MORE INFORMATION?

CHECK OUT THESE RELATED TITLES:

	QTY	PRICE	TOTAL

Inside CorelDRAW! 4.0 Special Edition. This updated version of the #1 selling tutorial on CorelDRAW! features easy-to-follow lessons that quickly help readers master this powerful graphics program. Complete with expert tips and techniques—plus a bonus disk loaded with shareware—this book is everything CorelDRAW! users need. ISBN: 1-56205-164-4   ____ $34.95   _____

Inside CorelDRAW!, Fourth Edition. (covers version 3.0) Tap into the graphics power of CorelDRAW! 3.0 with this #1 best-seller. This book goes beyond providing just tips and tricks for boosting productivity. Readers will also receive expanded coverage on how to use CorelDRAW! with other Windows programs! ISBN: 1-56205-106-7   ____ $34.95   _____

CorelDRAW! Special Effects. Learn award-winning techniques from professional CorelDRAW! designers with this comprehensive collection of the hottest tips and techniques! This full-color book provides step-by-step instructions for creating 30 stunning special effects. An excellent book for those who want to take their CorelDRAW! documents a couple of notches higher. ISBN: 1-56205-123-7   ____ $39.95   _____

CorelDRAW! 4.0 Now! Users who want fast access to thorough information, people upgrading to CorelDRAW! 4.0 from a previous edition, new CorelDRAW! users—all of these groups will want to tap into this guide to great graphics—now! Developed by CorelDRAW! experts, this book provides answers on everything from common questions to advanced inquiries. ISBN: 1-56205-131-8.   ____ $21.95   _____

Name _____

Company _____

Address _____

City _____ State ____ ZIP _____

Phone _____ Fax _____

☐ Check Enclosed ☐ VISA ☐ MasterCard

Card #_____Exp. Date _____

Signature _____

Prices are subject to change. Call for availability and pricing information on latest editions.

Subtotal _____

Shipping _____

$4.00 for the first book and $1.75 for each additional book.

Total _____
Indiana residents add 5% sales tax.

New Riders Publishing 11711 North College Avenue • P.O. Box 90 • Carmel, Indiana 46032 USA

Orders/Customer Service: 1-800-541-6789
Fax: 1-800-448-3804

CorelDRAW!
for Non-Nerds
REGISTRATION CARD

Fill out this card to receive information about future Non-Nerds books and other New Riders titles!

Name _____ **Title** _____

Company _____

Address _____

City/State/ZIP _____

I bought this book because _____

_____

I purchased this book from:
- ☐ A bookstore (Name _____)
- ☐ A software or electronics store (Name _____)
- ☐ A mail order (Name of Catalog _____)

I purchase this many computer books each year:
- ☐ 1–5   ☐ 5 or more

I currently use these applications: _____

_____

_____

_____

I found these chapters to be the most informative: _____

_____

I found these chapters to be the least informative: _____

_____

Additional comments: _____

_____

☐ I would like to see my name in print! You may use my name and quote me in future New Riders products and promotions. My daytime phone number is: _____

New Riders Publishing 11711 North College Avenue • P.O. Box 90 • Carmel, Indiana 46032 USA

- Fold Here -

PLACE
STAMP
HERE

New Riders Publishing
11711 North College Avenue
P.O. Box 90
Carmel, Indiana 46032
USA

Become a CNE with Help from a Pro!

The NetWare Training Guides are specifically designed and authored to help you prepare for the **Certified NetWare Engineer** exam.

NetWare Training Guide: Managing NetWare Systems

This book clarifies the CNE testing process and provides hints on how best to prepare for the CNE examinations. NetWare Training Guide: Managing NetWare Systems covers the following sections of the CNE exams:

● NetWare v 2.2 System Manager

● NetWare v 2.2 Advanced System Manager

● NetWare v 3.X System Manager

● NetWare v 3.X Advanced System Manager

ISBN: 1-56205-069-9, **$59.95 USA**

NetWare Training Guide: Networking Technology

This book covers more advanced topics and prepares you for the tough hardware and service/support exams. The following course materials are covered:

● MS-DOS

● Microcomputer Concepts

● Service and Support

● Networking Technologies

ISBN: 1-56205-145-8, **$59.95 USA**

OPERATING SYSTEMS

INSIDE MS-DOS 6

NEW RIDERS PUBLISHING

A complete tutorial and reference!

MS-DOS 6

ISBN: 1-56205-132-6

$39.95 USA

DOS FOR NON-NERDS

MICHAEL GROH

Understanding this popular operating system is easy with this humorous, step-by-step tutorial

Through DOS 6.0

ISBN: 1-56205-151-2

$18.95 USA

INSIDE SCO UNIX

STEVE GLINES, PETER SPICER, BEN HUNSBERGER, & KAREN WHITE

Everything users need to know to use the UNIX operating system for everyday tasks

SCO Xenix 286, SCO Xenix 386, SCO UNIX/System V 386

ISBN: 1-56205-028-1

$29.95 USA

INSIDE SOLARIS SunOS

NEW RIDERS PUBLISHING

Comprehensive tutorial and reference to SunOS!

SunOS, Sun's version of UNIX for the SPARC workstation version 2.0

ISBN: 1-56205-032-X

$29.95 USA